ADVANCE PRAISE FOR

Spirituality, Ethics, Religion, and Teaching

"Robert J. Nash's *Spirituality, Ethics, Religion, and Teaching: A Professor's Journey* tells the story of a common journey of all teachers in an uncommon language. When I was his student, he always encouraged me to respectfully learn the other's language and create my own bricolage. We continue our conversation about the teacher's journey, now as colleagues, and the journey continues to soften from the complexitites of our praxis into spiritual shades, hues, hills, and valleys."

Ernest Nalette, Ed.D., Associate Professor and Chair of Graduate Studes in Physical Therapy, Ithaca College, New York

"The work of the professor is, to most people, a mystery; the stereotype of the academic is characterized by a cold, hyper-rational person who lives a lonely, esoteric life of the mind. In *Spirituality, Ethics, Religion, and Teaching: A Professor's Journey*, Robert J. Nash shatters this image and provides a window into the passionate world of teaching and learning in higher education. This highly personal and wonderfully inspiring scholarly work is both a portrait of the field of moral philosophy in education, and a more intimate 'letter of the spirit' by a postmodern, restless seeker of spiritual truths. When I walked into my first class with Robert J. Nash over ten years ago, I knew I was in the presence of a commanding intellect; what I now know, after reading this autobiographical narrative, is the depth of his passions for his students, for his evolving pedagogy, and for his own ongoing journey of faith."

Kathleen Knight Abowitz, Associate Professor, Miami University, Author of Building Community in an American High School

"A good teacher makes me think. A great teacher stirs my emotions, touches the soul of my humanity, and inspires me to learn. Robert J. Nash has always been a great teacher and this memoir demonstrates why. With intelligent philosophy and bold reflections of a life lived in education and lessons learned through education, Robert J. Nash offers a portrait of more than just his life as a 'teacher.' In addition to offering critical insights about educational pedagogy, he calls upon the reader to join him in the storytelling journey of learning."

Ray Quirolgico, University of SanFrancisco, California

Spirituality, Ethics,
Religion, *and* Teaching

STUDIES IN

EDUCATION & SPIRITUALITY

Peter L. Laurence and Victor H. Kazanjian, Jr.
General Editors

Vol. 5

PETER LANG
New York • Washington, D.C./Baltimore • Bern
Frankfurt am Main • Berlin • Brussels • Vienna • Oxford

Robert J. Nash

Spirituality, Ethics, Religion, *and* Teaching

A Professor's Journey

PETER LANG
New York • Washington, D.C./Baltimore • Bern
Frankfurt am Main • Berlin • Brussels • Vienna • Oxford

Library of Congress Cataloging-in-Publication Data

Nash, Robert J.
Spirituality, ethics, religion, and teaching: a professor's
journey / Robert J. Nash.
p. cm. — (Studies in education and spirituality; v. 5)
Includes bibliographical references.
1. Teaching—Religious aspects. 2. Education—Philosophy. 3. Moral education.
4. Spiritual life. 5. Nash, Robert J. I. Title. II. Series.
LB1027.2 .N37   371.102—dc21   2002003258
ISBN 0-8204-5848-1
ISSN 1527-8247

Die Deutsche Bibliothek-CIP-Einheitsaufnahme

Nash, Robert J.:
Spirituality, ethics, religion, and teaching:
a professor's journey / Robert J. Nash. –New York;
Washington, D.C./Baltimore; Bern; Frankfurt am Main;
Berlin; Brussels; Vienna; Oxford: Lang.
(Studies in education and spirituality; Vol. 5)
ISBN 0-8204-5848-1

Cover design by Dutton & Sherman Design

The paper in this book meets the guidelines for permanence and durability
of the Committee on Production Guidelines for Book Longevity
of the Council of Library Resources.

© 2002 Peter Lang Publishing, Inc., New York

Printed in the United States of America

TABLE OF CONTENTS

ACKNOWLEDGMENTS

I am deeply grateful to the College of Education and Social Services at the University of Vermont for granting me a sabbatical leave during the year 2000–2001 to write two books. The first, *Religious Pluralism in the Academy: Opening the Dialogue*, was subsequently published by Peter Lang Inc., in October, 2001, and it represented my take on the controversial issue of religious difference in higher education. I wrote about how the escalating reality of religious pluralism, coupled with intensely held political, geographical, ethnic, and racial beliefs, threatens to turn people against each other, sometimes violently, throughout the world and, lately, even in universities and colleges in the United States. I argued that, unless we learn to face this threat squarely and courageously in civil, cross-campus dialogue, religious difference could well become the latest obstacle to the full acceptance of pluralism in the academy.

I wrote the book well before the earthshaking, terroristic events of September 11, 2001 in America, and some readers have since called me "prescient." I prefer instead to call it simple common sense, as the indicators for religious conflict both here and abroad have been in the air for years. Americans are remarkably illiterate when it comes to understanding religious and spiritual difference. Not surprisingly, most know very little even about their own religions. I argued, among other things, in *Religious Pluralism in the Academy,* that educators needed to enlarge the multiculturalism curriculum to include the looming presence of religious diversity both within and without the American university.

The second book I wrote, the one currently in the hands of the reader, is what I call a scholarly personal narrative, or what, in my graduate Interdisciplinary Writing Seminar, I cryptically refer to as an "spn." I have wanted to write such a personal book for many, many years. Ralph Waldo Emerson once asserted that it is impossible to utter even a single sentence without unintentionally disclosing who we are, what we believe, and who and what we might like or dislike. This is simply to say that our sentences are not so much *by* us as *about* us. Although I have never been reluctant to use the first-person pronoun in my writing, I am becoming even more convinced that it is well-nigh impossible for me, or anyone else for that matter, to write what Raymond Hedrin calls an "impersonal, magisterial sentence."

This is a sentence that the academy purports to be without a trace of personal feeling or belief, a sentence totally devoid of interpretation, vulnerability, opinion, or of any other residue of self-revealing subjectivity. The imperative to become an impersonal authority in scholarship and research, sadly, is the omniscient, "objective" norm we impose on all our students during their years in the academy. For me, at this particular time in my professorial life, as I am entering the final years of a highly rewarding career, I find such a norm to be tedious and dishonest. More importantly, for myself, I find it to be a punishing, self-deceiving delusion. I long ago resolved never again to ask my students to write in such a way that I am simply unable or unwilling to do myself.

I arrive at this conclusion about the inevitability and centrality of the "I" in everything that I and my students do mainly as a result of my thirty-five years of teaching in the academy. In the pages to come, my debt to all my wonderful students through the years at the University of Vermont, particularly to my HESA, Interdisciplinary, and Educational Studies students, will become obvious. Evident, too, will be my indebtedness to my primary intellectual mentors of the last several years: Hazel Barnes, Theodore Brameld, Don Cupitt, Diana Eck, the Dalai Lama, Richard Rorty, and Bishop John Shelby Spong.

I am deeply grateful for the opportunity that the University of Vermont has given me to take a series of sabbaticals in order to earn additional graduate degrees in my newly developing areas of intellectual interest, as well as to undertake the research and scholarship that has produced a number of scholarly articles and books. This time off is a privilege because it always seems to come at a time when I am contemplating a significant change of direction in my thinking, teaching, writing, and consulting. How fortunate I am as a university professor to be able to take advantage of the perquisite of a paid leave to do what I love to do without the day-to-day demands of having to be on the job. I am fully aware that nobody else in my family or circle of friends outside the university is ever granted such a privilege.

I wish, also, to thank Peter L. Laurence, Director of the Education as Transformation Project at Wellesley College, for encouraging me to write these two books for his and Victor H. Kazanjian's series on Education & Spirituality for Peter Lang. I wish, too, to thank my excellent senior editor at Peter Lang, Heidi Burns, Ph.D., for all her supererogatory, technical work on my two books. Although I have never met her in person, I feel that she genuinely understands who I am as a result of what she has read of mine. I want, as well, to thank my wisest, most honest critic and soul-mate of forty-three years, Madelyn, for volunteering to be the first person to read this manuscript. As usual, I found her observations to be compassionate, candid, and challenging, and, in the end, whatever its worth to the reader, I believe that my book has been vastly improved as a direct result of her efforts.

I would like to thank Mike Waggoner, Editor of the Journal of Religion & Education, for permission to use sections of previously published material from the Spring issue, 2001, in Chapter 5.

Finally, I express my enthusiastic gratitude to my two daughters, Mika and Kayj, for being willing, at a moment's notice, to talk with me about the art and craft of their own teaching. We have shared many a story with each other about our soaring successes and grinding failures in the classroom. Also, without the forbearance of my three grandchildren, Cody James, Chaney Lee, and Mariposa Marie, I would not have had the peace and quiet during my sabbatical necessary to complete all my writing projects. I take this opportunity now to apologize to each of them for the trips to McDonald's, Dunkin' Donuts, and Rocky's softserve ice cream stand that they missed because their "dee-dee" was just too busy with his writing to join them. Lastly, I am grateful to my parents, James and Myrtle, for being unrivaled examples of uncompromising integrity, unflinching candor, and, best of all, hypocrisy detectors of the highest order. May this book be worthy of every single person that I mention in the preceding paragraphs.

INTRODUCTION

My passion is teaching. I am a college professor who has been going strong since 1968. My successes have been many, but so have my failures. I have had the good fortune to receive much national recognition for my scholarship. Moreover, my elective courses frequently fill up on the days they are initially announced. Thirty-plus years ago, I developed the first courses in applied ethics, moral education, and character education ever offered in a college of education in this country. I also created a graduate course in religion, spirituality, and education that I believe is unique in America, in that it draws practitioners from all the human services, in addition to educators; furthermore, it is offered by an educator in a professional school rather than by a theologian or philosopher in a religious studies department. I have also been a co-creator of three major interdisciplinary graduate programs. One of them, the Higher Education and Student Affairs Administration Program, is acknowledged by professionals in the field to be among the top five in the country. Some have called me a pioneer. I call myself incredibly lucky.

I mention these successes, not because I am boastful, but because I am grateful. I mention them, too, because in these pages I intend to pull no punches about my more obvious weaknesses as someone who has a huge passion to teach and what some have said is an ego to match it. I am grateful, because I am one of those very fortunate persons who has found a profession that is a near perfect fit for someone of my particular temperament, taste, training, and talent. I have tried a number of other professions during my adulthood that have been less than satisfying to me. Thus, I think I know what works for me and what does not. My wish for all my readers is that, like me, they too might discover the ideal match between who they are, what they believe, and what they do.

The book before the reader is a first-person reflection on what I have learned about being a teacher for almost thirty-five years in a "public ivy" university. It is a personal narrative of pedagogical and intellectual musings. It is not a *how-to* book. Rather, it is a *tell-why*, recursive series of intellectual and spiritual reflections on what I have come to value about teaching and learning during my many years in the academy that I love. I intend to tell a very loose chronological, and a very selective autobiographical, story in these pages of hard-won intellectual and spiritual growth as a teacher. I hope to do this always with grace and generosity.

I am a philosopher by temperament and training. Thus, I am deeply sensitive to the transformative power of ideas. My way of touching the reader's heart is to begin first with the reader's mind. This, I believe, is what good teachers everywhere should strive to accomplish at all levels of schooling. I am idealistic enough to think that even though I am a college professor, what I have to say about teaching and learning, spirituality and philosophy, morality and character education, ethics and higher education will have considerable appeal for teachers and learners everywhere.

Because I am a philosopher, I confess to being an unabashed lover of wisdom and knowledge. This is the actual meaning of the word *philosophy* (G. *philosophia*). For me, philosophy is both a content and a process. Philosophers love knowledge, to be sure, but the best of them strive to be passionate seekers of knowledge rather than self-satisfied possessors of it. Ours is a love affair with the pursuit, rather than the acquisition, of wisdom. We are in love with the open-ended journey of discovery, with the endless cycle of questions that this search provokes, and with the ultimate mystery that surrounds the existence of each and every human being. Therefore, we tend to experience a special empathy for those students and colleagues who are fellow seekers and lovers; and for those who are not, we see it as our particular mission to whet their natural appetites for self-understanding and personal meaning.

To teach as a philosopher is to fall in love over and over—day after day, semester after semester, year after year. The story that unfolds in these pages will be intense at times. I like to think of myself as someone with an ardent passion to teach. In fact, I will argue that, in my opinion, passion is one of the necessary preconditions for successful teaching and learning, and for successful living as well. To this end, I will recount some of the life-changing, intellectual, and emotional insights that I have gleaned from students and colleagues, scholars and mentors, throughout my own career. My narrative is, in part, one professor's account of building a lasting community of friends. It is about developing enduring relationships with so many kind and bright people, including, not least, all those authors whom I have never met personally but whose words have changed my life.

Equally important, my story will be about the struggle to create a spirituality of teaching, no easy task for a postmodern, agnostic skeptic like myself. For me, a spirituality of teaching has much more to do with an open-ended journey to create multiple meanings in my life that are able to sustain, and elevate, me professionally than it does with simply trying to apply the principles of conventional religion and New-Age spirituality to the practice of education. This means that one of the major tasks in this book is to reframe traditional notions of religion and spirituality, as well as correct conventional misunderstandings of postmodernism. My approach to both spirituality and postmodernism is capacious enough to countenance a postmodern spirituality. In my own case, I do not believe this to be oxymoronic. However, I am still working on it.

My story will not be a particularly intimate one. Neither will it be retaliatory. I have no great personal secrets I wish to disclose or professional scores to settle. I am a relatively happy, sixty-something, bourgeois liberal, whose professional life has been, on the whole, enormously fulfilling. I do, however, have an intellectual and spiritual journey to narrate that, at least to me, has been an exciting, fluctuating adventure. I am presumptuous enough to believe that my odyssey, though unique in its personal details, will touch a responsive chord for many of my readers. Writ large, my story is every teacher's story, in that it tells of the joys and sorrows, the ups and the downs, the satisfactions and the dissatisfactions that keep us coming back for more, year after year. The narrative that educators will encounter here is one that I am convinced many have lived in their own fashion at their own levels of teaching. Teaching, in my opinion, is the most noble and humbling, exalting and dispiriting, profession of all. While it carries with it the grave risk of inadvertently injuring, or even killing, the hearts and minds of students, it also does something far more redemptive. It offers all of us the magnificent opportunity of saving hearts and minds because its intellectual and emotional impact can be both magical and life-transforming.

CHAPTER ONE

The Passion to Teach...
and to Learn

Passion is the exhilarating experience of being carried along by a power greater than controlled conscious willing.
——Rollo May, *Love and Will*, 1969

My vocation is the spiritual life, the quest for God, which relies on the eye of the heart. My avocation is education, the quest for knowledge, which relies on the eye of the mind.... But—unable to blink one eye, shut them both, or live in a blur—I have been forced to find ways for my eyes to work together, to find a common focus for my spirit-seeking heart and my knowledge-seeking mind that embraces reality in all its amazing dimensions.
——Parker J. Palmer, *To Know As We Are Known:*
A Spirituality of Education, 1983

RETIREMENT IS OUT OF THE QUESTION...FOR NOW

I have, all of a sudden it seems, reached the age of retirement as a professor. Even so, to paraphrase Dylan Thomas, I refuse to go gently into this good night. I have practiced my craft—teaching—at the high school and college levels for almost four decades. Nothing surprises me anymore in the classroom, even though everything continues to delight me. A very insightful graduate student once said to me: "You claim to be a religious agnostic. I think I know why you have the luxury of holding this position. Your work as an educator is actually a religious vocation because it gives you a sense of transcendence. Your church is the university. Your sacrament is teaching. Your community of saints is made up of your students. And your prayer is when you carry on intense, revitalizing, give-and-take conversations in the classroom. Am I right?"

Yes, this student is correct, and I blush at being so transparent. I am not at the point in my life when I am willing to withdraw gracefully to a life of monitoring the stockmarket, sailing, traveling, golfing, volunteering, or running for the local school board. As worthy as all these activities are, the truth is that I live to teach, to be with students, to read their papers, to advise their theses and dissertations, to write and to learn, and, yes, even to engage in the incessant political maneuvering with my colleagues that tries the patience of so many college professors. I am that strange breed of professional animal who is a proud, lifelong teacher. What is more, I am a happy one, at least most of the time. I was not always this way, however. I have only gradually, at times painfully, grown into my contentment.

I first entered the profession of teaching at the high school level, in the year of 1962, in a major suburb of Boston, Massachusetts. While I hated the emphasis that administrators and teachers in this large, suburban, working-class school put on routine and discipline, or, in their words, "keeping resistant students in line by enforcing the rules," I, nevertheless, found much to love in the challenge of teaching a bunch of distracted adolescents the joys of English. I remember glowing for days afterward, for example, when "Liz," a very troubled sophomore, came up to me after class and said: "Wow, this stuff called poetry that we've been studying for the last month is really cool. Would you mind reading a little poem I wrote last night in memory of my little brother who died of leukemia last year?"

Or when "Ken," the president of the school's National Honor Society, exclaimed that he had just been accepted to Boston College on an academic scholarship and that, thanks to my course, he was declaring himself to be an English major. Ken eventually went on to earn a doctorate in English, and he is today the chairman of his department at a very prestigious university. What is more, Ken's books on postmodern literary theory are well known in the academy. I beam with pride whenever I announce to my students that I knew the author when he was a high school English whiz. I also point out that he was a very competitive basketball player. To this day, I enjoy telling my students the tale of suffering a broken nose during a pickup basketball game when I foolishly attempted to challenge Ken during one of his signature, hard-driving layups to the basket. To compound my physical pain, *I* was the one who was charged with the personal foul!

Of course, I vividly recall my terrible disappointments in that school as well. Noteworthy among them was a junior, "Paul," who sat for days at a time in the back of the classroom, glaring sullenly at me, and never opening his mouth. Throughout the term, I continually asked him to stop by after school to talk with me, but he never appeared. I later learned that he dropped out of high school. When he returned his textbooks to the assistant principal, the words scribbled in large boldface on the cover of his English text were these: "Mr. Nash is a fucker! I hate him, and I hate English." When Paul did make a connection with me a year later, it was in an angry letter. The words were meant to taunt and hurt me, and they did: "High school was bullshit! So were you. I'll bet I'm making more money driving a truck cross-country than you are teaching your crap. You know what? I don't need poetry or grammar to make it in the world. When are you going to get an honest job, make some real money, and do something useful for a change?"

Then there was "Millie," a trailer-park child old beyond her years, a senior, already a divorced, teenage mother, and the daughter of two severely depressed, alcoholic parents. Millie was also brilliant, the possessor of a near-photographic memory and a fertile, creative mind. I took it as my solemn mission to raise her educational aspirations. I cajoled her throughout her senior year to take the SAT exam, and to apply to colleges. She managed to gain admission to Northeastern University, a cooperative education college that would have been a wonderful fit for her. There, she could have worked for her tuition and studied at the same time. She was also accepted to Smith, an exclusive women's college in Massachusetts, which came up with enough financial aid for her to get through at least the first two years.

Millie was killed in an automobile accident shortly after her high school graduation. Her blood-alcohol level was almost three times the legal limit, and she was also six months pregnant. Her older sister later told me that she had no intention of ever going to college, despite what she was telling me and her friends. According to the sister:

> Millie liked and respected you very much, Mr. Nash, but she felt tremendous pressure to gain your approval. She told you what she thought you wanted to hear when all along she really wanted you to be her friend. She was so deeply lonely and needy to have an adult confidante she could trust. All you ever talked about with her was how important it was to have a college education. She could never understand why you weren't interested in

her personal problems. These, I think, are what turned her to booze and eventually killed her.

I left high school teaching forever, knowing that I had failed with too many Pauls and Millies. I left mostly to lick my wounds, and to figure out why teaching had been such a bittersweet experience for me. I hated the public school bureaucracy. I could not understand the sarcasm in administrators' voices whenever they talked about teachers and parents, or the cynicism in teachers' words whenever they referred to administrators or, sadly, to their students. More personally, why did it seem that for every soaring success I experienced in the public school classroom I also suffered an offsetting and dismal disappointment? Why was it that on some days I could not wait to get to school in the morning, while on others I yearned to call in sick? Why was it that so many of my colleagues deep-down, intensely disliked teaching, yet still chose to stick it out year after year—complaining, conniving, and gossiping, and, in the process, casting a pall of gloom and discontent over all the rest of us? I wondered: Were my ambivalence and my doubts about my work and my colleagues normal? Was all of this professional misery somehow inevitable?

I decided, after much soul-searching, to return as a fulltime student to the university, to find refuge in the books, papers, and solitude that I had always loved. I began my doctoral studies at Boston University in philosophy and educational theory with high hopes. Experiencing a crisis of religious faith, I wanted to deepen my formal understanding of existentialism, a very popular 1950s and 1960s philosophy which I taught my honors classes. I had enjoyed assigning my honors students a number of readings by such authors as Albert Camus and Jean Paul Sartre. These writers rarely failed to touch something vital in the hearts of my bright, questioning adolescents, and, not coincidently, in my own heart as well. At the time I was struggling with the age-old philosophical problems of good and evil, freedom and determinism, creation and chance, theism and atheism, the individual and the community, and with the starker realities of coming to grips with my own human finitude. I vaguely sensed that existentialism might be able to provide some answers, or, at least, some ways of asking the right questions about such difficult philosophical puzzles. I hope to describe some of my learnings on these topics in the chapters to follow.

I also wanted the systematic opportunity to examine the ins and outs of educational theory. I needed to look objectively at what I could have done as a high school teacher to be more effective and to gain a greater peace of mind. Teaching was still my obsession. In fact, it was behind everything that I thought about during the three wonderfully reflective years that I spent at Boston University. The combination of philosophy and educational theory hooked me from the start. I knew almost immediately that I would become a philosopher of education. I also knew that I would someday return to teaching—not in the public schools but in the university. Moreover, I knew that I would make my academic home in a professional school, a college of education, rather than in a philosophy department.

This academic home is where I have resided for over three-and-a-half decades, and I have never once regretted my choice. It is here in the university that I have gained a deep sense of vocational satisfaction, along with a modicum of spiritual peace. As will be apparent in subsequent chapters, though, I am still restless when it comes to matters of the spirit. Most of all, however, I have found in teaching something that I can do every day of my life with a special gusto, with what some of my students today love to call "passion." Sadly, this term is so often used in the helping professions that it is fast becoming a cliché. It is a word that, in my opinion, cries out for thoughtful deconstruction and reconstruction. This will be one of my aims in the pages that follow.

PASSION, EROS, AND THE CLASSROOM

I cannot think of another human undertaking that is as painful or as joyful, as mundane or as spiritual, as the profession of teaching, unless it is being a parent or a lover. Ironically, the root of the word *passion* (Latin *passio*) conveys these two antithetical meanings: a powerful fondness or enthusiasm for something; and suffering, endurance, and pain, as expressed in the Christian Gospel narrative of Christ's passion and crucifixion. It will be one of my hypotheses in the chapters to come that effective teaching, similar to effective parenting and loving, requires considerable passion. This reality, though, sometimes turns out to be a mixed blessing, because passionate educators always run the risk of oscillating between the extremes of a soaring exhilaration and a grinding depression as a result of what happens in their classrooms. I remember an educator once remarking somewhat irreverently to me that teaching is a lot like dying and then being reborn: When things go badly in our instruction, we die a little bit, but when things go well, and inevitably they always get better, we experience a resurrection better than Jesus Christ's. I also recall another teacher, less eschatalogical, saying that "when my teaching is successful it's better than sex and chocolate; but when it's a disaster it's worse than unexpected airplane turbulence and root canal surgery."

I, for one, do not know how anything truly worthwhile can happen in a classroom unless teachers experience a powerful fondness, indeed even something akin to a lustful enthusiasm, for teaching, learning, and subject matter. In this sense, teaching is an erotic activity. I am not talking about being sexually attracted to some students, although this is more of a reality in teaching than most of us would care to admit publicly. We are, after all, naturally libidinal creatures for whom sexual energy can, and ought to, be transformed into something wholesome and creative in our teaching. Rather, I am referring to eros in the way that the Greek writer, Hesiod, did: Eros was the god who emerged from Chaos, a being who drew all things together into an order. In this sense, eros is the supreme creative and binding force in the universe, and, in my estimation, in the classroom as well.

Eros is the unapologetic love of beauty, relationship, and truth that I believe ought to underlie everything that we do with students. It is the major source of inspiration for our continual search in life for meaning and purpose. It is the primordial human energy that attracts us to each other and binds us together in affection and generosity. It is the moral and aesthetic force that enables us to live the good and beautiful life. Eros fuels the passion for knowledge, relationships, and practice, and it has the potential of turning a dull classroom into something dynamic and memorable. Eros is clearly a synonym for the way that I understand spirituality.

bell hooks (1994), the transgressive black educator, believes that it is only our passions that make us whole, that "expand rather than diminish the promise of our lives." hooks does not think it possible for us to bridge the "world outside and the world inside the academy" unless we are willing to display an erotic passion both for ideas on their own terms and for students on theirs. She says, "To restore passion to the classroom or to excite it in classrooms where it has never been, we teachers must find again the place of eros within ourselves and together allow the mind and body to feel and know desire" (p. 199). How else, I wonder, is it possible to get beyond those awful, desiccated times when the classroom venture gets hyper-stressful or hypertedious? In my estimation, many supporters of the back-to-basics and standardized-testing movements in the schools, especially in the upper grades, including the colleges and universities, attach very little value to passion. For them, this is a dangerous emotion teachers must keep securely in check. After all, or so these critics reason, if physicians and lawyers must struggle to keep their feelings under strict control in order to make the tough professional decisions their work requires, why should teachers be any exception?

I have even heard a well-known teacher educator, who is a devotee of a no-nonsense approach to teaching what E. D. Hirsch, Jr. (1987) calls background knowledge, announce to a large conference gathering one day that, whereas empathy, enthusiasm, and warmth are certainly desirable in working, say, with younger students, they are "contraindicated" with older students. According to her, the best high school and college teachers must strive to become "more authoritative and objective and less affective." They must do this in order to make the unbiased, professional judgments nec-essary to control unruly behavior, as well as to transmit and to measure the acquisition of core subject matter more efficiently. Sadly, to me, this per-ception stereotypes teachers and students at all levels. It limits the expres-sion of feelings to teachers of elementary and middle-school children and relegates critical thinking to teachers of high school and college students. It bifurcates the heart and head by making passionate professionals appear unaccountable, anti-intellectual, manipulated by their feelings, uncool in the literal sense, that is, interested only in pandering to the hot emotions of their undisciplined charges.

It is revealing to note that the ancient philosophers thought of pas-sion as a type of madness that people must assiduously avoid. The ancients would never have agreed with Rollo May's (1969) assertion in the epigraph that introduces this chapter that often "controlled conscious willing" can actually be a hindrance to experiencing the deepest forms of love, freedom, and power. For May, to be completely caught up in love for a person or an idea can oftentimes be incredibly liberating and empowering. It can also be profoundly inspiring.

In contrast, the Stoics considered passion to be a fatal misunder-standing and an enemy to reason because passion leads too frequently to loss of control, frustration, weakness, and unhappiness. Who in their right [rational] mind would want to be out of control, frustrated, or unhappy? Later, Christian theologians, following Plato and Aristotle, taught that what makes humans most divine is their reason, whereas it is their passions that threaten to engulf them and sweep them away. Immanuel Kant disdained the passions as bothersome "illnesses," diseases to be cured rather than gifts to be celebrated. When the Enlightenment thinker, David Hume, made the outrageous declaration that reason is, and ought to be, "the slave of the passions," philosophers at the time were shocked.

Passion as Artful Madness

What Hume meant, of course, was precisely what I believe is a prerequisite for passionate teaching: While reason is obviously necessary for stimulating a student's intellect and even for touching a student's heart, it is rarely sufficient. Reason without strong feeling is unlikely to motivate either teachers or students to reach beyond their more narrow self-interests. Hume's "natural human sentiments" must always accompany rational calculation, if teaching is ever to hit the mark of inspiring students to reach beyond themselves in a strictly nonutilitarian way. I prefer to think of passion as a kind of artful madness, whereby teachers skillfully direct their own intense excitement for learning to the furtherance of one primary goal. This is the goal of generating an intense excitement in students for the intellectual and emotional work that both sides must undertake together if anything truly breathtaking is to happen in a classroom.

In fact, as both Blaise Pascal, a seventeenth-century philosopher, and Friedrich Nietzsche, a nineteenth-century thinker, knew so well: Every passion contains its own quantum of reason. To paraphrase Pascal's more ironic language: The heart has reasons which reason knows nothing about. The passionate teacher, then, is someone who vividly understands that heart and head are intricately linked in the teaching-learning venture; that agony and ecstasy, insight and ignorance, feeling and thinking are ubiquitous and always precarious bedfellows. When I speak of the passion of teaching, then, I describe a paradoxical awareness that, for teachers and learners, what is ultimately at stake in teaching is staggering, even though what happens day-to-day in the classroom might appear to outsiders (and to some insiders) to be merely humdrum and customary.

When I speak of passionate teachers, I think especially of those teachers who are unavoidably, helplessly, in love with their work. I think of teachers who feel intimately, indeed amorously, about their subject matter, their students, and the whole magical experience that sometimes transpires whenever learners and teachers come together in the confined, artificial space called a classroom or a seminar room. I think of teachers who are so deeply in love with ideas that they cannot wait to share an exciting insight garnered on their own time—perhaps something learned from a conversation with friends, or from reading a particularly challenging book, magazine, newspaper, or journal article, or from attending an engrossing lecture, film, or play. Nel Noddings's (1993) words to describe this exuberant, personal giving are poignant:

> There ought to be gifts freely given in education. Aristotle once said that teaching does whatever it does "as to a friend." In the discussion of religious, metaphysical, and existential questions, teachers and students are both seekers. Teachers tell stories, guide the logic of discussion, point to further readings, model both critical thinking and kindness, and show by their openness what it means to seek intelligent belief or unbelief. Students long for gifts of this sort from their teachers. (pp. 134–135)

Passionate teachers are those who have thought long and hard about the nature of knowledge, about what makes students of all ages want to learn even when they are most surly and resistant, and about what young people really need to know, and do, in order to be good and decent human beings—of no imminent danger either to themselves or to others. I think, also, of teachers who experience the same kind of breathless excitement that Aristotle did when he reached the startling conclusion that ultimate knowledge resides, not in some distant Platonic World of Ideas, but in the fresh, uncensored questions of eager and curious children and young adults. How then, Aristotle asked, can a teacher ever dismiss out of hand any student's wonder, no matter how seemingly impertinent, naive, off-track, stupid, irreverent, or subversive? Finally, I think of teachers who, by virtue of the incredible intellectual, emotional, and physical energy they expend while working at their profession, eagerly await vacation breaks as a time for necessary spiritual rejuvenation. However, these are the same teachers who soon grow bored with the time off and begin furtively to look at the calendar with the anticipatory excitement of starting yet another school term or school year. Away from their classrooms, they know that they are fish out of water.

TEACHING WITH COOL PASSION

I think of myself as a passionate teacher, albeit, on occasion I can be a strategically cool one. As I pass the middle of the third decade of my career as a university professor, I find that I am growing more passionate about my vocation almost by the hour. I know regretfully that the end of my work is in sight, but I also know that teaching continues to be the core of my life. As most teachers know, a vocation, in the religious sense of the term, is a calling, a summons by God or by some superior power to perform a particular, sacred function. I must confess that I have never been moved by this definition. It implies to me that the decision to teach comes from a force outside rather than from inside the person. Instead, I like the notion of teaching as a profession—this, also, understood in the religious sense. Professionals, like religious leaders, are obligated to profess, to make an open declaration that they believe in the worth of something with all their hearts and minds.

In fact, the comparative religions scholar Diana L. Eck (1993) goes so far as to say that "the word 'credo,' so important in the Christian tradition, does not mean 'I believe' in the sense of intellectual assent to this and that proposition. It means 'I give my heart to this'" (p. 195). By implication, for me, teaching is always more than an "intellectual assent" to some external administrative or practical imperative. Rather, it is an open avowal of the heart's commitment that nothing else matters quite as much as professing a special kind of love for students and subject matter. This is a love that is committed to helping students grow in the kind of self-knowledge which, in some cases, might ultimately lead to major personal and social transformation. This is the kind of love that says: I give my whole heart and soul to this undertaking. I can do no less.

Despite the high-sounding words in the preceding paragraphs, however, I am also a cool realist. I realize that I have failed, as often as I have succeeded, to profess, and to exemplify in my practice, my love for students and for learning. I must admit that nothing has the power to exhilarate or dispirit me as much as the act of teaching. The highs in my day-to-day, year-to-year work with students know no equal in any other area of my life, but, truth to tell, neither do the lows. I have walked away from some classes and courses thoroughly elated, and from others totally drained and dejected. More often than not, my students inspire me, but they can also depress me. There are occasions when I love my students, especially when they respond well to my intellectual entreaties, and when they treat each other, and me, with kindness, respect, and forbearance. Sadly, though, there are times when I dislike them, particularly when they are ungenerous toward each other and me, or when they are lazy, self-centered, and manipulative.

There are occasions when I would rather spend my free time with students, more so than with friends or colleagues, or, in some instances, even with loved ones. There are other times, though, when I desperately need relief from students (and, I am sure, they from me) because I am exhausted and empty. I cannot honestly give a single one of them another minute of my riveted attention. Their demands overwhelm me. During a recent yearlong writing sabbatical spent at my home, I purposely scheduled several leisurely breakfasts with my students at a nearby restaurant, mostly at their initiation. I did this because I genuinely missed my classroom contact with them.

I was honored and touched that so many of them chose to linger a bit with me during their zealously guarded free time. Listening to them share their out-of-classroom joys and sorrows, their hopes and fears, with me over a bowl of granola or a western omelet, I realized that I felt closer to them as real people than I ever had in a seminar or in an office. (I will speak of this experience at greater length in the last chapter.) However, in all honesty, I would not have chosen to do this nearly as often during a typical semester of teaching, advising, and university service. I know from years of experience that revivifying periods of time away from students are absolutely necessary if the time spent with them is to be mutually productive and satisfying.

As a teacher, although I am passionate, I suspect that my passion is a bit cooler and more tempered than Rollo May's, whom I quote in this chapter's epigraph. On the one hand, I am not as willing as he, at least not yet, to subordinate my critical, rational faculties to a "power greater than conscious, controlled willing." I am, after all, trained as an analytic philosopher. On the other hand, however, I find it impossible at this stage of my career to teach in an impersonal or dispassionate manner about what have been the scholarly loves of my professional life—moral philosophy, ethics, educational theory, and religious studies. I am struggling to this day to achieve some kind of a balance between hot passion and cold dispassion. I have learned the hard way that a teacher's unrestrained cool passion can sometimes intimidate and overwhelm students; ironically, so too can an uncontrolled hot passion. Either way, students are silenced.

According to the seventeenth-century philosopher, Thomas Hobbes (1962), "hot passions unguided are for the most part mere madness." While I do not agree a whit with Hobbes's attempts to justify the existence of an authoritarian state by urging people to relinquish their personal freedom in order to gain civil security, I do respect his warning about the dangers of unguided hot passions. Thus, I believe that something tantamount to a cool passion is the best compromise. It is what good teaching is all about, because, at least for me, this paradoxical combination best balances the forces of heart and mind, affect and cognition, personal investment and critical detachment, as well as private disclosure and professional formality.

I believe that I have been at my best both as a teacher and scholar whenever I remain calm yet cordial, controlled yet responsive, independent yet relational. I have been at my worst when my teaching and writing have been so frenzied and ideologically driven that they border on the frantic and politically self-serving, or so imperturbable as to appear chilly and distant. I am striving in these, my later years to be a teacher and a scholar whose cool passion speaks to both impassive and impassioned students. While I want to be cool, I also want to be perceived as warm and responsive. In the sixth decade of my life, I crave connection. As a professorial elder, I have become, in Erik Erikson's word, "generative." I pursue affiliations with students that are mutually caring, supportive, and affectionate. I believe that deep down these are the essential conditions for intellectual and spiritual growth, both theirs and mine. I will talk in greater detail about these types of connections, and their potential to enhance pedagogy at all educational levels, in the chapters to come.

For now, however, it is important for me to acknowledge that what has kept me passionate about my teaching, in addition to my insatiable love of knowledge and my wish to infect others with it, have been the wonderful relationships that I have formed with students for lo these many, many years.

I continue to correspond with hundreds of them. I have attended their weddings and, sadly, their funerals. I have met their parents, partners, and children. I have seen some of them become college professors in my own disciplines. Others have gone on to become teachers and administrators in fine schools and colleges throughout the country. Also, I am in the rare and enviable position of having observed several generations of students come and go in my classes, a few even from the same family. Some of my older students from the 1960s are now grandparents whose grandchildren have already made an appearance in my classroom. I have observed up close the human chain that links what colleagues call the "community of scholars," and what the Quakers call the "society of friends." I am delighted to be a living link in this unbroken chain.

Always I am reminded of Parker Palmer's important observation that the literal meaning of the word *truth* has little to do with correspondence, revelational, or coherence theories of knowledge. It has everything to do with faith and trust, encounter and engagement, and dialogue and connection with others. The Germanic root of the word *truth* is actually *troth* as in *bethrothal,* an entering into a faithful and lasting relationship with persons. Thus, etymologically, truth, like teaching, is first and always relational: It aims mainly to secure trust and initiate a relationship with others. My single most significant objective as a teacher through the years has been to help my students get to the point in private and public conversations where they, and I, are ready to relinquish the dogmatic dimensions of ourselves. We endeavor to do this in order to grow into some kind of binding connection with each other. The actual Latin derivation of the word *religion* (*religio*) means to bind people together in community, to fasten human ties. This communal pursuit of truth requires an uncommon humility, a luminous generosity, and, above all, a limitless capacity for self-transcendence.

SPIRITUALITY, *EPEKTASIS*, AND POSTMODERNISM

I begin this section with an honest personal disclosure, a truth-in-packaging statement regarding my own take on spirituality. Like Parker Palmer (1983) in this chapter's opening epigraph, I believe that I am a spiritual person "forced to find a common focus for my spirit-seeking heart and my knowledge-seeking mind..." (p. xii). In contrast to him, however, my peculiar brand of spirituality is neither Christian nor Quaker. In fact, it is not even theistic or pantheistic. Rather, it comes closest to what the sociologist of religion, Robert Wuthnow (1998), calls a "spirituality of seeking." If I were forced to give it a name, I would call it a kind of restless, existential agnosticism, punctuated by what the fourth-century theologian, Gregory of Nyssa, called, in Greek, *epektasis.* This is a *straining forward* toward mystery, toward a luminous darkness, toward an unsatiated desire for a meaning beyond meaning.

I will readily admit that there are times when I want the elusive biblical peace that "surpasses worldly understanding." I also crave the stillness in the center of it all that is uniquely Taoistic. Moreover, I understand well the supreme importance of cultivating the compassion and achieving the quieting of my voracious worldly cravings that are distinctively Buddhist. While I have never been truly comfortable as a conventional religious practitioner, I have always been an eager student of religion and spirituality. I have been fascinated with issues of meaning and emptiness, faith and doubt, transcendence and immanence, the secular and the sacred, the ineffable and the expressible. In my own way, I have been involved in a lifelong process of *epektasis.*

So too are most adults I know. I believe that the majority of students of high school and college age are as well, even though they may not openly show it or know it. Another more common phrase for *epektasis* is *searching for meaning,* a meaning better understood in secular terms as *hope* and *purpose,* or *raison d'etre.* I honestly do not know of a single human being who is able to live a coherent and hopeful life without a sense of expectation or purpose, a reason for being alive.

At this time, as I prepare to live out the final third of my life, I prefer the word *trust* to *faith.* In spite of my lingering agnosticism about all things supernatural, I do have an uneasy assurance, a hopeful expectation, that my life is good, and that I can be both loving and loveable. I know that there are reasons why some (but not all) things happen which I will never be able to comprehend. I am hopeful that the principles of honesty, integrity, compassion, and social justice mean as much to millions of others throughout the world as they mean to me. I also trust that the ineffable mystery that encompasses and suffuses my everyday life is real, as real in its own way as the numbing ordinariness that also characterizes that same, everyday life.

Moreover, I trust that, in some way, this mystery shapes, defines, and transforms the meaning of my life. However, I must be willing to listen to it, to allow it to find and touch me. Somewhere, somehow, I trust that there is warmth, joy, love, and purpose at the center of my existence. I cannot demonstrate any of this to those who have their doubts, of course, but at the middle of my sixth decade on this good earth, I no longer have a need for converts in my classroom, or anywhere else for that matter. You see, I have nothing left to prove in the spiritual realm, because I am still in glorious pursuit of *epektasis.*

I do not come to these beliefs easily, though. My own straining toward mystery is a continual struggle. I am a devout postmodernist. This is to say that I am a narrativist in my view of the world. I believe that each of us lives in a series of stories, particularly when it comes to religion and spirituality. These narratives are always cultural and historical in origin. I just cannot accept that there is some Final Answer as to whether the Ultimate Truth of any or all of these narratives exists outside of a humanly constructed culture. While the metaphysical itch to locate a Final Answer is important to me, and I scratch it whenever I can, what is more important is to engage in an ongoing, vibrant conversation with colleagues and students about just this sort of itch.

I do know, however, that if our individual spiritual narratives were indeed connected to some Transcendent or Divine Reality outside of us, it is highly unlikely that we could formulate a universally accepted method of determining which spiritual story was the True Account of meaning-making. I do not deny the possibility of Ultimate Transcendence, Objective Religious Truth, or Universal Spirituality. I only assert that, in my experience in particular, and in the historical record in general, it appears more than unlikely that anyone will ever be able to construct or discover Ultimate Religious Meaning, except through peculiar interpretations or mediations. These, in turn, are irrevocably blurred by the personal, historical, and cultural contingencies that shape our humanness. I, for one, shout an enthusiastic *yes!* to the existence of this multiplicity of spiritual and religious narratives.

In William Butler Yeats's words, we can never escape the "rag and bone shop of our messy lives" (cited in Natoli 1997). I know of no spiritual story that definitively transcends the rags and bones of particular times, places, and psyches. Thus, in the end, we are left with two options: telling our rags and bones stories to others, and listening to theirs as well; or keeping our stories to ourselves and compartmentalizing our private and public lives. As a teacher, I believe that the former is the best educational choice for those of us who choose to spend our time together in a learning community.

The contradictions in my spiritual worldview will become glaringly apparent in the chapters to come. At times I labor heavily in the midst of my *epektasis*. I grunt and I gasp. I huff and I puff. Trained as a philosopher, I am a certified, postmodern skeptic. I could easily be the one who occupies the first Endowed Chair of Official Unbelief at my university. I wrench and I twist whenever I enter the spiritual realm. I know well how to pull and tug at religion and spirituality, both in my private life and in the seminar room—especially in the seminar room. In all my years as a teacher, I have learned when to bear down with my students and when to loosen up. I am learning how and when to challenge them on spiritual matters and how and when I must yield to them. Each semester, my inner life undergoes both subtle and dramatic changes. I become the taught as well as the teacher, the sought as well as the seeker. Most of all, however, I am learning that my work as an educator, and my life as a parent, husband, and still-evolving adult, are, in large part, framing how I think and feel about spirituality.

At this point in my life, spirituality is the name I give to the never-ending struggle that for each one of us is inescapable: the need to provide satisfying answers to life's most insistent questions about meaning. For Parker Palmer (1983), quoted earlier, spirituality is the "quest for God." For me, God is only one, tentative answer that some of us give to such questions as:

- What am I?
- Why am I?
- Where am I going?
- How should I act?
- What is worth knowing?
- What do I stand for?
- What should I believe?

- What should I hope for?
- Why should I believe?
- What is worth dying for?
- Whom should I love?
- Whom should I help?
- Who is my neighbor?
- To whom or what should I belong?
- What is the source of my joy?
- Why do I and others suffer?
- Is social justice truly possible?
- Why should I be moral?

Also, for me, God is better understood as an aesthetic concept rather than a theological one; as a poetic expression rather than a philosophical proposition; or as a story to be narrated rather than a doctrine to be believed.

A SPIRITUALITY OF TEACHING

I will attempt to make the case in upcoming chapters that constructing a *spirituality* of teaching is a prerequisite for fostering a genuine and lasting *passion* for teaching. What I mean by this is that I do not believe an invigorating passion for the demanding work that we do as teachers is possible without a spirituality of education to ground us and to deepen our commitment to the profession of teaching. A spirituality of teaching attempts to help students formulate their own soul-satisfying answers to the questions I ask above. Walter Kaufmann (1961), the existential philosopher, comes at spirituality in a similar way when he talks about *ontological privation*. He chooses to use the term *ontology* rather than *spirituality*. For him, ontology is the technical branch of philosophy that deals most adequately with the questions I raise in the previous section regarding being, existence, ultimate meaning, mystery, and human finitude. He says: "We all experience ontological privation, whether we are aware of it or not: we need to rise above that whole level of being which is defined only by our psychological and physiological needs and their satisfaction; we need to love and create" (p. 423).

In my opinion, the chief implication for educators of what Kaufmann is saying is this: Teachers and students have a fundamental human need to create meaning by loving and creating, and by pursuing higher levels of aspiration. The person who is content only to spend inordinate amounts of time trying to gratify psychological and physical desires is also someone who is frequently restless, unsatisfied, and bored. To deny or to ignore one's ontological privation—to be oblivious to the spiritual questions that I ask above—is to settle for a life lived only in the present, hedonistic moment. The consequences of ontological privation, both for teachers and students, can be disastrous. According to Kaufmann, an inability, or refusal, to rise above the physical and material routines of our everyday personal and professional lives means that our fundamental need for love and creativity goes unfulfilled. Whenever this happens, we burn out or we dry up. Worse, some of us become aggressive, hostile, and alienated. We get paranoid, or we grow numb.

This book, therefore, is one educator's humble attempt to speak to teachers at all levels, teachers-to-be, and students everywhere, who want desperately to experience a deeper and richer meaning in the important, day-to-day work that they do. I want especially to reach the minds and hearts of those teachers who might be restless, unsatisfied, even bored. I hope to say something worthwhile to those educators who refuse to settle for a life superficially lived. I want to speak to teachers in schools and colleges who are concerned more with the search for a lasting meaning and less with the pursuit of a frenetic careerism. I wish for my words to reassure the hopeless, and to revitalize those who have grown numb and lifeless. I have been there many times during the dark nights of my soul. My aspiration is that my own passion for teaching, and particularly for my subject matter, might become infectious, might somehow prevent at least a few other teachers from drying up or burning out. It is my firm conviction, born out of the struggle to come to terms with my own troubled *epektasis,* that a spiritual approach to teaching is the only way to keep from dying to ourselves and to one another.

CHAPTER TWO

Meeting My Mentor
The Passion for Politics

The entire purpose and process of education should be reconstructed. [We live] in a time when timeworn curriculums, traditional teaching and learning practices, indeed much of the inherited structure and function of education, [are] outmoded. Education, more than any other institution created by the only culture-building animal on earth, has the responsibility and opportunity to bring to all the children and adults of all countries the full import of the fearful and promising age in which we live…. The worst failure that educational leaders could commit today would be that of denying these millions the privilege of demonstrating their eagerness to transform education into an unconquerable agency of cultural change—change directed toward the single most compelling goal of our age: world civilization.
—Theodore Brameld, *Education as Power,* 1965

We shall not cease from exploration, and the end of all our exploring Will be to arrive where we started, and know the place for the first time.
—T.S. Eliot, *Little Gidding,* 1936

MY INITIAL ENCOUNTER WITH THE MOST FAMOUS PHILOSOPHER OF EDUCATION IN AMERICA

I met Theodore Brameld (1904–1987) in the early fall of 1965, my first year of doctoral work at Boston University. Who was this man, Theodore Brameld? For starters, he was one of the twentieth-century's leading educational scholar-activists. Born and raised in the Midwest, holder of a Ph.D. in Philosophy from the University of Chicago, and profoundly affected by a broad cultural-political movement called social reconstructionism, reaching its zenith from the 1930s to the 1960s, Brameld became an educational mover and shaker, along with such internationally renowned thinkers as George Counts and Harold Rugg. Of all the social reconstructionists involved with the famous *The Social Frontier: A Journal of Educational Criticism and Reconstructionism,* Brameld, in my estimation, was the thinker who built social reconstructionism into a carefully elaborated, systematic philosophy and anthropology of education.

Brameld chose to become a faculty member in the field of education, rather than in academic philosophy. Like John Dewey, he felt that philosophy needed to be more than an abstract, isolated field of study. Done well, it needed to be directly applied to the analysis and resolution of pressing social problems. Therefore, Brameld (1971) decided to cast his lot with the educationists, because in his words, they were "closer to the firing line of the human condition... dealing with such issues as severe economic dislocation, world wars, virulent nationalism, and racial and class exploitation..." (p. viii). He went on to teach at three large, urban universities, finally ending his long career at Boston University, where I studied with him. He often said to me that he never regretted his early choice to spend his entire career teaching in schools of education. Having made a similar choice in my own career, neither have I.

Brameld was a prolific author. Not only did he write more than a dozen very important books, but he wrote often for scholarly journals. He was a cofounder of the international Philosophy of Education Society. He was one of the first so-called public intellectuals as well, occasionally writing for lay magazines and newspapers in a jargon-free language that nonspecialists in educational philosophy could readily understand. He was a world traveler and lecturer, a scholar-activist who actually changed the face of education in such places as Puerto Rico, Korea, Japan, and Russia. He was a tireless public advocate for workers' rights, a national teachers' union that would incorporate the American Federation of Teachers, the National Education Association, and the American Association of University Professors, the United Nations Charter for Human Rights, and a radically restructured United Nations Educational, Scientific, and Cultural Organization. Brameld also worked hard for democratic decision making in all institutions, nuclear disarmament, social justice for all racial and ethnic groups, the teaching of controversial social issues at all levels of schooling, and some type of democratically conceived, internationally constituted world government, long before these became popular causes for Critical Pedagogues, multiculturalists, and global educators.

I remember vividly my first scheduled office meeting with Theodore Brameld. My intention, against all the well-meaning advice I had received, was to ask him to be my doctoral advisor for the length of my program. During my preliminary conversations with his colleagues and students, I found that some of his colleagues thought of Brameld as far more preoccupied with his own scholarship and worldwide consulting junkets than with the mundane tasks of advising doctoral students and helping them to write defensible dissertations. Several of his students found him to be overly demanding in the classroom and not at all adept at drawing out people. In a seminar, he was more comfortable lecturing at students rather than conversing with them. I recall a former advisee of his telling me that Brameld was a "self-righteous ideologue," and unless I were ready to agree wholeheartedly with his political and educational philosophy, which tilted distinctly leftward, I had better seek the support of someone else on the faculty.

Thus, on that crisp, fall morning in September, 1965, I waited anxiously outside Brameld's office door, fearful that he would immediately see right through me, and quickly dismiss me for the intellectual charlatan he would find it very easy to detect. Asking him to be my advisor was a huge risk for me to take because if he had said no, feeling rejected and unworthy, I would have walked away from the university for good. Here I was, a working-class, twenty-something, first-generation college graduate from a nonprestigious state university (once a teachers college), who had never once been outside the New England area. I was approaching an internationally famous scholar who often jetted off to Puerto Rico, Korea, Japan, and Russia as easily as I made the five-mile daily jaunt to Boston University from my home in West Roxbury, a working-class, ethnic neighborhood in the city of Boston.

When he finally called me into his office that morning, I stammered something inane like "Hello, Professor Brameld; I would like to study with you, because you come highly recommended." For years afterward, I wished I could have retracted that vapid greeting. The fact was that I had read much of Brameld's work when I was a master's student in English at another university. I was inspired by his educational vision, personal integrity, and philosophical brilliance. Having had no background at all in philosophy, at first I found his ideas dense and difficult to navigate. After a while, however, the complex concepts began to make sense. He was a clear and passionate writer, and I wanted, not just to understand him, but to be like him.

During that first meeting with Brameld, I tried awkwardly to tell him what I liked about his thinking. My effort was mostly in vain, though. His overall bearing was daunting: authoritative and professorial. Fiftyish, with an unlined face, and completely white-haired, Brameld leaned back in his chair, peered at me with bemusement over his reading glasses, and never once made a single, overt effort to draw me out. It was clear that if I had something on my mind, it was my responsibility to present it to him. His time was obviously precious, too valuable to spend with the likes of me, or so I thought. I grew more and more nervous, and so I bloviated. I tried too hard to impress him. Unfortunately, even though I got to know Brameld quite well during the three years I spent studying with him, I always remained a little tongue-tied in his presence. I never really felt that I belonged in his august company. This, of course, was my own peculiar problem, a reflection of my lifelong anxiety over not being good enough to move in the company of internationally renowned scholars with impeccable Ivy League credentials.

Sensing my nervousness during this initial meeting, graciously and discerningly, Brameld tried to put me at ease when I had finished making my case to work with him. He said:

> I'd be pleased to have you as my advisee. I've been looking over your résumé and your statement of purpose. I'm impressed. You've taken the trouble to read much of my material. You comment on some of my work very thoughtfully and, what I admire most is that you are critical at times. You are obviously not an apple-polisher. This is good. I don't like devotees. They bore me. I'd be pleased to have you as my advisee. You need to know, however, that you don't have to be a True Believer to work with me. Just read carefully, listen patiently, and make up your own mind about the validity of my ideas. Believe it or not, I look forward to learning as much from you as you do from me. I need my students to keep me honest. For now though, stop looking like such a frightened animal about to become a hunter's prey.

I left Brameld's office feeling great relief. Not only was I about to embark on an intensive intellectual journey with the leading philosopher of education in the country, but I knew I would like this man as a person. Happily, I sensed that he might like me as well. While I could hardly be aware of it at the time, and despite many philosophico-political fits and starts over the next three and one-half decades, Theodore Brameld was about to change the course of my entire life. I went on to take every graduate-level course that he taught at Boston University, he was my program advisor for all my time there, and he was the major inspiration and official sponsor for my dissertation—"A Philosophical Examination of the Educational Ideas of Ten American Anthropologists."

Also, I spent two weeks in Puerto Rico (the first time I had ever been out of this country) in connection with one of his seminars, "Educational Anthropology," where he and his students did original field research. As a result of that seminar, I published my first scholarly article detailing my findings in the prestigious *Journal of Education,* thanks to Brameld's influence with the editorial board. Later, he also used his influence with George Spindler, a very important educational anthropologist at the time at the University of Wisconsin, who published a revised, reduced version of my dissertation as the first chapter in his widely used, edited volume, *Education and Cultural Process,* in 1974.

Brameld was an unusually generous advisor and mentor, even though his academic standards, at times, seemed impossibly high. I remember waiting eagerly and fearfully for his initial feedback on the first draft of my just completed dissertation. He called me on the telephone and said simply:

> Robert, you use too many adverbs, you could have cut the size of the dissertation in half, you need to shorten your sentences which go on forever, and, in places, you end up merely *typing* when you should be *writing.* Oh, by the way, it is also the best dissertation I have read since I arrived at Boston University, and I will do everything that I can to help you get it published, after substantial revisions, of course.

Also, of no little importance, Brameld lobbied colleagues hard in other universities for my first teaching position. In this connection, I often went to professional conferences with him during the three years that we spent together. I enjoyed rooming with him and getting to know him as a compassionate and witty human being who also knew how to kick back and have a good time. Brameld knew everyone in the world who was a player in educational philosophy, it seemed, and he was always eager to introduce me to his colleagues. He made me feel that I was his professional equal, even though I knew that I was but a brash, albeit insecure, neophyte, looking to establish myself in a discipline that he himself had dominated for years. Brameld was very important to me at a formative stage of my life. In fact, he was always more than a simple advisor to his students; he was a living political and scholarly legend, and he was a faithful crusader on their behalf. Most of Brameld's students went on to become frequent publishers, speakers, and activists of one kind or another, due largely to the example that he set.

EDUCATION MUST ALWAYS AND EVERYWHERE BE POLITICAL

Remember that Brameld was writing mainly in the 1950s, 1960s, and 1970s. Some of his educational thinking was undoubtedly influenced by the ideas of progressive educators such as John Dewey, whom he greatly admired. Some of it was influenced by what he actually saw going on in too many schools and colleges: harried and burned-out teachers, and artificial disciplinary boundaries that prevented students from seeing the interrelationships between and among the various bodies of knowledge. He witnessed boring and repetitive drill and memorization and a dearth of hands-on, collaborative research and student/teacher action projects. He found curricula at all levels of schooling that were deadening because they were filled with irrelevant subject matter and slanted toward a narrow career training.

He also saw, via his firsthand field research, a number of run-down, long-neglected, inner-city schools, with their woefully unqualified teachers, their beaten-down minority students, and an all-too-predictable school ethos that expected failure, and, in fact, delivered it. In the suburbs, and in the elite private schools, he saw an intensive teaching-to-the-test so that students could get into the best colleges. Much of Brameld's educational thinking was obviously a product of his strong commitment to democratic process in every cultural institution, but particularly in the schools and colleges. Furthermore, some of his educational thinking was a function of his own training in social philosophy, when he was a graduate student of the symbolic interactionist, George Herbert Mead, at Chicago.

What I remember most keenly about Brameld's example, however, were the philosophical questions that he continually raised, both in his teaching and in his writing. He taught me that these questions were absolutely central to all levels of schooling. He wanted teachers to ask similar questions of themselves every single day of their lives:

- What are the larger purposes for which we are educating?
- When all is said and done, why do we keep on doing what we do in the schools and colleges of this nation?
- Why do we go back to our jobs day after day, month after month, year after year?
- What drives us, what sustains us, what do we care about, what makes it all worthwhile when, at the end of the day, we put our feet up and reflect on the meaning of our work and our lives?
- Is it education's chief role to be system-maintaining or system-transforming?
- How is education both a creature and a creator of the larger culture, an instrument and an impediment to advance the interests of those in power?
- Is it possible for the schools and colleges to be both system-maintaining and system-transforming and retain even a vestige of moral integrity?
- Is it possible for educators to reconstruct school and college cultures so that students' and teachers' needs take priority over bureaucratic imperatives?
- How can we enlarge curricula at all levels of schooling to deal with education's long neglected areas—values and the search for meaning?

To this day, I include some form of these questions, along with the ones that I ask toward the end of the previous chapter, in every syllabus that I construct. They are the backbone of each course that I teach. I make it a point to smuggle them into informal conversations with students, perhaps during a coffee session or on a walk from my office to the library. I also raise them openly in my lectures and seminar exchanges. To my colleagues' chagrin, I even push them at faculty meetings, but always with caution for fear of offending. I know that I drive many of my students crazy because these types of inquiries force them to go beyond the usual four Ts of educationists—training, testing, technology, and technique—for answers to the difficult educational decisions they must make on a daily basis.

In retrospect, I only wish that I had been given an opportunity in my own training to encounter these questions, both before and during my public school teaching experience. Not only would they have helped me to confront personal and professional issues around my own spiritual deprivation, but they would have helped me to place the successes and failures of my teaching in a larger, more realistic, institutional, and societal context. What I was and was not able to accomplish while teaching in my high school was a consequence of a much bigger nexus of sociopolitical and educational influences than I realized were operating at the time. I was not a lone wolf or free agent in the classroom, existing independently of the influence of others. I was actually an integral part of a complex network of persons, structures, traditions, and activities that both enhanced and impeded my development as a classroom teacher. What was becoming more obvious to me was that these same phenomena also influenced my students' development as well.

Regretfully, I had never learned how to connect in any serious manner with my colleagues at the high school where I taught. They, too, were cut off from one another. We just did not have the framework or the vocabulary to talk about modifying or transforming the structures that held us all back in the work that we did with students. All we ever did with one another when we got together was to carp and cavil about administrators, parents, and students. In retrospect, I realize that I never once confided in any genuine way to another colleague. I kept my most deeply felt disappointments and failures with students to myself. My colleagues and I did not know how to build a community. We did not see the world of education whole. What we did know all too well was how to perpetuate a culture of grievance and disparagement that only ended up exacerbating our personal and professional problems.

While I know that Brameld would have vigorously denied it, in my opinion, the types of questions he forced me to ask were profoundly spiritual in nature. It is true that, at one level, they were political, but, at another level, they were good for the soul. These kinds of questions, today, bring my students and colleagues face-to-face with what Walter Kaufmann (cf. Chapter 1) called our "ontological privation." They bring us back to existential basics. They remind us of our human finiteness but also of our limitless capacity for transcendence. They are laden with ideals. They elevate the usual methodological discourse in schools of education by emphasizing questions of purpose, meaning, and values. They are calculated to get students to think deeply, sometimes to grow angry, but always to reexamine the reasons why they chose to become educators in the first place. I will discuss in greater detail in subsequent chapters just why I believe that, at their core, questions like these are, indeed, spiritual.

Brameld's signal passion as a teacher was his unwavering, day-in and day-out commitment to politicize education at all levels of schooling. As an educational theorist, he was a macropolitical visionary. He saw the world tall, and he had little patience for those who only saw it small. When he looked at society, he saw the poverty amidst the abundance, the tyranny amidst the freedom, and the hypocrisy amidst the idealism. He looked at schools and colleges and found too many of them to be empty, fact-disseminating machines without a principled core. What education he saw there was predominantly what he called "transmissive" and "essentialist." Educational institutions appeared to be more interested in restoring the intellectual legacy of the past, or in training people to become personnel for jobs that ended up buttressing a reactionary status quo. This status quo, he believed, favored the empowerment of the few—the privileged—and the economic marginalization of the many—the oppressed—particularly the working class in this country and throughout the world.

Brameld found it impossible to disentangle schooling at all levels from what he called the "cultural dislocations" (by which he meant "crises" or "sharp discrepancies" both in the United States and elsewhere around the world) that pose "intolerable contradictions" in the way that people live their lives. He wanted to get the schools and colleges directly involved in examining, as well as in working together to solve, these cultural crises. From his Cold-War perspective of the 1950s, 1960s, and 1970s, Brameld saw worldwide institutions infected by "chronic instability, confusion, bifurcations, and uncertainties." A product of his time, he hated the totalitarianism of the Soviet Union. However, he also saw much in the United States that was totalitarian, albeit implicit, but still equally insidious in its own way.

For starters, Brameld (1971) identified several "disabling dualisms" not only deeply embedded in American life, but also in other societies throughout the world (pp. 24–37). He wanted the schools and colleges to play a part in ameliorating these "disabling dualisms" by becoming more overtly political, more concerned with constructing curricula that spoke to the global issues that threatened the well-being of humankind everywhere.

According to him, some of these dualisms were:

- an out-of-control self-interest at odds with the widely heralded Western ideals of social interest, interdependence, and international cooperation;

- troubling incidences of inequality, finding expression in subtle and not-so-subtle acts of bigotry, discrimination, and stereotyping, in obvious conflict with the Western rhetoric of equality and justice for all;

- a drift toward planlessness and a reliance on the invisible hand of capitalistic markets and technology to lead us all to the good life, at a time when national and international planning are necessary in order to avert drastic stock market swings, irrational technological exuberance, and an increasing distance between the haves and the have-nots;

- disturbing expressions of nationalism and parochialism at a time when internationalism might be the only way to avoid worldwide wars, global economic instability, genocide and ethnic cleansing, and nuclear holocausts;

- an alarming absolutism in religion and politics throughout the world when experimentalism, tolerance, cosmopolitanism, pluralism, and open-mindedness are necessary to overcome the temptation of totalitarianism, with its authoritarian prohibitions of free speech and democratic self-governance, repudiation of shared decision-making, and stifling of free expression in the arts and humanities.

Here is Brameld (1971) at his rhetorical best:

Frustrated as human beings have so often been by life-denying customs, by ignorance and superstitions, by cleavages in loyalty and other values, they have never approached anywhere near full command of their own energy, creative intelligence, and strength. They have been ruled over far more frequently than they have ruled. They have been starved, hoodwinked, exploited, cajoled, intimidated, frightened far more often than they have been decently fed, well informed, respected, encouraged, and aroused. With all the weaknesses that remain for human beings to conquer, the next development in human evolution will be the mature social development of humanity itself. This is the foremost task of education throughout the world today. (pp. 36–37)

Brameld believed that how people are taught to think is how they will act. For him, educators at all levels of schooling, and in an age-appropriate way, ought to be about the business of helping their students to develop the purposes, knowledge, perspectives, and skills to "build the new social order." It is only when educators are willing to think tall that they can begin to prepare their students to live small (in their local communities) and tall (in the world at large) in the most effective democratic ways. Brameld (1965) lived his entire life holding what he called his "one indispensable conviction": "Democracy, more than any form of society devised thus far by human beings, is capable of providing the greatest happiness for the largest number of people on the earth" (p. 223).

Brameld's zeal for a "world civilization" was unremitting. He believed that without some type of international order, without some form of world community, without some persistent, centralized effort on the part of international leaders to locate, affirm, and strengthen the universal values that could bind all civilizations together, then the "disabling dualisms" mentioned above would eventually destroy any hope for world peace. He wanted educators to be unashamedly utopian in their aims, by playing a pivotal role in creating political models for a new world order. Some overarching concept of world civilization, in Brameld's plan, was a way to integrate curricula that, for most of the twentieth century in which he lived, had remained thematically scattered and philosophically rudderless. He urged that the schools and colleges throughout the world ought to encourage students to talk openly and honestly about all the "disabling dualisms" which he spent a lifetime describing in his scholarship.

Finally, in response to those critics who accused him of being a utopian ideologue, of teaching a set of intractable, a priori, political blueprints, a golden calf that he wanted all of us to worship, Brameld (2000) had this to say:

As I regard it, the utopian mood never aims at ultimate perfection. Such an aim only invites rigid-minded faith in some form of spurious salvation either in heaven or on earth. I see no contradiction between the requirement of far-reaching cultural portrayals based upon substantial knowledge of all of the sciences and the arts, and the equal requirement of adequate room for radical corrections or additions to these portrayals. (p. 171)

Was I Really a Social Reconstructionist or a Skeptical Deconstructionist?

All of this represented pretty heady politics for the son of a very conservative, Irish, Boston policeman, and a stay-at-home Republican mother who voted enthusiastically for Barry Goldwater, and who also admired the anti-Communist "patriotism" of Senator Joseph McCarthy. My political worldview, if I were even to call it that, was mostly local, grassroots, and instinctively libertarian when I started my studies at Boston University. Politically, I thought very small, and I had no concept of what a tall politics might be. Mine was more the political heritage of Mayor Curley's ethnically provincial, Boston outlook on the world than it was of John F. Kennedy's Harvard-inspired, geopolitical worldview. By upbringing, I was a provincialist, not a cosmopolitan. I was state-college, not Ivy League, in my understanding of the purposes of education. I was working class, not ruling class, in the way that I thought about the helping professions. I was South Boston Irish Catholic, not North Shore WASP, in my religiosity.

To his credit, Brameld always refused to pigeonhole me. In fact, in all the time that I knew him, he never once asked me about any details of my past. Rather, he had faith that, whatever my background, I still had the ability, if I desired, to reconstruct my previous political and educational beliefs. In his estimation, I was a blank political slate awaiting enlightenment. With this attitude of acceptance and gentle persistence, Brameld got to me. His passion for building an international world body of some kind—where nations made the continuing commitment to live side-by-side in cooperative exchange in order to learn from one another's successes and mistakes in religion, history, art, culture, education, politics, and economics—was contagious. Brameld had a way of making all of his students feel a sense of educational and political urgency, and, most of all, he convinced them that their work was important. After all, if the schools and colleges were to become the central agencies in constructing a more humane world, then educators would become, in theory, the world-builders rather than the world-conservers. We would be educational and social reconstructionists!

Alas, I found it easier to be a one-world activist while I was Brameld's student than I did during the more nitty-gritty, career-building years following graduation from my doctoral program. While in graduate school, my classmates and I, many of them from working-class backgrounds like my own, saw ourselves to be on a prophetic mission to bring peace and justice to the aggrieved peoples of the world. The demonizing of the Soviet Union as a result of the Cold War, the relentless stockpiling of nuclear arms by the two superpowers, and what many Americans saw as a dangerous American adventurism in Southeast Asia, all conspired to turn many politically liberal students into campus radicals. We despised Richard Nixon, whom we viewed as the reactionary devil-incarnate. We marched proudly against the Vietnam War and for civil rights. We wanted to bring down the ignominious President Lyndon Johnson and his bureaucratic henchman, Robert MacNamara. We cheered loudly for Bobby Kennedy and Eugene McCarthy, vocal opponents of the war, and either of whom we believed would make excellent American presidents. We gladly stumped for Bobby and scrubbed for Gene.

We attended endless peace vigils and anti-government protests. I remember demonstrating on the campus of Boston University against the Vietnam War on a hot and humid weekday afternoon. The temperature in the sun had crept above 110 degrees. A profusely sweating policeman on the other side of the barricades approached me and my fellow war-resisters with sympathy and with bottles of ice-cold soda pop. The policeman was my father on a special work detail, and while he knew very well who I was, I pretended not to know him. Along with my friends, I arrogantly refused his gift. To this day, my father and I have never discussed the incident at any length, and whenever I bring it up, he abruptly changes the subject. It is obvious to me that he was deeply hurt by my supercilious behavior. For my part, I still experience a gnawing regret about the way that I treated him. I had put a political cause ahead of a family relationship and, at least for me, this was drastically out of character. I had denied a very important piece of my personal narrative in the same way that Brameld had by never asking me even one question about my story. I felt like a Judas Iscariot denying any knowledge of his Jesus.

My peers and I frequently lashed out publicly against American capitalism, and what we saw as the greedy corporatization of the world's economies. We criticized the nationalism of patriotic, middle-class Americans as being destructively ethnocentric. We stood in solidarity against the racism, sexism, and classism that we found evident everywhere, including the university, government, media, even the churches. We were absolutely convinced that the worldwide power struggle for market supremacy, initiated and orchestrated by the United States, commodified and cheapened every aspect of human existence. We indicted the schools and colleges for being system-maintaining and intellectually hidebound failures, preoccupied only with some mediocre, curricular, and instructional tinkering at the margins.

When I left the exciting, politically charged zeitgeist of Boston University in the late 1960s, I found myself reverting more to my working-class personality type. I realized after a while that temperamentally I was just not cut out to be a political reformer. I was less the social and political reconstructionist and more the philosophical deconstructionist. I loved doing the philosophical analyses required for any kind of thoughtful social and cultural reform, but I resisted practicing the day-to-day activism necessary to bring about major (or even minor) political change. This is where I find myself at the present time: politically sensitized to be sure, wavering inconsistently between a unique kind of postmodern libertarianism and a progressive liberalism. Always, however, I am more the detached observer and critical analyst than the in-your-face protester and social change agent.

I am still thinking small, but, I hope, not parochially. I am more comfortable attempting to affect individual attitudes instead of changing public policies. My driving mission, among other educational priorities, is to understand why a conservative politics speaks so convincingly to some people, while a progressive politics speaks more persuasively to others. My first instinct is to look for what makes people tick, what makes them so different in their passions and in the defining, personal stories they tell. My second instinct is to try to locate the common or overlapping philosophical and political grounds that people inhabit. I want to reconcile opposing worldviews wherever possible, rather than to dichotomize, and condemn, them. My natural tendency is to expose and resolve conflict rather than to let it fester and conflagrate. In my teaching, I encourage compromise over certainty, and consensus over condemnation.

For these reasons, I continue to be suspicious of imperious Critical Theorists and Critical Pedagogues on the left as well as doctrinaire, essentialist educators on the right. Each, in their own ways, end up disparaging and alienating their opponents. Each tend to be black-and-white, all-or-nothing in their worldviews. I miss the educational point of it all, even though I think I understand the hot passion in the contrasting political positions of both groups. How, I wonder, is it possible to be so certain that one or the other side possesses the whole truth? I left the Catholic Church in my youth for precisely this reason: All Truth was said to reside in Rome, to be dispensed and enforced by an infallible papacy and a loyal magisterium, encoded in a set of dogmatic principles, practices, and traditions. *(Extra Ecclesiam, nulla salus. Outside the Church, there is no salvation.)* At the present time, no dissent is acceptable to the Catholic Church hierarchy once Truth has been certified as Absolute and Inerrant by Papal Fiat. I could not live my inner or outer life within the prison of such uncompromising authoritarianism.

To this day, I find that I am personally attracted to dissenting Catholic theologians like Mary Daly, Hans Küng, Charles Curran, and Matthew Fox rather than to triumphalist conservatives like Pope John Paul II, John Cardinal Ratzinger, and Eternal World Television Network's Mother Angelica. While I reject outright the opposing theologies of both groups—each of which I find narratively displeasing and spiritually arid— I empathize more with the alternative-truths spirit of the dissenters. I readily acknowledge, however, that both groups can be equally polarizing in their views and equally rigid. How to stand up for what one believes without standing on top of others and crushing them is a question that I have spent many, many years exploring in my own teaching and scholarship.

In later chapters, I will talk about my attempts to construct what I call a "moral conversation" in order to deal openly, respectfully, and yet critically with genuine differences of opinion and belief in the classroom. I must admit that, as hard as he tried, Theodore Brameld was unable to conduct what today I think of as authentic moral conversations in his seminars. He never quite found the *media via* between fervent conviction for the cause and open-minded compassion for the difference of opinion. I identify painfully with his struggle, as later examples of my own failures (and successes) to discover the same *media via* will show.

I am, mainly, a pragmatist. I wonder how all those educators I know who are on the firing lines every single day would react to Brameld's large-scale utopian political expectations. Can the elementary school teacher who lives in my hometown, or the professor who teaches down the hallway from me, or the dean who sits in her office struggling to hold on to tenure lines that are in imminent danger of disappearing in the latest round of strategic budget cuts, afford the luxury of being big-picture educational reconstructionists? What if some educators are beaten down simply trying to tread water, striving to remain afloat each day and each semester in a profession that literally grinds down its practitioners? What if some educators are most at home with thinking small, teaching small, and administering small? What if, by temperament and choice, some are content mainly to create cooperative, life-affirming communities in their individual classrooms, colleges, human-service agencies, and even in their homes? Can they also be part of the reconstructionist revolution, without accepting the entire macropolitical agenda?

In my opinion, Brameld, if he were alive today, would applaud our individual efforts while reminding us that what we do in our individual classrooms, families, and communities inevitably contributes to the "whole complex of human dynamics through which every culture seeks both to maintain and to innovate its structures, operations, and purposes." He would urge us to keep our eyes on the larger prize: self-determination for each and every one of our students, regardless of their differences. He would also urge us to lobby for full democratic participation in all kinds of decision making, both for our students and their students as well, here and throughout the world.

Whenever we read Brameld's *Education as Power* (2000), I always ask my students the following pivotal question: To what extent do you think that Theodore Brameld, and other philosophers of education like him, ask too much of educators? Do you think that we should be taking on the work of politicians and change-agents for democracy, stumping for some grand conception of world order, when the demands on our time and energy seem positively overwhelming? Already, in addition to everything else that we educators do, we are asked to be multicultural advocates, social workers, guidance counselors, classroom management experts, home-school coordinators, interagency professionals, substitute parents, and conflict-resolution specialists, among sundry other vital functions.

Moreover, what if we do not agree with Brameld's politics? How will we be treated by the revolutionaries if we are seen as heretics in a reconstructed world democracy? Will there be room for a loyal opposition in Brameld's reconstructed world order? Do we need to be one-world advocates in order to support Brameld's overall philosophy of education? I am always struck that, as I ask these questions, I recall with some surprise and disappointment that Brameld himself never thought to surface them in his own teaching. I wish he had. I think that we would all have been richer for the exercise. For many years, my own resolve as a teacher has been to activate the voices of both the loyal and the disloyal opposition in my classroom. On some level, I suspect that Brameld would probably approve of my approach. I continue to ponder, though, why he was reluctant to subject his own true beliefs to the critical scrutiny of his students.

It was easy for me to be a youthful political activist on an urban university campus when the only real thing at stake was getting the next research paper written in time for class, or currying the favor of my doctoral advisor who was supervising my dissertation. My frenetic political activity in the 1960s never quite rang true to me, even during the period when I was caught up in the righteousness of it all. At least for me, it seemed too convenient, safe, and self-soothing. Frankly, it was an unearned assertion of moral superiority. It represented what the theologian, Rheinhold Niebuhr, once called "easy grace," a momentary passion with nothing to lose and with little staying power.

While I am convinced that, at the time, my classmates and I were genuinely sincere in openly declaring our social reconstructionist sentiments, and particularly in our anti-war activity, truth to tell, my own heart was never fully into the public expression of these political enthusiasms. To this day, I remain a skeptic concerning all types of True Belief, whether political, educational, religious, or ethical; whether on the right or the left; whether codified in the name of democracy, John Dewey, God, or Natural Moral Law.

I cannot help but think that, if he were alive today, my old mentor would challenge me on what he would see as a dangerous political vacillation that leads nowhere, an indecision that is in fact, counterreconstructionist. He would probably be right.

SOCIAL-SELF-REALIZATION

I have a reputation as a teacher at being good in drawing out students, in leading nonjudgmental discussions, and in keeping my opinions to myself unless asked directly for them. What I bring to the classroom has been shaped by three central ideas in Brameld's writing and teaching: social-self-realization, defensible partiality, and consensual validation. The first, social-self-realization, was, for him, the supreme goal of education.

Throughout Brameld's lifetime, he expressed a passion for universals, for those common purposes and objectives, if any, human beings might share, regardless of where, when, and how they lived their lives. This is one of the reasons why he turned to anthropology at the beginning of his career to supplement his philosophical training. He wanted to study other cultures in order to find these universals. As a result of his worldwide travels and extensive empirical examinations of other cultures, Brameld believed that certain physiological, psychological, and social needs were constant across all cultures. These included the needs for security, satisfying work, love, and play, belonging to communities and enterprises larger than the single individual, democratic self-determination, artistic and other forms of imaginative expression, and self-transcendence. He included all of these universal needs within his umbrella term, *social-self-realization*. Here is Brameld's (1965) shorthand definition of this term: "the desire of most human beings for the richest possible fulfillment of themselves both personally and in their relationships with other human beings through groups and institutions" (p. 93).

Although *social-self-realization* is a lofty term, somewhat abstract and awkward sounding, for Brameld, its practical implications for educators were huge.

- First, if it were to become the all-encompassing rationale and goal for education, it would influence everything that teachers included in a curriculum at all levels of schooling. It would force educators to look always at what people have in common rather than at how they are different. Knowledge, training, and skill development would be aimed foremost at helping people of all races, creeds, classes, and cultures to build a more satisfying life for themselves and others based on their similar needs and drives.

- Second, it would change the way educators look at themselves. Now they would start to believe that they are "members of a truly great profession because it is a profession of great purpose," engaged in doing a great work. Their morale would rise, and the important yet tedious details of their work would seem less burdensome.

- Third, teachers' instructional methods would now be guided by larger sociopolitical purposes calculated to bring people together rather than drive them apart.

- Fourth, subject matters would now be assessed according to the extent to which they furthered the social-self-realization of students, as well as all those whose lives were being touched in some way by these students, including family and friends.

While I never admitted this to Brameld, I have always harbored a genuine ambivalence regarding the concept of social-self-realization. On the one hand, I appreciate the idea of being committed to a goal such as social-self-realization. Brameld is saying that each of us is a social being as well as an individual being. In fact, without the former, realistically there can be no notion of the latter. This, of course, is a basic principle of postmodernism: Our affiliative contingencies define us in some very important ways. To think of individuals as "group-unsituated," "above-the-historicist-fray," "context-independent" free agents is to construct a narrative that bears little resemblance to how people actually develop and live their lives. I have written a great deal about individualism and communitarianism in educational thinking. Most of what I have written leads to Brameld's conclusion that individuals are most likely to become genuinely self-realized according to the extent to which they claim membership in a number of what the Harvard social philosopher, Michael Sandel, calls "constitutive," "sentimental," and "instrumental" communities (1982).

On the other hand, however, as a postmodernist, I have my serious doubts about the existence of what Brameld refers to as "human universals." To say that human beings everywhere share certain "psychological" and "social" needs does not seem very helpful to me because psychology and sociology are interpreted in so many different ways by so many different people. Human needs are as socially constructed as are notions of gender, race, social class, nationality, and ethnicity. I do not deny that people everywhere are similar in some ways. For one, their basic, human physiology does not differ that much, although interpretations of what constitutes fundamental physiological needs, and how these ought to be satisfied, differ from culture to culture. The imperatives of religion, politics, education, and geography, among others, always frame how we ought to deal with so-called, objective, physiological realities. Think, for example, of sex drives, diet, exercise, child rearing, and health care. I have had enough students from other cultures, even from subcultures in the United States, bring me up short whenever I am tempted to universalize what to me is self-evident truth, but to them is merely peculiar to the middle-class, mostly white, American university culture that I know.

Thus, I remain cautious whenever educational or political leaders, no matter how well-meaning, claim that their culture's needs ought ipso facto to be another culture's needs, on the grounds that these needs are "universal." I am convinced that claims of universality can too easily serve the interests of some powerful group's religious or political agenda by deliberately obliterating important differences between and among people and cultures. For this reason, I am very sensitive to the concern of some countries that America has no divine right to force democracy on nondemocratic governments, in the name of some universal need that people everywhere have to determine their own political destinies. I, myself, believe strongly in the value of democracy because this is the way I was raised.

For example, I have a philosophical ideal of human rights, and a conviction about what might violate those rights, that is very important to me. However, would I be willing to wage all-out war with those nations who are in continual transgression of these rights? Would I be more willing to stop short of war by supporting an international boycott against the exportation of essential resources and services to those nations? What if these actions meant inflicting inevitable collateral damage on civilians in those countries, particularly on the elderly and children? In the absence of some internationally agreed-upon, transcendent political authority, some all-encompassing religio-political grand narrative, why should others accept as a metacultural truth what I do? What if they have been raised to believe just as strongly as I that their systems of government are right and good for them?

Under the aegis of the United Nations, the United States has intervened throughout the world to stop bloodshed and to bring peace to troubled regions. Some of these interventions have been genuinely humanitarian, and some have been motivated by raw self-interest. Also, some interventions have been highly selective—e.g., the Gulf War—given the sheer geopolitical reality of American interests abroad. Therefore, what leaders consider to be a moral mandate to intervene in the affairs of other nations in the inviolable cause of human rights is a social construct, morally benevolent for some, but morally malevolent for others. No nation, like no individual or group, ever operates with an immaculate political perception that is morally flawless or independent of politics.

It seems to me that Americans need to tread lightly here. For example, many countries throughout the world deeply resent what they call the "imperialism of democracy" that they believe drives the international political agendas of the United States and other Western nations. Some countries, such as China, Iran, and Iraq, see Western talk of democracy as nothing more than an all-too transparent cover for transporting the evils of modernism, capitalism, and globalism to cultures struggling to be free of these demons. In our own country, the current Bush administration in Washington assumes that helping others in local communities is work best done by faith-based Judeo-Christian charitable organizations. This claim is made on the grounds that all Americans have a universal need to believe in something greater than themselves, if they are to find the will to change their troubled circumstances. Therefore, Judeo-Christian human service organizations are, at some levels, better equipped to transform people's lives than secular organizations.

I ask, who says so, and how can any political administration be so sure? I would also ask Brameld why the need for a world-community is a universal need. If it is, why, then, are there so many fervid nationalistic governments in the world that reject outright the very notion of a world-community? Other questions that arise for me in this connection are the following:

- Is the best way to teach for social-self-realization to build curricula around so-called universal human needs?

- More controversially, is a respect for diversity a universal human need, one that transcends individual cultures, times, politics, and geographies?

- If so, then what do we do with nations that pride themselves on their ethnic, racial, or religious homogeneity?

- Do we pluralists respect this type of diversity?

As a postmodernist, I am pleased to call myself an admirer of democracy, and a philosopher of pluralism, somebody who loves to encourage the free and open-ended circulation of multiple stories, philosophies, beliefs, and practices in my classroom. As yet, though, I am unwilling to claim any kind of universality for my love of pluralism. Does this mean, then, that I will always be something less than a social reconstructionist in my teaching?

Defensible Partiality

Defensible partiality (1965) was one of Brameld's favorite classroom strategies. It was a process he devised in order to force his students to think outside of what today I would call the "dogma box." He did not want his students to be content simply to parrot clichés about their overall educational or political purposes, or to fall back on their unexamined dogmas and doctrines to justify their professional practices. Brameld wanted everything put on the table in the classroom so that teachers and students alike could subject their "partialities" to the rigorous examination of others. His way to keep his own constructs from becoming rigid with his students was to demand compelling evidence, sound reasoning, and excellent argumentation in order to back up one or another of his truth claims. He expected no less of us.

Brameld insisted always that our partialities be defensible, that they be constantly exposed to public inspection, to the free and critical flow of communication. Nothing must ever be taken for granted. Brameld (1965) believed that, unfortunately, educators in this country and elsewhere were teaching concepts such as capitalism (what he thought of as "competitive enterprise motivated by the desire for profit" [p. 160]), communism, and many of the world's religions, through indoctrination rather than through a rigorous process of defensible partiality. Here is Brameld on the meaning of defensible partiality: "What we learn is defensible in so far as the ends we support and the means we utilize are able to stand up against exposure to open, unrestricted criticism and comparison. What we learn is partial in so far as these ends and means still remain definite and positive to their democratic advocates after the defense occurs" (p. 157).

What Brameld means is that, if we are being true to the principle of defensible partiality, we can never disregard the impact of sound, honest criticism of our educational ends and means. We need to be on guard always to avoid becoming dogmatic, or impatient with people who may genuinely and convincingly disagree with us. The only alternative to the use of defensible partiality in our teaching is indoctrination, which Brameld felt was nothing more than "card-stacking propaganda."

In this regard, Brameld made what I think is a useful distinction between prejudices and convictions. Prejudices were opinions and attitudes hastily, illogically, and emotionally shaped. Convictions, by contrast, were opinions and attitudes carefully, logically, and consciously shaped, but, more importantly, they were beliefs exposed to rigorous public scrutiny, debate, and critique. Defensible partiality was Brameld's way of trying to keep his pedagogical means consistent with his political ends (full democratic participation for all involved constituencies).

Defensible partiality is a process that I find very useful in my own teaching. In my ethics courses, I often say to my students that good ethical decision making in our professions is all about defensibility. We must be able to defend (give sound reasons for) the decisions we make, and these need to stand up to the public scrutiny of a jury of our peers. I also remind them that declarations of belief are rarely conversations about belief. Genuine conversations about our convictions, as opposed to declarations of our prejudices, require a self-critical and self-correcting, mutually respectful, back-and-forth, open-ended process of inquiry. This is what my notion of moral conversation is all about, and, without a doubt, Brameld's influence on my construction and use of this communications process is incalculable.

I still waver though. Is it really possible to subject our pet political, religious, and educational convictions to Brameld's rigorous process of defensible partiality without, at some point, accepting the fact that real compromise, or maybe even relinquishment, of our most heartfelt ideals might be necessary? Brameld himself believed so fervently in his reconstructionist political convictions, for example, that there were times in his courses when I was honestly reluctant to challenge them, even though he invited me and others to do this all the time. I am more than willing to admit that this was probably more my problem than his. Still, his convictions were so strong and well thought out that few people in his seminars were willing to take him on. Because we rarely challenged him, we never learned just how far Brameld was willing to go in making concessions and changes in his own partialities. In fact, in all the time that I studied with him, I always felt that Brameld, deep down, held so fast to certain partialities of his— e. g., world government—that, despite his rhetoric of open-mindedness, the convictions were really sacrosanct.

How, then, I ask teachers today, does one keep one's defensible partialities from unwittingly turning into ossified doctrines? How do we avoid intimidating, or worse, silencing, students with the force of our most profoundly held convictions? Is it possible that what we might perceive, at times, to be a unanimous endorsement by our students of our political, religious, or educational convictions is actually an expression of their reluctance (read fear) to take us on, so passionate and self-righteous are our positions? The line between enthusiastic and informed conviction and card-stacking proselytization and bullying is very thin for all of us. How, then, can we stand up for the things we believe with all our hearts and minds without standing on top of, and suppressing, those who believe differently and far less strenuously? Brameld, particularly in the middle and later stages of his career, grew acutely aware of this danger, but I do not think he ever came up with an answer. Neither, by the way, have I, but I am still trying.

Consensual Validation

Consensual validation (Brameld 1965) is closely related to defensible partiality. It is an attempt on the part of the teacher to secure some type of cooperative agreement from others on the ends or purposes that will direct the work of the group. For Brameld, it is the best way to resolve differences peacefully and ecumenically. Brameld warned that consensual validation must never be forced, however. Due process is always to be respected in the sense that dissension in a group must be given a full voice. Consensual validation as a way to reach both short- and long-term political and educational goals is a practical necessity, in that it keeps conversations from deteriorating into an endless spinning of wheels. It also recognizes that any kind of conversation needs a terminus somewhere along the way if it is to be constructive.

Consensual validation, while attractive as a democratic goal, and no matter how useful in coming to agreements, must never become a substitute for a Final Truth. I have seen too many conversations in my own classroom terminated prematurely because students felt the need to arrive at some kind of quick consensus, to tie up the loose ends, even though an agreement might have been artificially forced. Another point to remember is that consensus in and of itself has little to do with whether we have arrived at Truth because truth has nothing to do with how many people support its claims. Whole nations, similar to whole classrooms, can be wrong, because numbers alone do not constitute Truth. A consensus may point the way to a truth, but, in itself, it is not The Truth.

In my own teaching, I sometimes strive for group consensus in ethical decision making, or in setting up ground rules for how a group will undertake a moral conversation together, or in assessing the morality of a particular ethical practice. Sometimes, however, group consensus is impossible to achieve. At times, it is simply contraindicated, because some controversial topics are best left unsettled, some ideas are best left in a muddle, and some readings lend themselves to multiple interpretations, beyond the reach of a larger consensus as to their precise meanings. How, for example, is it ever possible to reach an authentic group-consensus in pluralistic local communities around such divisive educational topics as creationism, prayer in public schools, the posting of the Ten Commandments in public places, vouchers, standardized testing, sex education, multicultural education, and character education? I think that Brameld is well aware of the trouble spots in achieving any kind of group consensus. I must confess, however, that at this time in my life, as group consensus has become a less important, explicit goal to me as a teacher, it has finally become achievable in certain settings and under certain carefully qualified conditions. I no longer feel the need to force it. Instead, I have learned to accept it as a gift when it happens, but also to accept it as a gift when it does not.

I have had much success in stimulating thoughtful conversations about
pluralism, truth, ideology, discourse, and dissent whenever I ask the following types of questions about consensual validation:

- How do you avoid equating consensual validation with Truth? Or
  are the two equivalent in your thinking?
- Where, in the work that you do, is there space in your own consensual validations for otherness, difference, or even heresy?
- To what extent do you allow the apostates in your groups to modify, perhaps even change, some of your group's consensual validations?
- Isn't the antipathy aimed at political correctness by some students
  fueled by their skepticism that so-called consensual validations in
  the academy on matters of race, gender, ethnicity, and sexual orientation might be just another name for group-think or political
  coercion with a happy, democratic face?

VALUES AND EXISTENTIALISM

Listen to Brameld (2000) on the need to "axiologize" education at
all levels of schooling in America:

> The time is already well passed when we can afford to indulge in the lux-
> ury of cluttered curriculums, in spurious academic aloofness rationalized in
> the name of objectivity, in confused if not often obsolete codes of moral con-
> duct, and in stultifying ambitions to grasp the dubious goals of success and
> status at whatever cost to our personal and communal integrity. For the grim
> truth is that nothing less than the life of mankind as a whole is now in pre-
> carious balance. To reassert that values are education's most neglected
> problem is really to insist that we no longer have any genuine choice but to
> bring the nature and meaning of values out of the shadowy background and
> into the spotlight of sustained concern on every level of learning from
> kindergarten through the university. (p. 148)

I learned how to be a values educator as a result of my contact with
Theodore Brameld. In my own case, this has been Brameld's lasting intellectual legacy. Thanks to him, I realize that before I am anything else as a
teacher, I am an axiologist. This is a philosophical term that refers to
someone who studies values in order to determine their meaning, origins,

types, criteria, and knowledge status. Less technically, however, I am proud to admit that I am not just someone who examines values from a distance. I am also a teacher whose driving mission is to engage students at middle and upper levels of schooling in vigorous values conversations. I am a values provocateur, as several examples in the chapters to come will verify. The following sorts of questions, in addition to the previous lists of questions that I have enumerated earlier, usually guide my axiological provocations in the seminar room:

- What should we know?
- How should we live together?
- What moral principles should guide our lives?
- What spiritual commonalities should bind us together?
- How can we treat each other more humanely?
- What should we value?
- What should we believe?
- How can we build a more peaceful and just world?

One of what Brameld (2000) famously called his "values frontiers" was *existential humanism*. He urged teachers to bring values like this one "out of the shadowy background and into the spotlight of sustained concern on every level of learning" (p. 100). Although Brameld's understanding of existential humanism remained resolutely atheistic and centered on the here-and-now, he encouraged educators to emphasize the following principles among others:

- Abstract categories and neat conceptual systems fail to grasp the fundamental mystery of human existence. There is always something more, something beyond human comprehension.
- Educators need to raise questions with students about the "human predicament," dealing with such issues as alienation, anxiety, inauthenticity, dread, sense of nothingness, and anticipation of death.
- While the universe has no rational direction or creative scheme, and though, in some senses, it is meaningless and absurd, there is still more to life than meets the rational eye.

- In spite of the "death of God," and the loss of a Transcendent Moral Authority to ground values and ethics, people still need to be responsible for their actions as well as for the actions of others.

I would add to Brameld's existential principles the following principles of my own, with their educational and religious analogues:

- Death is inevitable and final, and, despite our denials and evasions, it awaits all of us someday. Educators need to help students cope with, and overcome, the anxiety and avoidance usually associated with this reality. Students must understand that they are not immortal, and they will not live forever, that aging and dying are necessary dimensions of being fully human, and that life truly begins when one's finitude is fully grasped. Therefore, the one question worth asking every single day is this: Given the fact that I will die—who knows when? possibly tomorrow, possibly in a thousand tomorrows, possibly in ten thousand tomorrows—how then do I choose to live my life right now?

- How can we solve the dilemma of using our hard-won freedoms from the older, dominating religious and political myths in order to re-create ourselves and our world in the absence of traditional gods and authority figures? If, as some existentialists claim, there are no final, unimpeachable answers to be found in the consoling, metaphysical fictions of the past, where, then, do we go to learn how to be free and purposeful in our daily lives? How do we avoid the despair of meaninglessness that, for some, leads to what Albert Camus once called the "metaphysical revolt." This is the choice to commit suicide, or to live an escapist life of nihilism, hedonism, or consumerism, as ways of coping with the loss of the older metaphysical certainties. Knowing that, in the end, each of us is condemned to make meaning, what are the most effective ways to make the wisest choices in our own, and others', best interests? How can educators help young people use their personal freedoms to become independent agents in the world, but agents acting always with prudence, compassion, and responsibility toward others?

- As one of the prices to pay for the personal freedom gained from the breakdown of the older authoritarianisms, how can we help students to deal with the inevitable isolation and solitude that form the unique destiny of each and every human being? Better still, in the face of this unavoidable isolation and solitude, how do we inspire students to reach out to others in order to form relationships and community, the necessary preconditions for finding happiness and fulfillment in a self-constructed world?

- Finally, existentialism confronts each of us with a double paradox. We need to find or create a meaning in a life that has no intrinsic meaning. We must also understand that meaning-making is more a by-product of living a life of activity and purpose than something consciously sought as a fixed product. If this double paradox is valid, how, then, do educators encourage meaning-making in the face of what some now-disillusioned students reared in traditional religions will see as ultimate meaninglessness? Also, how do we convince students that, often, the finding of meaning is indistinguishable from the process of pursuing it? Meaning is not an external goal to be pursued but the aftermath of an activity to be enjoyed for its own sake.

Existential humanism has been the necessary precursor for post-modernism in my own life. Moreover, it has irrevocably shaped my personal pursuit of a spirituality that I can live and teach in good faith. I could be mistaken, but, in my opinion, Brameld showed signs that he was starting to understand, after years of wrestling with questions of deeper meaning in his own life, that although egalitarian decision making was a vital part of living and learning in a democracy, life as a whole must include something more than believing in a progressive politics. I like to think that I might have been at least a minor influence in this subtle change of direction in his thinking. Perhaps, through our many, personal conversations about the ultimate inability of a progressive (or regressive) politics to confer lasting meaning on people's lives, Brameld began to expand his thinking about values and philosophy to include elements that were not always rational, logical, or susceptible to precise social planning. I would be honored if this had been the case.

In my own estimation, life can never be fully explained by referring only to the social and cultural contingencies that help to shape it. While social determinists and critical theorists might concur with the existential humanist that indeed "existence precedes essence"—that is, class interests and judgments always come before, and influence, so-called "objective" or rational judgments about the truth of existence—nevertheless, the two depart in a major way. For the existential humanist, there is, according to Brameld (2000), a "fundamental, unrational, primordial self" that precedes all sociological and cultural contingencies, including class interests. Moreover, the existential humanist, in Brameld's words, is "trying to help us face the truth that there is something dreadful about reality. This dreadfulness centers in the mystery and inevitability of death" (p. 128).

At the present time, a postmodern philosopher like Richard Rorty, another major influence on my own thinking, and one of the main reasons why I have come to embrace a postmodern view of the world, would challenge the existential humanist. He would energetically repudiate the assumption that any self could ever be pre-existent, capable of transcending its context and contingencies, or even that there is anything resembling a primordial self that is not socially constructed. He would also say that if there is something "dreadful" about reality, it is only because people have imposed this particular narrative structure on what the American philosopher, William James, once called the "blooming, buzzing confusion" that characterizes their lives.

Brameld appeared to believe otherwise, and even though today I am a Rortyian through and through, as will become evident in the pages ahead, I cannot help but side with Brameld on this point. This is the spiritual part of me that always seems to lie dormant beneath my postmodern posturings. Rorty can be arrogantly, even disdainfully, antispiritual in much of his writing. Not I, however. Partly in response to those critics who attacked him on the pretext that his philosophy of educational reconstructionism was excessively rationalistic and triumphantly utopian (the same type of criticism that Rorty often receives), Brameld set out in some of his later writings to demonstrate that his philosophy of education did indeed possess a tragic sense. Influenced by the work of existentialists like Heidegger, Tillich, and Unamuno, Brameld frequently spoke in his later years of the depth and significance of being, in the midst of the utter finitude of human life. He spent some of his final years trying to add a dimension to his social reconstructionism that "deepened the meaning of being, the meaning of both subjective and objective reality." In my opinion, he was only partly successful in achieving this goal.

It is becoming clearer to me that I am taking over, in my own way, where Brameld left off. I am trying to deepen the meaning of being in my teaching and writing, often with mixed success, however. The dumb, indomitable, quotidian reality of human life, with its incessant nowness and ordinariness, often overpowers any meaning that a deeper sense of being might have for me. I am an instinctive materialist, a pragmatic realist, someone who lives mainly in the here-and-now. My taste for the physical world, with all of its diverse sensory delights and challenges, but also with its comfortable routines and satisfying commonplaces, can frequently be a much greater lure for me than the metaphysical. However, at times, my desire for a meaning that transcends the material present and the consolations of the ordinary can also be intensely seductive. Despite these apparent contradictions, I persevere, nevertheless, in attempting to understand the mystery of being that often grasps my students but eludes me.

I listen with envy to many of them express, both in private and in public, their complete wonder over the incomprehensible miracle of their existence. I am touched by the transcendent sense of joy they experience in their contacts with nature, pets, and children. I am inspired by the serious commitments they make to public service, to enduring, loving relationships, and, increasingly, to religious communities where they might be able to find the spiritual meaning that too often gets away from them in the day-to-day stresses of the career rat race. I am struck by their desire to find something that they can believe in, something, in the words of Diana Eck, that they can give their hearts to. I am haunted by the comment of one of my students, a postdoctoral fellow in educational philosophy, who said to me one day: "I have had upwards of twelve years of post-secondary education, most of it in the humanities, and only once in any classroom was I encouraged to talk honestly and openly about the sense of mystery and depth that I frequently experience in my own life. Ironically, this occurred in an undergraduate course on socio-biology. Thank you for giving me this opportunity, on the eve that I am about to enter the ranks of the professoriate."

Richard Rorty, the Critical Theorists, and other contemporary post-modernists could stand to take seriously Brameld's own late-life insight that there is more to life than simply coming to grips with the impress of our cultural contingencies, or unmasking the reactionary political pretensions of those in power. I am convinced, along with Brameld, that we live, too, within the imprint of a mystery so vast that, at times, it dwarfs our immediate sociological predicaments. The trouble with postmodernism is that it remains oblivious to the ultimate riddle of what it means to be human. As a teacher, I make my best connections with students whenever I temper my postmodernism with the tragic sense of existentialism. Existentialism gives postmodernism a depth that it sorely needs, if it is to speak with conviction to many of today's aimless, yet desperately searching, Gen-Xrs and Millennials. The existential lesson for postmodern educators everywhere is to encourage students to live courageously, purposely, and actively in the face of all of life's perplexities, particularly in response to the ever-widening sense of anomie that leaves so many young people today feeling helpless and hopeless.

VALUES AND RELIGION

Possibly Brameld's most controversial proposal for rejuvenating the value dimension of education in America was to encourage teachers to deal openly with religion at all levels of schooling, in a manner that was neither subservient, dogmatic, nor propagandistic. In the 1960s when he first broached this particular "values frontier," the proposal was thought to be highly controversial. In some ways, I think that it is even more controversial today. For Brameld, moral and character education was incomplete if it refused to tackle religious issues head-on. Although Brameld himself remained a lifelong skeptic toward institutionalized religion, he still understood how important the life of the spirit was to human beings everywhere. His own view was that human beings, not a God or a Supreme Force, ought to direct the course of their own lives. They should make their own rules and laws, in cooperation with one another, while eschewing any supernatural "quest for certainty," to use John Dewey's (1960) phrase. This hope in the value of collaborative human effort to build a better, more peaceful world, despite so much of the counterevidence of history, represented Brameld's nascent spirituality.

As a secular humanist with strong, still evolving, existential leanings, Brameld (2000) held that if life was to be made better for all peoples, then human beings "needed to build it through their own struggles, their own aspirations, their own scientific and creative powers" (p. 123). From his reconstructionist perspective, the Ten Commandments were actually cultural constructions that people shaped out of their experiences, in order to invent a better way to live productively and peacefully with one another. For Brameld, teachers who frequently engaged in the debate around the proper place of religion in American education usually lined up on one or the other side of the conservative-progressive divide. Brameld's own preference, based on his belief that education was "primarily modification" rather than "transmission," was progressive. He often declared that what human beings actually needed was less faith in a supernatural creature who supported the status quo and more faith in their own powers to upset the status quo in order to create a better world.

Despite his own partiality for a scientific or secular humanism, Brameld was convinced that human beings would never succeed in grasping the full meaning of their existence. Even with the remarkable breakthroughs in astronomy, cosmology, and physics, Brameld realized that we still knew relatively little about the nature and destiny of the universe. In the 1960s, when Brameld's reputation reached its zenith, there was not a shred of direct, incontrovertible evidence that life actually existed on other planets. Today, the same holds true. Thus, while we possess great scientific power to comprehend and control nature and human nature, there is still an enormous amount that we do not know about the mystery of existence. At this point in history, we can only continue to investigate its enigmas, while marveling at the variety of religious approaches that people have taken since the beginning of human time in order to understand and appreciate it.

To this end, in 1965, Brameld came up with a thoroughly radical proposal: The schools must allow students to study in depth the "great religious approaches to life and the universe—Oriental, Occidental, humanistic, theistic" (p. 165). Along the way, students must also learn that while religions have, throughout human history, been sources of enormous hope in the presence of fear, hatred, and ignorance, they have also failed to deliver fully on their promise to create a world of universal love and compassion. At the present time, a number of prominent educational philosophers (see Nash 1999, *Faith, Hype, and Clarity,* for complete documentation) are just beginning to make a similar case. Like Brameld, they believe that students need the time and space in schools and colleges to study the great existential and religious questions. In my opinion, however, none have said it with more élan than Brameld.

Brameld (1965) favored a critically robust dialogue on religion. He was insistent that teachers should encourage students to understand, compare, criticize, and argue about the virtues and vices of the greater and lesser religious orientations with one end in view. This was to arrive "at their own free agreements or disagreements as to which, if any, of the major religious philosophies offers them the most help and the richest promise." The following comments remain trenchant, and necessary, even today, as some experiments to teach about religion in the public schools and colleges of America take either an innocuous or a dogmatic form: teaching the Bible as benign literature, or teaching the Bible as The Revealed Word of God.

> Nor do I believe that it is at all improper for education to be imbued with the quality of religiosity—certainly not if one defines that word in such nonsectarian terms as the total devotion of any person to the search for life's highest values. What *is* improper, of course, is any kind of education that allows religiosity to overcome the completely equal requirement of critical and constant readiness to examine *every* commitment and to correct *every* weakness that such examination may expose. (p. 165)

I intend in a later chapter to discuss my own take on teaching about religion and spirituality. Thus, I will wait until then to present my thinking on this issue in more detail. Suffice it to say here, however, that without Brameld's pioneering proposal to discuss the world's religions in public school and college classrooms, I never would have entered this arena on my own. Thanks to him, I realized that I could be a postmodern skeptic about the influence of institutionalized religion in my own life and still encourage the open exploration of religio-spiritual values in the classroom. Brameld helped me to see that religious commitment is one way of searching for life's highest values. As such, the topic of religion deserves a place in the classrooms of every public school and university in the United States.

Furthermore, Brameld's firm conviction that while religious dialogue must always begin with genuine respect, as a credible subject matter it must also allow for dispassionate, critical examination, along with a commitment to "correct every weakness" that comes out of such an open-ended discourse. We expect to do this with other content in the curriculum, so why not with religion? We make a decision not to neuter or to indoctrinate the ideas that we teach in other academic fields. This dual objective—respectful investigation and constructive critique of religions—although, in my experience, far more challenging and complex than Brameld thought, has consumed a large portion of my teaching and scholarship in the university, especially during the last decade. I regret that Brameld himself never got around to implementing the "values frontier" of religion in his own teaching. I could have learned from both his successes and failures. It took me almost three decades even to get up the courage to construct a formal course offering in this area. In retrospect, and even though I have spent thirty-plus years surreptitiously smuggling this material into a number of other courses, I realize that I am still fumbling with how to teach this content fairly and effectively.

"THE END OF ALL OUR EXPLORING
WILL BE TO ARRIVE WHERE WE STARTED"

Because I lost touch with Brameld during the later years of his life, I was always curious as to whether he himself had ever come to embrace a belief in some kind of transcendence, some kind of meaning beyond political or scientific meaning. While at Stetson University in Florida, in the year 2000, speaking at a conference sponsored by Brameld's Society for Educational Reconstruction, I did something I had been wanting to do for many years. I took the risk of violating Brameld's privacy during his final days by asking his Japanese-born widow, Midori Matsuyama, if her husband had died a spiritual person. I know that he had suffered from a variety of debilitating physical ailments during the last year of his life. She appeared startled by my question and did not answer immediately.

Later that evening, just before dinner, she whispered to me in her very gentle way: "Robert, Ted was always looking for something more in his life. He never stopped growing. He often tried to meditate, and he was strongly attracted to Zen Buddhism. But he died a convinced scientific humanist to the core. I hope that you are not disappointed." No, of course I am not disappointed. In fact, in re-reading Brameld today, from my own perspective as someone who is both a secular humanist and a tireless spiritual seeker, I find in his writing, particularly in his later work, a profound sense of spirituality, even though it is mostly tacit. I sometimes wonder, though, if I too will live the last years of my life as Brameld did: maybe wanting what William James once referred to as the "More" but settling for the "less" that, in all likelihood, is what there actually is.

After I completed my formal studies with Brameld, our personal interactions were on-again, off-again when I left the Boston area. Toward the end of his life in the mid 1980s, our relationship—beyond his according me the great honor of asking me to do an essay review for the *New York Times* of what he thought was the capstone book of his whole career, *Patterns of Educational Philosophy,* published in 1971, and which I somewhat arrogantly turned down because I was busy with more "important" things—was practically nonexistent. Today, I deeply regret not doing that review; even more, I am remorseful over losing touch with my old mentor for the last decade before he died. I never had a chance to tell him about the career-long impact he had on my teaching and writing, even when I was trying to forge my own intellectual identity and independence. It has only been during the last few years that I have become aware of his lasting influence on me. After all my exploring, to repeat T. S. Eliot's words in the title that heads this section, I have indeed arrived at the place where I first started.

Although I have rarely used Brameld's exact vocabulary in my writing and teaching, I have dealt at length with many of the same issues he did, and from an eerily similar perspective. All of my scholarship, for example, is rooted in a stance of progressive liberalism. Better still, using Brameld's language, I come out of a cultural interpretation that today I would call a postmodern reconstructionism. This is a creative reconfiguration of Richard Rorty's neopragmatism, Jurgen Habermas's neoliberalism, and Brameld's social reconstructionism. Rorty aestheticizes and ironizes public conversation. Habermas rationalizes and politicizes it. Brameld democratizes and internationalizes it. I also promote a view of education that is more transformative than transmissive, one that challenges, deconstructs, and looks for more democratic alternatives to established politico-educational arrangements, rather than one that simply accepts, and adapts to, them.

As a professor, I am first and foremost a values educator. I have developed a number of courses in several disciplines that push students in many human service professions to examine closely, and when necessary to amend, their axiological biases. While some of these courses may not be as overtly political as Brameld would have liked, they would, I think, please him very much. I have spent the last decade of my life in higher education attempting to create both a *modus operandi* and a *modus vivendi* for people in a number of professional venues to communicate respectfully yet candidly with each other across their ideological differences. The purpose of this is to find some common philosophical and political ground that we all can stand on, if only for a little while. Brameld's influence on this communication process, as I mentioned in a previous section, has been large.

I have also arrived at another place where I first started, and this is closer to my own social and religious upbringing. I know today that I am both a social reconstructionist *and* a postmodern constructivist. I acknowledge, too, that I am a bundle of contradictory philosophical, educational, political, and religious tendencies, none of which is pure or absolute, and each of which is seriously, but not fatally, flawed in some way. On many days, I am a social utopian, a pluralist whose politics of difference can be very passionate. On other days, I am a cultural conservative, a libertarian whose convictions can be equally as fervid. On most days, I rejoice that I am long since free of organized religion's suffocating influence. However, there are also those days when I envy the metaphysical certainties and consolations of the churched-up True Believers who manage to find their way to my courses. I struggle to make sense of this philosophical-religious mishmash, and I openly, sometimes defiantly, share this personal conflict in the seminar room with my students, as well as in publications with my readers.

Of one thing I *am* certain, though: I will carry a piece of Theodore Brameld—ambivalences and all—with me into the remaining years of my teaching, as well as into my retirement. As I close this chapter, I can only say, rest in peace, old friend, and thank you for your patience in helping me to arrive, finally, at the place where I started, but in my own way and in my own time. Per your example, I will continue to allow my own students the same time and space to find themselves.

CHAPTER THREE

Becoming A Constructivist
The Passion to Teach About Morality

Critics of moral relativism think that unless there is something absolute, something which shares God's implacable refusal to yield to human weakness, we
have no reason to go on resisting evil. If evil is merely a lesser good, if all
moral choice is a compromise between conflicting goods, then, they say, there
is no point in moral struggle. The lives of those who have died resisting injustice become pointless. But to us pragmatists moral struggle is continuous
with the struggle for existence, and no sharp break divides the unjust from
the imprudent, the evil from the inexpedient. What matters for pragmatists
is devising ways of diminishing human suffering and increasing human
equality, increasing the ability of all human children to start life with an equal
chance of happiness. This goal is not written in the stars, and is no more an
expression of what Kant called "pure practical reason" than it is of the Will
of God. It is a goal worth dying for, but it does not require backup from
supernatural forces.
—Richard R. Rorty, *Philosophy and Social Hope,* 1999

In the end…what matters is our loyalty to other human beings clinging
together against the dark, not our hope of getting things finally right.
—Richard R. Rorty, *Consequences of Pragmatism,* 1982

ARRIVING AT THE UNIVERSITY OF VERMONT AS A MORAL EDUCATOR

I believe that I left Boston University a more consistent and committed existentialist than Brameld. From his perspective, he rightly used existentialism as a tool to strengthen and deepen his ideal of achieving a global,
democratic social order. Existentialism, for him, humanized (and spiritu-
alized) the quest for political solutions to age-old human conflicts, to the

social dilemmas of existence that have confounded human beings since their origins. For Brameld, existentialism was a very important, philosophical means calculated to bring about a greater socio-political end. He never took his utopian eyes off what for him was the greater ideological prize: a democratic world community. Existentialism was his way of tempering a dream of achieving absolute political perfection. He reasoned that if there is always a tragic, inexplicable dimension to human life, then utopian political arrangements, no matter how desirable, will always fall short of ultimate perfection. Despite this reality, however, we must forge ahead, in good existentialist fashion, to push Sisyphus's heavy stone of hope and expectation up the hill.

In contrast to Brameld, at the time, I allowed existentialism to get into my soul's fiber, to completely define my way of viewing and being in the world, to become almost a philosophico-spiritual end in itself. I was less interested in what existentialists call the problem of "intersubjectivity" than I was in coming to terms with my own conflicted subjectivity. Existentialism became my primary way of constructing meaning. It gave shape, focus, direction, and reason to my life. Its emphasis on self-creation, chance, choice, freedom, courage, finitude, anxiety, and the tragic sense of life thoroughly demolished my early Catholicism as well as my working-class view of reality.

Existentialism helped me to make sense of failure, evil, suffering, responsibility, and loneliness, at least for a while. I no longer blamed others for my weaknesses and sense of powerlessness. I no longer looked to the distant heavens for supernatural assistance. Existentialism helped me to understand that, whether or not I liked it, *I, and only I,* was the determining agency in the living of my own life. Thus, I had to accept the responsibility at all times to choose wisely and to live authentically and courageously. I had to live my life this way, even though there might be cowardice, corruption, compromise, and chaos all about me, as there so often is in the American university, as well as in most other corporate entities.

As an existentialist, I soon became a convinced moral constructivist, which I will describe in later sections in this chapter. I did not use this particular term at the time, however, because it was unavailable. The existentialism of the 1960s and 1970s in the larger culture had not yet begun to transmute into the postmodernism of the 1980s and 1990s in the universities. So, I started calling myself a cultural relativist instead. I still agreed with Brameld that the best political system might indeed be some form of international arrangement where world leaders worked together to locate a politico-moral consensus that could assure some peace between and among different nations and cultures. Unfortunately, though, this grandiose political ideology did little to nourish, or to settle, my restless spirit. Besides, I often got the impression that some internationalists I knew cared less for the existential plight of concrete individuals, particularly those individuals who belonged to the white working class, than they did for humanity in the abstract.

Also, to me, Brameld was irritatingly unclear as to whether democracy or world government were, as Rorty says in the epigraph that introduces this chapter, "written in the stars," or whether they were the product of Kant's "pure practical reason." I suspect that, if Brameld had been exposed to the French brands of postmodern theory dating from the late 1970s, 1980s, and 1990s, and developed by such thinkers as Jean-Francois Lyotard, Michel Foucault, Jacques Derrida, and the American, Richard Rorty, he might have blinked at many of its claims. For one, he would have vigorously challenged Rorty's assumption that all moral choice is but a compromise between conflicting goods, or that evil is really just a lesser good. If this were all that political activism came to, then, as Rorty predicted, Brameld would have failed to see any point in moral struggle.

I am sure, though, that Brameld would have enthusiastically agreed with Rorty's desire to diminish human suffering and increase human equality. However, he also would have insisted that this goal be grounded in a moral *terra firma* considerably more firm than Rorty's politics of neopragmatism and postmodern irony. In retrospect, I believe that Brameld was, in some ways, a closeted moral objectivist, a perspective I will also explain in the immediate sections to come. Because I was struggling at the time of my doctoral work to transcend the cultural provincialism of my working-class upbringing, Brameld's political cosmopolitanism was seductive. However, it came with a price. It entailed, among other things, that I accept a political worldview which, in some ways, was no less objectivist or absolute than the childhood religion and morality that I was in the painful process of repudiating. Of course, I did not have these insights about my ambivalences during my time at Boston University. These have been slow to develop, the result of several decades of teaching, reflecting, and writing at the University of Vermont.

I was recruited to my current university position three and one half decades ago with the expectation that I would become my department's moral philosopher. My first professional assignment directly out of graduate school was clear-cut: Develop courses in character education, moral education, and applied ethics for a department top-heavy in methods courses but bottom-light in theory and philosophy. In the late 1960s, there were very few models for such courses anywhere in the country. Thus, my course constructions and classroom pedagogy were mostly of the trial-and-error type. I will talk in this chapter about my current stance and approach as a character educator, and, in the next, about the challenges of putting together what I have been told is the first graduate-level, applied ethics course in a professional college of education in the United States. I will concentrate more on course content and philosophical perspective than I will on instructional processes, although, when relevant, the latter will also be a prominent feature of my account.

For the most part, however, these two chapters will be about the challenges I have faced in forging a perspective toward the teaching of morality and ethics, along with the impact that my evolving spirituality of education has on this teaching, that continues my narrative from my Boston University days. The place where I am right now can be summed up in this way: I have lurched, in fits and starts, from a tentative moral objectivism to a more settled, yet still tenuous, moral constructivism in my thinking about character education, applied ethics, and religion and education. Mine is a philosophy of moral and spiritual education very much in process. The end is still in doubt.

"WHAT MATTERS MORE THAN GETTING IT RIGHT IS CLINGING TOGETHER AGAINST THE DARKNESS"

I have never met Richard R. Rorty in person, but I feel that I know him as well as I know any human being. I have sent graduate students to the University of Virginia to study with him when he was a humanities professor at large there. Educated at Chicago and Yale, a former professor of philosophy at Princeton, Virginia, and currently Stanford, winner of a famous MacArthur Genius Award, and one of the two or three most influential living philosophers in the world, Richard Rorty is someone whose academic reputation and intellectual achievements are prodigious. Predictably, though, few educationists, and others outside the discipline of philosophy I have met know anything about him. Sadly, many would not see his relevance to professional education. In contrast, here is what a well-known fellow philosopher says of Rorty (Brandom, 2000):

> Richard Rorty is one of the most original and important philosophers writing today. He is also one of the most influential beyond the confines of professional academic philosophy.... Dazzled, as one cannot help but be, by the boldness of his conjectures and recommendations, the breathtaking scope of his generalizations, the erudite innovativeness of the connections he discerns between disparate aspects of the culture, and the sheer stylistic brilliance of his prose, it is easy to lose sight of the subtlety and complexity of Rorty's views. (p. xx)

I believe that I have read everything Rorty has ever written, although I can never be sure. As is sometimes said about him, he rarely has a thought that he does not publish. Whenever I use his books in my courses, students come up with the usual, contradictory complaints: He is too hard for them—nonphilosophers—to understand. His language is specialized and technical. His arguments are cryptic. His reasoning is complex. His observations are impractical, too critical, and irreverent. He leaves readers hopeless and desperate for something to believe in. He cannot be taken seriously, because it is hard to know when he is actually being serious and when he is simply being ironic and frivolous. He is a relativist and a subjectivist, maybe even a nihilist. He is a postbourgeois elitist. He is an out-of-touch, 1930s socialist. He is really a closet libertarian who hides behind the rhetoric of democracy and postmodernism. He is actually a poet dressed in a philosopher's garb. He is a self-important philosopher posing as a populist. He has no vision. He is too idealistic. He is a wolf in sheep's clothing. He is a sheep in wolf's clothing.

When I first read Rorty, around 1980, I, too, failed to make much sense of him. I mostly agreed with the sentiments of my students. After my total immersion in the political ideas of Theodore Brameld, and then subsequently, after digesting the writings of dozens of existentialist authors, both atheistic and theistic, on the issues of meaning and responsibility, I found Rorty's thinking to be shallow and beside the point. It was clever and full of élan, to be sure, but it seemed more concerned with style than with substance. I did recognize, however, that long after putting his books away, I reluctantly found myself still carrying on spirited, albeit imaginary, dialogues with him.

While I was able to refute some of his arguments, most I could not. He was clearly getting under my skin as well as inside my head. The more I read Rorty without self-defensiveness and reflected carefully on his insights, though, the more he seemed to meld the best of social reconstructionism and existentialism. In fact, I can say that the aphorism of his that I chose to title this section guides most of my work today in character education, religion and spirituality, and ethics. Actually, it is the principle that underlies much of my teaching, advising, and scholarship. Moreover, it even provides the preliminary framework for my politics: "What matters more than getting it right is clinging together against the darkness" (Rorty 1982, p. 157).

Rorty was the first postmodernist that I ever studied in any systematic way, and, after a while, I found myself avidly using his ideas in my teaching and writing. His books—especially *Philosophy and the Mirror of Nature* (1979); *Consequences of Pragmatism* (1982); *Contingency, Irony, and Solidarity* (1989); *Truth and Progress* (1998), and his more recent *Philosophy and Social Hope* (1999)—triggered for me a Copernican intellectual revolution. At the time, I did not realize that I was becoming a Rortyian, let alone a postmodernist. My conception of moral conversation/unbounded dialogue, which I will frame in this chapter, is a pedagogical construction inspired, in large part, by his ideas (as well as by Brameld's). For this gift alone, I am very, very grateful.

Rorty believes that the best metaphor to use in the pursuit of knowledge is not vision but conversation. Objective truth, if it exists, is unknowable; thus, any systematic attempt to know such a truth is to play God. For Rorty, the world is an alien place and essentially unfathomable, except as we attribute our attitudes and descriptions to it; except as we create stories to understand and explain it. Objective truth is nothing more than knowledge that we arrive at by consensus, and that we agree upon through vigorous conversation. Furthermore, when we can no longer reach a consensus on knowledge, we ought either to agree to disagree, or we should abruptly change the subject.

The ultimate political ideal for Rorty is solidarity, and the way to get there is through robust conversation, exchanging stories, and looking for overlap and commonality in the unique and different politico-religio-moral vocabularies that people use to talk about what really matters to them. Grand political or religious visions, for Rorty, always manage to kill the creative impulse. They tend to homogenize difference and turn people into zealots for One Immutable Truth. Historically, they have produced societies marked by compliance, contestation, conformity, and, worse, endless suffering and humiliation. The chief way to arrive at a human solidarity that encourages eccentricity, heresy, and the practice of compassion is for educators to remain neutral, or at least agnostic, on the ultimate questions of morality, meaning, and whatever the truths of human existence might be. Who, Rorty questions, really knows for sure how anyone else ought to live a life?

Rorty is very critical of what he calls "systematic philosophy." This is the futile attempt to find self-evidently true beliefs that has set the intellectual agenda for philosophers, theologians, and metaphysicians for at least 3,000 years. He has spent much of his career challenging those thinkers who believe that absolute knowledge of one kind or another can be grounded in something called an "essential human nature" or a "transcendent divine nature." For Rorty, no truth claim ever corresponds to an objective, metaphysical reality. There are no fixed, indubitable foundations, only endless permutations of narratives, interpretations, perspectives, and cultural conditionings. Truth is always local rather than universal, contingent rather than absolute.

Any claim to truth, whether moral, religious, political, or educational, is but a particular social construction, made by particular people, living in particular communities at particular times, and telling particular stories. The claim that there exists somewhere outside the human universe an irrefutable core of unchanging, transcendent values or morals overlooks a stubborn fact of life: Language, socialization, and culture are everything. One's take on truth and value depends on how one is raised, where one has lived, and the unique vocabulary that one has been taught to use.

Rorty is convinced that democratic institutions are those best suited to increase equality and reduce suffering. However, as he says over and over, there will never be an airtight, metaphysical connection between people's

political views and their views on morality. There is simply no way in a secular pluralist world to "hold reality…morality, and political responsibility…in
a single vision." Here are Rorty's (1999) personal thoughts in this regard,
and I find them to be searingly honest. "I am not the person to come to
if you want confirmation that the things you love with all your heart are
central to the structure of the universe, or that your sense of moral responsibility is 'rational and objective' rather than 'just' a result of how you were
brought up" (p. 20).

When I first read these words I was put off. Rorty's language seemed
sarcastic, and somewhat fatalistic. Try as I might, however, I was unable
to negate either the philosophical or the pedagogical validity of the deeper
insight that lay behind them: As a teacher, I can never confirm once and
for all the truth of what my students believe with all their hearts and
minds, no matter how much some may want this comforting approval. In
the absence of a self-evident Divine Warrant or a Final Authority, who ever
could? At best, I can only listen, affirm or challenge these beliefs, and then
get out of the way and let good sense, temperament, and taste run their
course. In contrast, I think that Brameld would have been horrified at Rorty's
intellectual dispassion and resignation. He probably would have dismissed
Rorty as being overly deterministic, smug, anti-democratic, and counterreconstructionist. To Brameld, Rorty's political vision would be thin not
thick. It would lack the capacity to solve large social problems and to promote grand visions. It would, in short, be system-preserving rather than
system-disturbing.

I would respectfully disagree, in part, with Brameld. In my case at
least, a steady dose of Rorty leads to a constant rethinking of what one takes
for granted. Some students have told me, after reading and comparing the
two authors: "Richard Rorty is no Theodore Brameld." This is true, and
this, in my estimation, is just the way it should be. Rorty lives in an age that
no longer accepts Brameld's mid-twentieth century assumptions that a grand
political vision is always a salvific force; or that democracy is the one-size
political system that will fit all; or that the search for cultural universals should
be the predominant work of the social sciences and humanities; or that large-
scale, social blueprints are needed in order to solve the world's complex,
human problems. While both Brameld and Rorty are left-leaning in their

politics, anti-dualistic in their epistemologies, and committed to decreasing human suffering, Rorty departs in a significant way.

Democracy for Rorty is mainly a process whereby people can attain an appropriate combination of unforced agreement with tolerant disagreement. His is a thoroughgoing utopia of cultural pluralism. In my opinion, Rorty is far more willing than Brameld to let the political chips fall where they may, depending on where people might end up in their conversations with each other. At this particular period in my life, I find that I am more aligned with Rorty than with Brameld on issues of politics and morality, particularly when it comes to teaching. The moral constructivism that I write about in this chapter and the next owes a great deal to Rorty's more laissez-faire approach to democracy and to character education, as the reader will soon see.

A NOT-SO-RELAXED DINNER PARTY AMONG COLLEAGUES

A short time before writing this chapter, I attended an end-of-semester dinner party with several academicians from my own and other universities—mostly philosophers, theologians, and educationists—along with their partners. The occasion was meant to be relaxed, somewhat festive, and a chance to get to know one another as real persons in a pleasant setting far from the academy. I found myself sitting next to a fellow ethicist and highly respected character educator who obviously had a bone of contention he had been wanting to pick with me over something that I had said a few months earlier in a public symposium on moral education at his Catholic college. What he took issue with was the following statement of mine, that, I admit, on second thought, was probably a bit more provocative in tone than if I were to assert it publicly on a Catholic campus today:

> I guess I would call myself a postmodern character educator. What do I mean when I use the term "postmodern"? Simply this: There is no objective, context-independent standard—either in here, out there, up above, or down below—to confirm once and for all what we need to call truth, reason, or good. Too often, metaphysical bottom or top lines function mainly as conversation-stoppers rather than consensus-generators. In the matter of character education, I believe none of us can ever prove conclusively that our preferred moral virtues are the ones that everybody else will need in order to conduct their affairs in the most praiseworthy manner. It is impossible for any one of us to step outside of our personal histories, cultural contexts, and

interpretive frameworks in order to gain a God's-eye view of the perfect way to live our lives. At most, we can only teach our students to respect each others' moral truths by trying to understand them on terms other than their own. This exercise—what Wilhelm Dilthey called *verstehen* (empathic understanding)—may actually be an insurmountable challenge for faculty and students, however, given our individual differences in tribal upbringing, talent, training, timing, taste, and temperament. Thus, I question whether an impartial, empathic understanding of morality is ever truly possible.

What I am suggesting is that we need to think about character education on the college level as a project that goes beyond the imposition of those pet religious, political, educational, or moral virtues which we are frequently tempted to call absolute or universal. Educating for and about character in a college setting means putting aside any preconception of an objectivist grounding for values and virtues. In contrast, I believe that the kind of character education that ought to go on in the secular academy is one where no single person, institution, or text are ever seen as having an irrefutable corner on moral or ethical truth. The ideal for all of us in higher education is to help students to settle their moral differences without having to thrust their metaphysical or political absolutes upon one another.

Character education, in my estimation, is most effective whenever it emerges from an honest exchange of opposing points of view in a free and open encounter. I believe that all of us—professors and students—must learn to live with the fact of moral plurality, and with the understanding that we ought never to demand absolute validity in our ethical conversations with one another. I can say with some assurance that in thirty-plus years of experience teaching courses in moral education, applied ethics, and character education to students of a variety of ages and backgrounds, I have never found an absolute moral validity that everyone could unanimously agree on. Nor, in truth, would I ever want to. Therefore, let a thousand, or even a million, approaches to character education bloom. Who can say for sure that any single one is unimpeachably right?

What concerned my colleague about this little outburst of mine was, in his words, my "indefensible philosophical stance as a moral educator." How was it possible, he asked, to teach ethics or character education "without adverting to objective moral principles or universal moral laws?" To him, I was simply another "postmodern relativist" whose moral position in the classroom verged on an irresponsible and dangerous nihilism. From his view, teaching for and about character made sense only if I had a "firm moral ground" on which to stand. All other approaches, but especially a postmodern approach, were "arbitrary, ungrounded, and woefully expedient."

It did not take long for several of the other dinner guests to register their enthusiastic support for his critique of my position. Much to my chagrin, I found myself the unwanted center of attention at the dinner table that evening, because I was being put in the position of expressing a very unpopular, almost renegade view on character education. Even the gracious dinner host had her say: "I do not know how anyone can call himself a character educator and be a postmodernist. It sounds to me as if this is another one of those pathetic little, politically correct oxymorons that we hear so much about in the academy."

One guest, a longtime associate in my own department, accused me of being intellectually incapable of issuing any kind of strong moral censure against Timothy McVeigh's bombing of the Oklahoma City federal office building in 1996, lethal student violence on public school campuses, or sexual harassment in the workplace because of my "subjectivist," "anti-principle" leanings. Another colleague upped the ante. She said that "some things are good or evil in themselves, because they are inherent in any objective view of morality and ethics." Her argument was that unless good and evil were somehow located in Kant's autonomous will, or grounded in Aquinas's natural law, or established by reference to God's inerrant biblical Truth, or verified by reason in the form of the scientific method or logic, then I could never condemn such atrocities as the holocaust, genocide, rape, and mass murder.

For good measure, one of my closest colleagues at the university added this fillip:

> I am sorry, but if you do not become an unequivocal moral compass for your students, then you are deliberately sending them the message that it is okay to become wishy-washy bricoleurs of right and wrong, patching together a moral code based on whether one thing or another feels good to them at any given moment. For God's sake, even the politically impotent, morally neutered United Nations constructed a Declaration of Human Rights in order to put itself on record as denouncing violations of human dignity.

Never mind that I sounded very defensive that evening. My responses, I am sure, grew increasingly flippant the more I felt my colleagues were piling on. I found myself referring to Richard Rorty's comment that, no matter how desperate we are to believe it, there is no built-in, moral reference point that all human beings share. I heard myself asking, somewhat snidely, why on earth they believed that we needed a metaphysical backup before we could assume a strong, committed position against all the moral evils they took such self-righteous pleasure in enumerating.

Because, like Rorty, I believe that there is nothing good or evil in itself, but only as we use language, consensus, pragmatism, and socialization to define it as so, this does not, therefore, make me an amoral subjectivist or a reckless relativist. I strongly believe that I too can stand passionately for what I think is right, without the need for metaphysical underwriters. Neither does my moral constructivism make me, heaven forbid, a "subjectivist," someone who expresses opinions or attitudes about right and wrong based only on his gut feelings, as one of my colleagues charged.

Somewhat vindictively, I pulled out my doomsday weapon with an intention to deliver the death blow to the prevailing objectivist argument that evening: What do we do in a secular pluralist democracy when one so-called objective moral truth is in irreconcilable conflict with another one? Is it not true that pro-life and pro-choice advocates in the abortion debate, or supporters and critics of same-sex marriages and capital punishment, for example, rest their cases on some ultimate version of objective moral truth? Moreover, I declared, didn't Hitler believe that his conceptions of the Third Reich, usurious Jewry, final solution, and master race, were grounded in objective truths of blood, race, ethnicity, geography, history, destiny, nationalism, and politics? Whose objective moral truth, therefore, is most objective? According to whose, and what, criteria? What truth ought finally to carry the day? In the end, isn't truth all about who uses the tools of persuasion most effectively?

To complicate matters, how do we convince the loser of the moral argument to gracefully accept defeat and withdraw, chastened yet transformed, from the conversation? Alas, the more I talked that evening the more my colleagues were convinced that I had gone off the deep end of postmodern moral skepticism, and perhaps I had. Little did I realize then that my nagging afterthoughts about that provocative dinner party would provide me with a number of compelling reasons for writing this chapter.

It took me a few days to understand that what the heated dinner-party conversation was really about was a frank difference of opinion between two distinct views in the academy on character education. The pivotal question amounted to this: Where is the best philosophical place to start in order to teach for and about character education—from a position of *constructivism* or from *objectivism?* Is teaching morality mainly about finding truth out there or constructing meaning from in here? Or is it somehow a dialectical combination of both approaches which, in the end, might be complementary in some ways rather than contradictory?

No longer is the question whether we in the American university ought to go about the business of inculcating values and virtues. Even a quick glance at a number of representative college mission statements will demonstrate that the question has already been answered in the affirmative. Every college in the United States, in some form or another, has gone on record as declaring that helping students become better human beings is a major aspect of the educational mission. Parents, boards of trustees, and the public-at-large expect no less. Besides, whether we admit it or not, we are always inculcating values and morals. This, in fact, is what we do as professors: We profess a strong belief in the worth or worthlessness of some things, either explicitly or implicitly. How could it be any other way?

What I assert in the paragraphs to follow I will try to do with great caution and humility, but most of all, with considerable respect for those of differing philosophical and religious perspectives who will inevitably oppose my position. If, as I truly believe, there is no possible way ever to have the final, indisputable word on matters of morality, religion, and ethics in the academy, then, to be consistent, I must acknowledge that my word is but one of many that deserve a fair hearing. Thus, I make no claims for universal or absolute moral truth in any of the statements to come. In truth, I am on a career-long quest to fashion a view of character education that is both defensible and honest. While I think of myself as a strong moral constructivist, I am also someone who has been on a three-decades-long journey to set reasonable limits to my constructivism. I honestly believe that after every sentence in this chapter, as well as in all the others, I can add a credible vice versa. I suppose, for some guests at the aforementioned dinner party, this acknowledgment will merely confirm their suspicion that I am a wishy-washy relativist. I disagree.

Moral constructivism is a postmodern concept which holds that there is no external, once-and-for-all, objective authority that grounds the truth of a particular morality or ethics. Moral truth is always a product of personal and group beliefs, attitudes, and cultural conventions, and, not least, of taste and temperament. Stated more simply: Moral constructivism is the view that prohibits looking to a sacred book, a definitive political system, an unimpeachable religious guru, or to a steel-trap, logical argument to certify any perspective on morality, religion, or ethics as absolute or airtight. For better or worse, at this time in my life, I simply do not believe that there is some super-legitimating stamp of approval for the moral, religious, and ethical behavior I find preferable in human affairs. To be sure, world government is nice—in the interests of peace, social justice, and cross-cultural cooperation even something worth working toward—but, in itself, it can never be the irrefutable, universal arbiter of what is good, true, sacred, and beautiful.

MY COMING OF AGE AS A MORAL CONSTRUCTIVIST

Plato, in the *Meno* (1956), raises the one question that has guided my work for all the years I have been in the academy. *What is the best way to teach the virtues?* How should we teach people to be good human beings? During my darker moments in the classroom, and like the young Thessalian nobleman, Menon, in the *Meno,* I often wonder whether teaching people to be good is even something achievable, because it might simply be in their natures to be either good or bad, regardless of the kind of moral education they receive. Earlier in my teaching, at times, I reluctantly agreed with Socrates that perhaps moral education and character development were indeed all about "divine allotment": Some people appeared to be "incomprehensibly" blessed by the gods to be good and some were not.

If this were true, I reasoned, maybe we needed to spend more time "searching out what virtue [was] in itself"; that is, perhaps we needed to be looking for some objective grounding, what Plato called *eidos,* a world of "innate ideas" or "forms," for those qualities of character that were admirable in and of themselves. Plato, Aristotle, Augustine, Aquinas, and Kant, each in his own way, were moral essentialists—believers in immutable, eternally perfect, moral norms. I thought that if this was good enough for these thinkers, considered by many to be the nonpareil character educators of all time, then it would have to be good enough for me. My students taught me otherwise, however.

As I have worked throughout the last three decades to define myself as a character educator, both in my courses and scholarship, my journey from a mild, but uneasy, form of moral objectivism to a stronger, yet qualified, form of moral constructivism intensified. I became increasingly aware of the presence, and, at times, the irreconcilability, of genuine moral difference and conflict in all my courses. If objectivism is the view that moral truth exists independently of language, culture, socialization, personal taste, temperament, and history; and, furthermore, that it is possible for one to find and know this independent, context-free moral truth; and that, once discovered, this truth must then become the unassailable foundation for all human conduct, then, as a teacher, I was clearly incapable of holding a position of moral objectivism. Whether in my ethics courses or in my character education seminars, it was virtually impossible ever to secure even a modicum of agreement from all of my students on those moral absolutes that Plato, Aquinas, or Kant, despite their significant philosophical differences, considered to be universal, unchangeable, and exceptionless.

For example, the so-called unquestioned law of God was out as a moral foundation because so many of my students were convinced atheists or agnostics. Thus, where did this leave the idea of divinely grounded norms? The so-called inexorable law of human nature was also out because students had such very different takes on whether human nature was even a coherent concept, given its extraordinary plasticity and multiple social constructions. Consequently, how could we ever refer to a universal human essence to validate our preferences for particular moral beliefs and virtues? The so-called ironclad laws of nature, reason, and science were likewise out because a conception of each of these is so intricately context-dependent, and driven by self-, cultural, and political interests. Therefore, what is left to confirm, once and for all, the indubitable truth of a particular way to live?

Philosophically, for better or worse, most of my students today are anti-realists regarding issues of morality and character: As they learn to be fluent in the language of postmodern theory, I find that they are less willing to accept the assumption that there are unchallengeable moral facts, truths, and virtues that possess a real life of their own, that exist totally separate from personal and social biases. Many of today's college students, particularly those majoring in the humanities and social sciences, are instinctual

Nietzscheans, even if they have never read one original word of this philosopher's works. They endorse, almost unquestioningly, Nietzsche's observation that objectivity is actually a figment of the scientist's, philosopher's, or priest's imagination. They agree with Nietzsche that, in the end, objectivity is reducible to the will to power.

For many of my students, being moral, knowing the virtues, and forming character are all about what Nietzsche (Hollingdale 1977) calls "perspective"; and, for him, the more perspectives "we allow to speak about one thing...the more complete will be our 'concept' of objectivity" (p. 69). Most of my Generation-X students are convinced constructivists on moral matters. Some of them insist that, at the very most, any notion of morality must be aesthetically and psychologically pleasing to them. Some ask for nothing else except that a theory of the virtues be pragmatic, coherent, and consensually agreed upon.

Others hold that propositions about what constitutes good moral character be recognized for what they are: location-, time-, and person-bound. They are quick to point out that Aristotle, for example, appears to have advanced a notion of moral character less interested in questions of access, rights, entitlements, liberties, and obligations than in constructing a gentlemanly moral code for the Greek aristocrat. Moreover, these students become suspicious whenever contemporary virtuecrats like William J. Bennett (1993), William Kilpatrick (1992), and Alan Bloom (1987) appear to privilege such compliant virtues as submissiveness; deference to authority, religion, and tradition; obedience and acquiescence, while ignoring the more robust and assertive political qualities necessary for a rich participatory life in a democracy. To these students, whom I call liberationists in my book, *Answering the "Virtuecrats"* (1997), it is no coincidence that virtuecrats like William Kilpatrick usually end up advancing a very conservative political agenda: one that openly blames Nietzsche and other postmodernists for so-called vices as far-ranging as western relativism, nihilism, fascism, Nazism, anti-Semitism, radical feminism, rock and rap music, values clarification, self-esteem education, and environmental fanaticism.

Today's students, with many important religious and political exceptions, are constructivists by temperament, as am I. They know, almost intuitively, that talk about moral character is always a social construction representing a particular thinker's or group's pet beliefs and attitudes. They understand all too well that John Rawls's (1971) "impartial" or "ideal" moral observer does not exist in the nitty-gritty, self-interested world that they inhabit. They realize that if character is the sum total of a person's virtues—including behavior, likes, dislikes, capacities, dispositions, potentialities, values, and even thought patterns—then, in their opinion, a far more complex theory of cognitive, moral, and personality development is required than the one that the classically oriented virtuecrats propose.

They also understand that particular virtues and vices are character traits that have no autonomous existence of their own, as some virtuecrats suggest. Rather, virtues and vices are always concrete developments of particular cultural and social traditions, upbringings, psychological states, and philosophical, political, and religious inclinations. Thus, there can never be a definitive, suprasituational construction of a standard of human flourishing or human decline. Neither can there ever be a foolproof method for resolving the dilemmas that occur when the virtues and the vices are in conflict with one another.

Shaping character in the schools and colleges, as in the home and church, is a complicated and demanding intellectual undertaking. In a society where there will always be competing conceptions of what is true and right, false and wrong; and in a culture where, to a large extent, the major shapers of moral character are the family, the popular media, the peer group, the shopping mall, the internet, MTV, video games, the athletic playing fields, and the workplace, my students have learned to become discerning moral "crap-detectors." They do not suffer gladly the simplistic objectivist solutions to complex social problems that they find in so many of the virtuecrats' writings. They are quick to agree with Warren Nord (1995):

> For better or worse, the moral character of students is shaped to a great extent by their families, by our culture, and by that predisposition to self-centeredness...that lies in the hearts of everyone. It would be naïve to think that public education can solve the moral crisis in our culture. It falls well beyond the competence of schools to eliminate the violence and drugs, the narcissism and psychopathology, of children raised in dysfunctional families and a corrupt culture. (p. 350)

IS IT POSSIBLE TO RECONCILE CONSTRUCTIVISM
AND OBJECTIVISM IN CHARACTER EDUCATION?

I often think about whether it is truly possible to be a moral constructivist, yet still be able to reject a self-referential, incoherent moral relativism. For example, any declaration of moral relativism, on the face of it, usually presents itself as *absolutely and universally* true rather than *relatively* so. This appears to be a blatant, indeed logically fatal, contradiction. The statement, "It is all relative," is as invariant and inflexible as its opposite, "It is all absolutely true." Also, if, indeed, it *is* all relative, why then is this assertion itself not relative? Why should it be an exception? Whenever I point out this obvious contradiction in class, few of my students fail to understand it. Surprisingly, however, few let it bother them. For many of them, logical incoherence is a kind of virtue, while the opposite is just another professor's attempt to impose a point of view on them.

Also, I wonder if it is possible to hold the view that, even though expressions of moral principles and virtues do in fact differ in many cultures and social subgroups, this fact alone does not preclude the possibility that there very well might be a core morality which, though not *absolutely* valid, is *empirically applicable* to very different social and cultural situations. In other words, could a character educator be a dominant moral constructivist with recessive objectivist leanings, without collapsing completely into philosophical confusion? My dinner party confreres mentioned above were obviously concerned that somehow I had fallen irretrievably into a bottomless pit of moral nihilism. I must confess that, at times, I feel some students in my courses have fallen into the same hole, and this perception disturbs me very much.

A prominent moral perspective, featured among a particular cadre of college students today, is what Alasdair MacIntyre (1984) disapprovingly calls "emotivism." While, generally, I believe that MacIntyre is prone to exaggerate the depth and breadth of emotivism among students that I have taught, I think he does make an important observation. Emotivism is the belief that "all moral expressions are nothing but expressions of preference, expressions of attitude or feeling, insofar as they are moral or evaluative in character." Consequently, for emotivist students, moral prescriptions are tantamount to saying nothing more than "what makes me feel happy and satisfied is good. Hooray!" "What makes me feel unhappy and unsatisfied is bad. Boo!"

According to MacIntyre (1984), emotivists draw the conclusion that there is simply "no established [objective] way of deciding between [competing] moral claims" (p. 12) regarding questions of right or wrong. Therefore, because the moral talk of character educators and other authorities is really personal-preference talk, then such talk must always be taken, if not with a grain of salt, then at most with a wink and a nod. Why then, my emotivist students ask, should anyone get so worked up about talk that, in MacIntyre's rueful words, is always "rationally interminable"? The next logical step for some of these students is to become moral cynics and nihilists.

Contra these emotivists, I have gradually come to the conclusion, after all my years of teaching a number of axiologically related courses, that I am *not* a moral relativist if relativism implies that I think all the virtues and vices are of equal moral worth, or that all the virtues and vices are merely arbitrary expressions of idiosyncratic preference. The empirical facts of cultural variance and individual difference throughout the world do not in and of themselves validate a belief in moral equivalence or moral nonjudgmentalism. The twentieth-century atrocities committed in the Nazi death camps, the mass slaughters at My Lai, Hiroshima, and Nagasaki, the continuing practice of slavery and genocide throughout the world, and the imposition of a system of apartheid on South African blacks completely destroy the pretensions of those who advocate a nonjudgmental, morally equivalent relativism. In this respect, Jonathan Glover's (1999) powerful and sweeping *Humanity: A Moral History of the Twentieth Century* is must reading for absolute moral relativists. I have taught long enough to be confident that some ethical decisions are more defensible than others, that some virtues and vices require decisive approbation and censure, and that some character education theories are more functional and sustainable than others. So too are some religions.

I *am* a relativist, however, if the only alternative to relativism is what I occasionally see as an extreme form of moral absolutism among some students and colleagues. I am not speaking here only about religious absolutists. I am also referring to those political, educational, and virtue absolutists who reside on both the right and left ends of the moral spectrum.

Moral absolutists believe in Background Truths that are presumed to be free from variability and error, that are underived, complete, and universally binding, that are, in Richard Rorty's (1999) words, "unwobbling in their pivots" (p. 15). In my seminars, I find that conservatives, liberals, and radicals of various moral-political stripes are equally capable of resorting to absolutist displays of certitude. Unfortunately, they sometimes do this as a stratagem to short-circuit open-ended, moral inquiry by trying to foster a sense of guilt among those of us whom they consider to be heretics and naysayers. Whenever this occurs in my classes, free and undominated conversation about morality and character gets stopped dead in its tracks.

Having said this, however, I must admit that I greatly respect those students and colleagues whose moral beliefs are rooted in some type of metaphysical or political ultimacy. They can be torridly passionate in their moral convictions, and, at times, I admire them for this. I have met far too many blasé or jaded Gen-Xrs and cynical Baby-Boomers who think that possessing strong moral convictions worth fighting, even dying, for is an illness to be cured rather than an ideal to be celebrated. The challenge for character educators, in my opinion, is two-pronged: to encourage the absolutists to articulate their most cherished moral beliefs passionately to the rest of us; but also to help them learn to make their case in languages and stories that speak effectively to those of us who might come from contrasting philosophical places.

In the next section of this chapter, I will talk about a postmodern character education aimed at cultivating those conversational virtues I believe are necessary for active participation in a pluralistic democracy. These virtues include, among others, capaciousness, compassion, flexibility, resiliency, narrative ingenuity, interpretive creativity, empathy, rapport, nonmanipulation, self-critique, confrontation, negotiation, openness to otherness, respect for plurality, patience, tolerance, and an inexhaustible sense of irony and humor.

However, at this point, the pivotal philosophical question still remains: Is it possible, or even worthwhile, to reconcile the contradictions that exist between constructivist and objectivist perspectives in teaching for moral character? For my part, I believe that reconciliation is possible but, at best, always tenuous. Moreover, I cannot think of anything that would enliven the conversation on character education better than a healthy, no-holds-barred dialogue on the strengths and weaknesses of constructivist and objectivist perspectives on right and wrong, good and bad, virtue and vice, religious truth and religious error. Actually, there is a moderate philosophico-educational view that stands between absolutist expressions of relativism and objectivism, between emotivism and absolutism, and it is the one to which I subscribe, at this particular stage of my career. Let me call it a character education that strives for pragmatic moral consensus through unbounded, dialogical encounter, or what I call moral conversation.

I start with the assumption that, though I am dubious (but open-minded) about the existence of a universal human nature (I do accept a universal human biology, however, as I mentioned in the previous chapter), or a beneficent Divine Being who alone is the Author of all morality, I still believe that people share much in common, despite their obvious cultural, philosophical, religious, and political differences. What most moral codes throughout the world seem to agree on is that the best way to create the good life for everyone—what philosophers call the promotion of human flourishing—is to display a respect for self and others, to practice compassion, to act responsibly, to work with, and in behalf of, others, and to insist on social justice for all.

These are universal moral ideals, not because they are emblazoned in some kind of natural law or inscribed in one sacred book or another, but because they are useful and life-sustaining. They actually confer survival benefits on human beings, as a number of respectable socio-biologists and evolutionary psychologists such as Edward O. Wilson (1998) and Robert Wright (1995) have argued. These moral ideals are pragmatic in that they set the stage for people to live together productively, happily, and peacefully. Louis P. Pojman (1995) has gone so far as to say that"… it may turn out that it is not science or technology, but rather deep, comprehensive ethical theory and moral living that will not only save our world but solve its perennial problems and produce a state of flourishing" (p. 17).

Our moral obligations to keep our word, tell the truth, respect the rights of others, prevent harm, honor due process, act responsibly, and strive for social justice are the inescapable, evolutionary requirements for constructing mutually fulfilling social orders. These are the moral principles that, despite their abrogation in many cultures, serve to forge a common bond among all human beings. Stripped to their basics, these ideals provide the moral groundwork, in Rorty's (1999) words, for "diminishing human suffering and increasing human equality, increasing the ability of all human children to start life with an equal chance of happiness" (p. xxix).

From another front, however, and unlike many character educators, I do not believe that ethical- and moral-stage theorists such as Lawrence Kohlberg (1984) or William G. Perry (1970) succeed in resolving the more glaring contradictions between objectivism and constructivism. These theorists' "universal moral ideals"—justice and commitment—are too abstract and restrictive to be of much concrete help in fashioning character education programs bent on "diminishing human suffering and increasing human equality." In Kohlberg's view, adolescent, white, middle-class American boys, ages 10–16, pass through "pre-conventional," "conventional," and "post-conventional" stages of moral development. These stages are hierarchical, invariant, and universal. The highest moral stage for Kohlberg, the "postconventional," is when the individual embraces, and attempts to live out, such principles as justice, autonomy, integrity, and empathy. In Perry's case, late adolescents progress from "dualism," to "relativism," to "commitment." The highest stage for Perry, "commitment," is when the individual develops a view of morality that is complex, situational, and based on a "pledge" to something larger than the self. Perry's stages of ethical development are "wavelike," less linear than Kohlberg's, but still presented as all-embracing, even, at times, as absolute.

As a character educator, I find moral development theory to be too pat and formulaic, too hierarchical and excessively linked to age and gender. I have a built-in bias against those character education programs predicated on an assumption that one size fits all, that proceed step-by-step to an appropriation of the virtues wherein some are presented as higher and others as lower. Many of my students think that developmental moral stages too often act as self-constraint traps and as self-fulfilling labels. They strenuously resist being forced to slot themselves at various points along a pre-established, moral plotline. I agree wholeheartedly with them. Most students are quick to recognize that these theories, falsely presented as the product of rigorous scientific research, merely reflect the moral biases of their creators—themselves highly educated, white, middle-class males who studied subjects, who, they hoped, would grow up to value what they did. Thus, moral development theory comes off to most of my students as being far more subjective than scientific, and much more prescriptive than descriptive. How could it be otherwise?

The trick for all of us who do character education is to resist the seductive temptation to locate once and for all some highest stage of moral development, one that alone contains the most preferred moral virtues. This is the classical objectivist approach to forming moral character. As a constructivist, I do not believe that there is a highest stage of moral formation that justifies the imposition of a particular bag of virtues. There is simply no moral frame of reference that is beneath or beyond the impress of our personal histories, languages, hermeneutics, cultures, and temperaments. Oh that it were so! This does not mean, of course, that some virtues are not preferable to some vices in particular situations. Neither does this mean that as a character educator I am incapable of teaching the virtues just because I am resolutely agnostic as to their ultimate origins or to their absolute validity.

TEACHING THE POSTMODERN VIRTUES:
SEEKING MORAL COMMON GROUND THROUGH DIALOGUE

I intend to lay my own moral cards faceup in this section. Democracy, despite its grave defects, is, for me, in principle, the most humane form of government the world has ever known. Holding this conviction, I realize that I am, indeed, John Dewey's and Theodore Brameld's political stepchild. I say this about democracy because, at least in theory, it thrives on freedom of individual expression and on the near-inviolable rights of self-determination and equal treatment. Democracy functions best when truth is considered to be nothing more than the unencumbered, nonmetaphysical outcome of a free and open encounter of equals who represent contrasting beliefs and goals. The kind of secular pluralist democracy I am talking about is what John Dewey saw as a vibrant experiment in cooperative living, a calculated risk that some early Americans took in order to avoid tyranny and to satisfy their needs for individual liberty and social justice. Thus, for me, the responsibility is great for all citizens in a democracy to learn to deliberate effectively in order to make morally defensible decisions on those controversial issues that affect their lives.

The best way to resolve conflict, I believe, is to talk openly about differences, to see things from contrasting points of view, to have more diverse resources from which to draw in order to solve complex personal and social problems. Therefore, the best character education is the one that helps citizens to dialogue with each other compassionately, peacefully, and productively. All of this, I submit, is a postmodern agenda requiring a set of distinctive virtues that will lead to a capacity for thoughtful deliberation with others, a tolerance for their rich complexity and difference, and a willingness to engage in highly creative problem-solving. Finally, I believe that a constructivist approach to character education is the ideal one for preparing students to live effectively in a secular pluralist democracy. Constructivism puts the onus on citizens themselves—not on governments, militaries, churches, despots, or gods—to create and shape a world, that, in Richard Rorty's words, is most likely to "diminish human suffering and increase human equality." How to get there, for the constructivist, is a matter of continual negotiation and conversation, and the end is always up for grabs.

I will go even one step further than Rorty, though: I believe that there is an ideal (*not* universal or absolute) core morality worth pursuing, and it is the one that I believe ought to undergird life in a secular pluralist democracy. I have already alluded to the contents of this core in the previous section. I will only add here that this common core ought to display a public moral language that is:

- *nonfoundational*—one that is ungrounded in particular, self-evident principles that everyone must accept.
- *multifunctional*—it should feature a moral language that is useful to all individuals and interest groups, regardless of their competing conceptions of the good.
- *nonexclusionary*—finally, it must be a public language that is an inclusive lingua franca usable by everyone, regardless of difference; one that patches together relevant ideals, principles, and virtues from a number of diverse, sometimes conflicting, moral vocabularies.

A nonfoundational, multifunctional, and nonexclusionary public moral language is a key in promoting reconciliation and healing division not just in a classroom or seminar, but in a democracy as well. In the words of Edward Tivnan (1995), this type of language is the one best suited to helping us "listen to the other side of the story." This public moral language is pragmatic and dialogical. Its primary aim is to solve problems, to serve as a tool to work out our differences with each other. It seeks to construct consensus out of discord.

It continually reminds us that character education ought to be an unending and open-ended, moral conversation "about how we can keep from stomping on one another's special projects of self-improvement" (Tivnan 1995, p. 258). The kind of character education that I am advocating regards morality, and all the virtues that accompany it, as both the process and product of a to-and-fro, consensus-seeking dialogue. This is a dialogue bent on reaching agreements between and among specific groups about what the content and purpose of character education ought to be. However, it also recognizes that on some occasions, moral consensus may be impossible to achieve. The dialogue I am advocating is always pluralistic in tone and devoid in content of ultimate moral and ethical trumps, as well as final, irreproachable moral high grounds.

While agreement and consensus are certainly important, character education dialogue also looks to achieve other worthy objectives. Diana Eck (1993) advocates a "culture of dialogue" in higher education that comes close to what I am promoting here:

> We do not enter into dialogue with the dreamy hope that we will all agree, for the truth is we probably will not. We also...enter into dialogue to produce real relationship, even friendship, which is premised upon mutual understanding, not [only] upon agreement.... A culture of dialogue creates a context of ongoing relatedness and trust in which self-criticism and mutual criticism are acceptable and valuable parts of the...exchange. (p. 22)

We need to set the rules beforehand that factitious agreement or fractious debate have no place in classroom dialogue. Rather, we are seeking mutual understanding, clarification, and the type of conversation that might result in self-criticism of our own strongly held moral views. We need to acknowledge at the outset that respectful, carefully conceived criticism is both acceptable and desirable.

Most significantly, however, we must understand that genuine moral dialogue, built on a foundation of respect, trust, and mutual exploration, of necessity, invites candor and critique. It does this because it conveys the message that a value-neutral approach really does not take the other's point of view very seriously. Conversation about morality and character is superficial without criticism and challenge. In my classes, it is frequently the moral absolutists (of all political and religious stripes) who are unable to tolerate honest criticism in dialogue. I have found that dialogue about morality without the opportunity to engage in critical questioning (I do not mean contrarian academic carping or sniping) narrows rather than widens the search for a moral truth each of us can live by.

There are no conversation-stoppers in the classroom dialogue I am proposing, only conversation-starters. Teaching the postmodern virtues presents a formidable challenge, because students must learn a whole new way of thinking about morality, truth, and communication. I would argue that the extent to which teachers are able to construct a dialogical/conversational environment in the classroom, one which fosters a spirit of respectful, open-ended moral inquiry, determines when we have really begun to teach, and do, character education. We are exemplifying the democratic virtues that we are explicating. What follows, then, is a brief account of what I consider to be the paramount postmodern virtues, along with an equally brief description of the dialogic process necessary to produce them.

A tolerance for the uncertainties and ambiguities entailed by the postmodern worldview, along with a willingness, nevertheless, to persist in educating for a democratic character. As I have been arguing throughout this chapter, the constructivist perspective assumes the absence of a common moral standard with which to evaluate the worth of a plethora of competing moral vocabularies, traditions, practices, and frameworks. Philosophers refer to this condition as "incommensurability," by which they mean that there is no objective and transcendent moral criterion which can finally and forcefully settle all of our disagreements over values. The problem with most current approaches to character education, as I understand them, is that each attempts to advance a particular moral vocabulary and a set of preferred moral virtues, as if both of these were part and parcel of a grand narrative accepted by, and normative for, everyone.

Unfortunately, grand moral narratives in the postmodern era have gone the way of most grand religious narratives: No matter how compelling and consoling to some people, all grand narratives break down at the local level. There is just too much philosophical, religious, political, and lifestyle difference among individuals and groups in communities through-out the United States for any moral metanarrative to carry the day for all. Alan Wolfe (2001), a sociologist, has spent years talking to Americans who prefer to live what he calls lives of "moral freedom." His exhaustive research documents the fact that most Americans seek to determine for them-selves just how they will achieve a good and virtuous life. Unlike their pre-baby boom predecessors, they are no longer willing to look to authoritative religious figures or institutions for easy answers to complex moral questions. For them, a life of integrity is all about exercising their autonomous rights to make moral choices consistent with their values.

Having said this, however, neither Wolfe nor I intend thereby to lay the groundwork for a despairing moral relativism or a narrow moral sub-jectivism. Instead, I am recommending just the opposite: Character edu-cators must proceed to teach the democratic virtues with a renewed humility and caution. We might try, for one, to get our students involved in helping to define those virtues that are most likely to encourage a bet-ter quality of democratic life for everyone. This objective entails, of neces-sity, that all of us, students and teachers alike, learn to work with, and integrate, a number of conflicting moral languages and stories in order to advance one major, democratic goal: the common good. The right of all individuals to pursue their diverse conceptions of the good life in their own best ways—what Wolfe calls "moral freedom"—is the basic tie that binds citizens in a liberal democracy. It is America's uncommon common good, and instead of destroying communal ties and responsibilities, Wolfe's research demonstrates that it has actually strengthened a sense of solidar-ity and commonality among all the people he interviewed.

It is my hope that, even though moral incommensurability is an inevitable fact of life in the postmodern world (despite persistent efforts by a number of religious, political, and educational leaders to resist or to deny it), people can still find a way to come together to build better lives for them-selves, their neighbors, and their fellow humans everywhere. Alasdair MacIntyre (1984), and others of his Thomistic ilk, does not think that this is possible without some transcendent moral standard that we can all agree on. I, however, am convinced that it is possible. Despite the persistence of moral incommensurability in the post-Enlightenment world, I believe that we can still be profoundly committed to the elimination of human suffer-

ing and to the advancement of human flourishing for all people regardless
of their differences. A good place for character educators to start is to recognize that conversation, critique, persuasion, and negotiation are the
virtues that must replace imposition and indoctrination in the classroom—
the classical forms of character training—along with the guilt-mongering
and sermonizing that so often accompany the latter.

*A capacity for engaging in moral dialogue that is open-ended, dialectical, com-
passionate, but, above all, humble and generous.* In my work as a character
educator, I always insist that students rely less on pontification and oratory
in their conversations with each other and more on an honest give-and-take,
a patient back-and-forth exchange of moral points of view. Tivnan (1995),
quoted earlier, tells us that "conversation is more likely to continue if we
can imagine the world from the other side of the barricade" (p. 258). His
point for character educators is to avoid narrowing the dialogue to one-
way declarations of our unassailable moral beliefs. It is to realize that no
matter how different our views, "we are all bundles of opinions and beliefs,
of theories and prejudices about how we and our world are or ought to be"
(Ibid.). This is simply to say that what we all have in common as we go about
the project of teaching for and about moral character is the fact that our
views are at one and the same time true and false, whole and partial,
strong and weak, each in their own ways. Thus, we need to listen to others as we would be listened to. We need to question and challenge others
as we would be questioned and challenged. Finally, we must pontificate to
others only under the condition that we want others to pontificate to us.

    I contend that, whether we are objectivists or constructivists, we are
each unique bundles of moral meanings, looking frequently to express them,
hoping to find others to confirm them, and wanting to live our lives in a
manner that is consistent with them. Mark R. Schwehn (1993) proposes
that four virtues in particular—humility, faith, self-denial, and charity—are
necessary for respecting, rather than changing, the meanings of others.
Humility presumes that we attribute at least a modicum of wisdom and
insight to others. *Faith* means trusting that what we hear from others is
worthwhile in some way. *Self-denial* suggests that, at some point, we need
to consider the possibility of abandoning at least a few of the meanings we
cherish in the name of intellectual integrity and honesty. Finally, *charity* is

all about attributing the best motive, and being willing to respond to serious differences of moral opinion with generosity and graciousness.

None of this, however, is to suggest that moral truth is an illusion, or that every view of moral truth is equally true or equally false. Rather, students need to understand that what might represent definitive or inerrant moral truth for some may represent just the opposite for others. Defective intellects, moral characters, or religious convictions (or lack of them) have little or nothing to do with why people actually reject one or another version of moral truth. Usually, a repudiation of a particular moral view has more to do with personal interpretation, socialization, and unique perspective than with a willful recalcitrance, ignorance, or sinfulness on the part of the gainsayer. The conclusion for character educators is inescapable: In order to engage in empathic moral dialogue, we must always work hard to detect even a little bit of truth in what at first might sound like the biggest bunch of nonsense. What constitutes truth and nonsense depends, of course, on *our* perspective, just as it does on *theirs*.

A heightened understanding that we do not live in a world where there are actual moral certainties. Rather, we live in a world where we actually construct stories which may or may not include moral certainties. It is self-evidently true, of course, that we live in a real moral world that we must negotiate every day. Ethical dilemmas abound—at home, at work, and at play—and they need to be resolved. At times, we are duty-bound to call some actions bad, some good; some dispositions virtuous, some vicious; and some decisions ethical, some unethical. However, this is a long way from saying that because we must make moral judgment calls with some definitiveness, even, at times, as though we possess a sense of moral certainty, that, therefore, moral certainty exists as an objective fact. If we are honest with ourselves, we will acknowledge that our conception of moral truth is largely a product of the way we were raised to think and feel about morality.

Most important for character educators, however, is the understanding that our moral truths unavoidably take the shape of particular stories that enchant us. What we might find narratively enchanting, others might find revolting, or merely vapid. It is unlikely that there will ever be a High Ground of Absolute Moral Truth for all to follow, because there will never be an All-Enchanting Moral Narrative that will appeal to everyone. In today's postmodern world, it is no longer acceptable to superimpose a religious exclusivity onto anybody's unique religious journey. So, too, it is unacceptable to superimpose a moral exclusivity onto anybody's unique moral journey.

The challenge for character education, then, is not to surrender to the lure of moral skepticism or cynicism. Rather, it is to approach narratives about character education with curiosity, modesty, caution, and when fitting, with a sense of humor. It is to realize that nobody ever makes moral judgments outside of a particular narrative. It is to listen carefully, and to learn how to exchange moral stories with each other with sensitivity, curiosity, and, when appropriate, with respectful criticism. Regarding the latter, it seems patently true to me that some moral narratives are more defensible, more desirable, even more ethically obligatory than others. I would argue, for example, that American democracy is a far more defensible, and moral, form of government than the German Third Reich or the political system of South African apartheid.

However, even though I would fiercely defend the morality of my preferred system of representative government, I must also acknowledge that all moral narratives, no matter how desirable, are infinitely contestable, because they are infinitely interpretable. Their meanings will always be indeterminate, with some people's moral bottom lines continually bumping up against other people's bottom lines. The result is that no people can ever claim to have spoken the final word on any moral issue. Stanley Fish (1989) is right: Interpretation and perspective do indeed "go all the way down." I like the ancient, most likely apocryphal, Hindu view of the world that I once read somewhere. According to this myth, the world rests upon an elephant and the elephant upon a tortoise. When the question is then asked of the Hindu, "What does the tortoise rest upon?" the answer is "Who the hell knows. Let's change the subject." This is to say that one person's rock-bottom, nonnegotiable moral premises are what another person might very well think of as begging all the really fundamental moral questions. Therefore, the question persists: Whose moral *down* down there is truly determinate? Who the hell can tell whether what one believes is really a moral stratum or a moral substratum?

I must acknowledge that every moral narrative contains serious internal contradictions. After all, it was the American system of government—

what many virtuecrats and I believe to be the most principled political narrative the world has ever known—that for decades condoned slavery, prevented blacks and women from voting, and established so-called "separate but equal" educational institutions for blacks and whites, along with a set of shameful Jim Crow laws in a number of other social settings.

Moreover, during the Second World War, the American government was the first government to use nuclear weapons against an enemy, resulting in the deaths of hundreds of thousands of innocent Japanese civilians in the cities of Hiroshima and Nagasaki. To this day, the United States still engages in extensive arms trading, props up repressive governments throughout the world whenever this policy is thought to advance America's oil and geopolitical interests, and builds huge nuclear stockpiles. What better opportunity for character educators to model the postmodern virtues in authentic give-and-take dialogue with students than to open up a frank discussion on the internal contradictions of democracy, or, for that matter, of religion, character education, or capitalism?

DIFFICULT LESSONS I HAVE LEARNED

Thanks to my students, I have learned many important lessons through the years as a teacher of character education. One of the more disturbing is that a postmodern approach to teaching about morality and virtue leaves a great deal up in the air—at times *too* much for some students. I have had students who are public school teachers summarily drop my courses in character education at various times throughout the semester whenever they realize that I will not be teaching them about specific programs guaranteed to inculcate the list of virtues they prefer. These students want practical, tried-and-true applications that they can use immediately in their classrooms. For them, if a course is idea-driven and critical-minded, then it is instrumentally sterile. Convoluted seminar discussions about moral constructivism and objectivism, incommensurability and emotivism, appear too ethereal, totally beside the point, for those educators who think of themselves as no-nonsense teacher-practitioners. As one of these teachers said to me: "I feel as if I've been floating in the ether for a whole semester. When will you ever come down to earth where the rest of us reside? What in the world will my high school students learn about being good human beings from engaging in philosophical conversations that go nowhere?"

Likewise, some students, on both the right and the left extremes of the religious and political spectrums, need more assurance and conviction from me that there are, indeed, certain virtues and moral perspectives that they ought to be transmitting to their own students. What looks to them to be an epistemology of moral incertitude makes them very nervous. These students dislike any teaching style they consider to be distractingly cavalier, too ironic and nonjudgmental for their tastes, particularly when it comes to imparting such important content as virtues and morality. For them, what constitutes good moral character ought to be self-evident. Regardless of their particular political or religious inclinations, these students know the good, and, therefore, I and others should know and teach this same good, too. My advocacy on behalf of a tolerance for uncertainty and ambiguity in moral conversations, and what to them is my blather about moral truth being somebody's special enchanting story, are gigantic copouts. I often hear versions of— "It's either right or wrong. Never mind all the shades in between. If we don't stand for something, we'll fall for anything, and so will our own students. Don't we get paid to teach and not to tease?"

Other students relish the manner in which I play the strengths and weaknesses of one character education initiative off another, and it does not take long for them to get fully into the spirit of the contest. These are the skeptics who claim that all morality is relative and flawed; therefore, it is all fun and games. Some of these students completely misinterpret my attempts to be evenhanded as my way of advocating a kind of moral equivalence about the validity of different theories of character education. Others spend an inordinate amount of time during discussions going on the attack, finding little or no value in any character education proposal. To them, character education is mostly worthless because it seems, in the end, to be so arbitrary and unprovable, little more than a blind leap of faith. Little do they realize that the peremptory and dismissive manner in which they dispose of beliefs they dislike is the loudest message they send to others about what virtues and behaviors are important to them. They are character educators without being aware of it; what is more, according to my criteria, they are poor ones.

Then there are the despairers. I am left to this day with the haunting image of an elementary education major (I will call him "Fred") whom

I once had in a course on character education. Fred was a Sunday school teacher of preadolescents in his local church, and a morally upright, very responsible co-captain of a varsity sport at the university. He often referred to himself as a "straight arrow." I liked him immensely. He seemed, in contrast to many of his peers, to be an island of moral probity and ethical sensitivity, and he was modest and unassuming. Still, there was never a scintilla of ambiguity about where Fred stood on the question of moral truth. For example, in the seminar, he loved reading William Bennett's *The Book of Virtues* (1993), but he openly challenged the relevance of his having to read Nietzsche's *The Genealogy of Morals* (1989). Nietzsche seemed to Fred to contradict everything that Bennett advocated by way of teaching the traditional virtues. For him, Nietzsche was a depressing nihilist, while Bennett was a responsible and hopeful Christian. Fred was well known among his peers at school because he refused publicly to participate in the party culture, with its attendant alcohol and marijuana mania that is so pronounced at my university. Fred could easily have been Bennett's poster boy for the traditional virtues.

As the semester progressed, however, I noticed that Fred grew increasingly bitter and withdrawn. He had little to say when the class got around to discussing my book, *Answering the "Virtuecrats": A Moral Conversation on Character Education* (1997). I attributed his silence to the possibility that he did not want to offend me with his disagreements. My primary intention in writing this book was to model the manner in which I wanted students to engage in open-ended, yet critical, conversations about character, morality, and ethics. I tried to reproduce in my writing the tone of Diana Eck's (1993) "culture of dialogue" around controversial issues. I thought that, both in my writing and in my participation in class discussions, I was exemplifying the kind of dialectical conversation on provocative topics that any democracy requires if it is to be viable. I honestly felt that, in my book, and in my seminar interactions, I had made an evenhanded effort to find both truth and error in contrasting character education initiatives, especially emphasizing the errors in my own view. Evidently, Fred did not see things this way. Toward the end of the semester, he wrote and signed a course evaluation that was blistering in its criticisms. Before our last class meeting, I asked him if he would be willing to go public with his critique of me and the course. He said yes.

Although angry, Fred's words were sincere and moving. I winced, not for my own sake, but for his. His peers were so eerily still during the short time he spoke that I could hear the rapid, irregular breathing of a few students who sat next to me. Here, as well as I can recall, is the gist of what he said:

I don't mean to be disrespectful, but I honestly don't know what the point of this course has been. I came here at the beginning of the semester wanting to look at what others were doing by way of teaching character education. No, this is not quite true. I wanted support for some of the things that I believed about morality. No, even this isn't exactly what I expected. I guess I'll come right out and say it: I wanted to take a course with at least one professor in this university who believed in something with his whole heart and soul without all the intellectual hemming and hawing. When I came in here, I thought that I knew how to work with youngsters. I thought that I was onto the kind of positive role model that they needed. I wanted to watch you, Robert, with your excellent reputation, work with us and maybe learn how to model some of your passion and your commitments. All you did was mix me up, though. I couldn't find one solid thing that you believed in, and, trust me, I listened closely.

What's the value in shooting down all these different approaches to character education in your book? As far as I can tell, your postmodernism is nothing more than a ticket to despair and a license to sit on the sidelines without taking a position on anything. First, you get us to look at the strengths in what you call "moral narratives," and then you get us to look at the weaknesses, and then you deliberately leave everything in a muddle. What am I supposed to do now? What are any of us to do? You let me down. I know you are basically a nice, well-meaning guy, but my mind doesn't work the way yours does. I need something to hold onto, something to love with all my heart, something that I can give to my students at church and to my friends here at the university. So many of my friends are totally lost, strung-out on drugs, and directionless. Hell, I feel so empty and stupid at this moment, and so disappointed, and so self-conscious, and so afraid that you will punish me with a lousy grade for what I'm saying....

Before he could finish, Fred started to tear up. I did too. He soon grew silent and dropped his head. He began to shake slightly. The class looked away in embarrassment. Many students stared at me, some sympathetically, others resentfully, but most seemed to be in shock. One student sitting near Fred gently rubbed his arm in a gesture of support and compassion. Fred eventually started to sob audibly, uncontrollably, and before long he fled the room. I never saw him again, despite my several efforts to contact him. He ignored all my e-mails and phone calls. Wretched memories of my high-school ordeal with Paul many years earlier came back to me. Was I destined to repeat my history of unintentionally hurting some students year after year, decade after decade? Nerve-racking questions about how and what I teach as a moral educator hounded me for days. Was a position of moral constructivism really the easy way out, as Fred charged? Was the best approach to teach character education to become a moral objectivist, if only as a pedagogical strategy in order to avoid disillusioning, and eventually losing, the Freds in my seminars?

To this day, I am not sure of the answers to any of these questions. I know that I am a good role-player in that I can be a convincing actor in support of every moral perspective that we study in class. I am constitutionally incapable of lying about my own passions, though, whenever someone asks me what *I* think beyond the subterfuge of my pedagogical impartiality. I honestly believe that, in the end, what is right and what is wrong for me and for others, what is vice and what is virtue, cannot be finally certified by any version of an inescapable, transcendent Truth. Moral truth is mainly a product of biological adaptation, utility, language, culture, politics, peculiar passions, aesthetics, and unforced democratic agreements. There are many tools that we can use to develop specific character education programs, and there are many languages and stories that we can use to reach consensus on what might enhance compassion, social justice, and human decency in all our human communities. I hope that, someday, Fred will understand that my personal suspicion of all those objectivist moral tribunals that claim the authority to settle the unsettleable questions once and for all is the outgrowth of my own history and has nothing whatever to do with him. I know well that my moral view is as fallible, and, yes, as valid, as anyone else's, including his.

I want Fred, wherever he is today, to know that I have learned from him. I need to continue to grow in generosity, respect, and sensitivity toward students who, like him, may not be ready for what, to them, looks like a shilly-shallying, postmodern dithering. I need to make it very clear early in my courses that I just do not have a God's eye view of morality or ethics to offer him or anyone else, nor will I ever. Finally, I hope that in his own teaching, if this is where he ended up, Fred has learned to look with understanding on postmodern freeloaders like myself. (I admittedly borrow much of my own sense of right and wrong from the Christian moral corpus—from what Catholic theologians once called the "substance" of the teachings, even though I reject the Christian formalities, or the "accidents.") More importantly, however, I hope that Fred has retained his wonderful passion for a moral and spiritual truth that he can give his heart to, that he can live his life by. I am convinced that he, his students, and his communities will be much the better for it.

How a Constructivist Perspective Is Changing My Teaching

I am convinced that, at least in my case, constructivism is helping me to become a more effective teacher and human being. At the end of a course, I find that I have fewer disgruntled Pauls and Freds than ever before. When I was flirting with a modified form of philosophical objectivism in my earliest years as a professor, I knew that I intimidated most of my students. Many of them liked my ideas, but many were also put off by my stern, pedagogical style. The majority of my students never got close to me; worse, very few even wanted to. I remember one student, whom I admired greatly, saying in a note she sent to me long after the course had ended:

> I took the moral education course with you because I knew that you would challenge me intellectually…to an inch of my life. But I also knew that I would never want to hang out with you outside of class. I did not trust that you could ever just kick back and take the time to know me on *my* terms instead of on *yours*. Students like me keep professors like you at arm's length, because on *our* turf you just make us nervous and self-conscious.

I was crestfallen when I received her note. Truthfully, while I got off on being admired and respected in the early days of my teaching, and, yes, even a little bit feared, I wanted my students to like me as well. How could they, though? As a quasi-Platonic objectivist, who believed that there were truths out there to be claimed through a rigorous, Socratic-like reasoning process, I often employed sadistic teaching techniques like the one I called the "argumentative hot seat." For years, this strategy became my pedagogical calling card. Most of my students detested having to undergo this ordeal.

Four times a semester, I required all my students to write extended argumentative essays on the material we were covering. On the days that papers were due, they had to present their arguments in a systematic way to the rest of us. So far, so good, but wait. The rules for this procedure were stringent, and, in retrospect, cruel. Each student presenter had to sit in a chair—the hot seat—separated from the rest of the class. The student then had to present the gist of the paper's arguments in a concise and authoritative manner, along with a number of pointed self-criticisms of those same arguments. When the presentation was over, then, on cue, the rest of us launched into action. Our assigned task was to ask questions calculated mainly to poke holes in the argument, to show the blind spots in the reasoning, to point out the *non sequiturs* in the logic: in short, to demonstrate the utter stupidity of the presenter.

The inhabitant of the hot seat had one responsibility. This was to answer every single question directly, without flinching, and, when appropriate, to acknowledge publicly the truth in the critique of the paper's overall argument. Whether the interrogators intended to or not, most, including myself, got into the activity with ghoulish enthusiasm. The scholarly quest for truth frequently deteriorated into a public degradation ceremony. With few exceptions, interrogators were not kind. The objective was to score points by making the hapless target in the hot seat look bad. At times, I actually saw students at the receiving end of the abuse openly perspiring and blushing. Some were reduced to stammering and stuttering. At first, I attributed this to a lack of practice in cooly and rationally debating the validity of their ideas. Eventually I realized that these were the panic behaviors of people in extreme distress. Knowing this, I still refused to rescue them.

I honestly thought that we were learning the art of effective, dialectical argumentation. After all, philosophers did this all the time at their professional conferences. We presented our carefully crafted papers to our properly wary colleagues, and then we waited for the inevitable, critical assault on our ideas. The dignified name for this was "rigorous scholarly interchange." My more insightful students called it for what it was: a "hot-seat mugging." If I had only been courageous enough to tell students about my own fear and dread on the day I was to deliver my first professional paper at a national conference, things might have been very different. On that terrifying day, I developed such a case of immobilizing anxiety over having to face an academic audience whom I imagined gleefully lying in wait to pick away at my mistakes that I spent almost an hour in the bathroom repeatedly vomiting. Even so, in spite of my own misery, here I was perpetuating the same type of torture in my classroom.

The more that I read postmodern constructivists like Rorty (e.g., 1989), Habermas (1988), Fish (1980), and Barbara H. Smith (1997), however, the more I understood that, in the classroom, there are some things far more important than arriving at, or demolishing, some elusive truth by abusing people along the way in order to achieve this questionable goal. The truth about Truth is this: It is bafflingly slippery, hardly objective, and, *mirabile dictu,* it always manages to end up confirming the prejudices of those truth-holders currently in power. Rarely, in my experience as a philosopher and teacher, have I seen professorial minds radically (or even minimally) transformed as a result of so-called rigorous "scholarly interchanges." With only a few conspicuous exceptions, at the end of the day conservatives tend to remain conservative, liberals remain liberal, postmodernists remain postmodernists, and skeptics remain skeptics.

In my own case, a change of mind from objectivism to constructivism came about very, very gradually, over a period of many decades. I can say for certain that this never happened as a result of intellectual warfare and professorial bombast in a classroom or a conference hall. Over time, I read opposing views to my own very carefully, at first privately, and then I started to assign these readings in my courses. I learned a great deal from mutually respectful conversations with students. I also engaged in many lengthy professional dialogues, both with objectivists and constructivists in my own university and throughout the country. I tried out constructivist ideas in my writing. Beneath the thin veneer of my tenuous objectivism, I was convinced that there had always lurked a constructivist waiting for merciful permission to be liberated. Eventually, after much soul-searching, I permitted myself to grow into myself. On some level, I had always believed that any claim to truth was inseparable from the attitudes, interests, and biases of the truth claimant.

The more cautious and modest I became about finding a once-and-for-all defensible truth for everyone, particularly in the areas of morality, ethics, and religion, the more I began to encourage the expression of the constructivist virtues in my classroom. All of these virtues can be consolidated into one constructivist nutshell: Each student's search for a usable and sustainable set of truths is always and everywhere an unpredictable, difficult, and challenging process. All students need our wise and sympathetic assistance, not our omniscient interference, in this demanding endeavor.

Just the way we do, they, too, need to form their own sets of values in order to inform their own lives in their own best ways. In the most important sense, of course, this is the point of any and all education, and, truth to tell, in most respects, we professors are merely beside the point.

All of us, students and teachers alike, are genuine seekers in the realm of values, ethics, and religion. Few of us have made up our minds once and for all on these topics, and few of us ever will. Therefore, we need to treat each other with exquisite respect and sensitivity. Critique and feedback, when appropriate, ought always to come out of a framework of generosity and compassion, and always with an intention to make the other look good. Spirited and candid conversations aimed at getting to the heart of some sustainable truths are more likely to occur when students and teachers feel safe and supported enough to speak their truths-in-process to others. I was learning the hard way that the receptive mode of listening and responding in a seminar is far more effective than the attack mode of adversarial discourse.

I recently received a gracious thank-you card from someone who took a course with me when she was an undergraduate, and fifteen years later enrolled in one of my graduate courses. I share this lovely note here, mainly because, for the first twenty years of my professoriate, I never once got a message even remotely like it. Not only would no student have ever taken the time to write me such a note, but, if one had, I would probably have rejected the sentiments as being anti-intellectual and brown-nosing. Today, however, such comments move me greatly. As an earlier victim of my infamous, hot-seat pedagogy, this student was gracious enough to remark on what she experienced as great growth in my ability to reach students in places in addition to their intellects. I blush only slightly in reproducing her comments.

> It is hard to know where to begin to say "thank you." Your class was truly a once-in-a-lifetime experience for me. I am not sure that I have ever been as engaged and passionate as I was for those three brief months in your classroom. I will forever be reflecting on the gifts you gave me during the course. I only wish that I could reciprocate in some way. If I could give you one thing, though, it would be this: to see yourself as a teacher who does so much more than expand the intellect of your students. Sometimes I suspect this is the major way that you see yourself. While I admit being in awe of your intellect, that is the least of the reasons why you changed and moved me the way that you did. You have an uncanny ability to wake up

the souls of those you teach. I know that I am not the only one indebted to you for that. Whether or not I ever see you again, you will be forever a crucial player in my spiritual journey. The words, *thank you*, are totally inadequate to express my gratitude. So I will just stop writing. I do have one question, though: How in the world did you manage to transform yourself without becoming a touchy-feely, anything-goes kind of guy?"

This student felt safer in my classroom, I believe, because I no longer feel the need to resort to techniques that barely mask the presence of academic aggression in my learning space. I am in pursuit now of dialogue with my students, not monologue or diatribe. My "argumentative hot seats" have been replaced by "conversational warm sites" for moral discussion. I think that I have become gentler and softer without losing my intellectual edge. I am deliberately trying to soften my previous hard edge without compromising those same high standards that I held years ago. Students still read and write voluminously in my courses, and learn to reason sharply, but now they do all of this without fearing for their lives. As a teacher, I will never stop working to balance my commitment to academic rigor with my desire to grow in spiritual compassion. I know that I still have a long way to go.

Although I never answered the note writer's last question, if I had, my response would have sounded something like the following:

> I am no longer interested in pitting students against one another. What kind of truth, if any, could ever emerge from such contestation? My classroom will never again become a gladiator's arena where the winner is the best debater or orator left standing, or, more appropriately, lording it over, the victim in the hot seat. There will be no more intellectual executions in my seminars. There will be no more students who are the real casualties of this type of intellectual aggression: the ones who sit silently week after week, either scared to death to get involved in the fray, or completely uninterested in playing the games that we all hate and fear but never openly acknowledge.
>
> There will be no more empty charades of scholarly name-dropping, textual nit-picking, and tedious logic chopping. At this time, I prefer to think of my classroom in the metaphor of what Deborah Tannen (2000) calls a "barn raising instead of a boxing match" (p. B7). In this image, my students and I become cooperative builders or co-narrators, not fighters. We work at constructing a group story that binds all of us together in a common edifice called a community of scholars rather than a "boxing ring" that leaves us only bruised and battered.
>
> The outcome of all of this is that we end up creating some important truths in our lives. One of these truths, in Michael Oakeshott's (1950)

words, is to learn to "taste the mystery without the necessity of at once seeking a solution" (p. 428). Another truth, in David Bromwich's (1992) paradoxical words, is this: "The good of conversation is not truth, or right, or anything else that may come out at the end of it, but the activity itself in its constant relation to life" (pp. 131–132). I think that Oakeshott and Bromwich are on to something: Their insights, for me, lead precisely to where character education should begin, and, ideally, where it ought to end: in a fondness for mystery; in a commitment to cooperative story-construction; in the tireless support of the other person's flourishing; in an ethic of do no harm and do much good; in an awareness that virtue and vice are constructs that people must decide, and act upon, collectively, but always starting from a base of compassion; and in a love of conversation for its own sake, absent all the usual off-putting, dialogue-stopping, ideological prerequisites.

CHAPTER FOUR

Real World Ethics
The Passion to Make the Right Decisions

If I accept the existentialist description of man and his relation to the universe, what sort of ethics naturally follows? If I am an existentialist, then what?.... The choice to be ethical embraces both the recognition that one is free and the acceptance of the responsibility which freedom entails.
—Hazel E. Barnes, *An Existentialist Ethics*, 1967

One can write [and teach] meaningfully about ethics without appealing to metaphysical certainties or any kind of absolute values, and about social responsibilities and community even if assuming individual self-interest as a starting point.
—Hazel E. Barnes, *The Story I Tell Myself*, 1997

A CHALLENGE TO CONSTRUCT A REAL WORLD ETHICS COURSE

The challenge to me in 1969 from the chair of my department was pointed, and the stakes were obviously high:

You need to develop a graduate course that is yours alone, if you are to establish your own niche here, do some original research, and eventually gain tenure. Your character education work is fine, but you are offering this content under the umbrella of an already existing philosophy of education course. Why not think about creating an applied ethics course, in addition to your work in moral education, as something that professionals can use in the real world? I know of no school of education in the country that has such a course in its catalogue. Yet so many of our students in the human services have asked for one. Have you ever taken a course in ethics during your graduate education? What do you know about the subject? I strongly suggest that you get retooled if this material is new to you, and then get on with

becoming our ethics expert. I would not like to see you have to move on
to another university after just a few years here, because you are a man without a specialization that we were able to use.

Thoroughly daunted, I managed to put off tackling this project for
a few years because I was content to teach moral and character education
within the aegis of a more general course in philosophy of education.
Unfortunately, this was a course which just happened to belong to the aforementioned chairperson, and I was the interloper. I was feeling safe teaching philosophy of education as moral education because I was able to be a
moral educator without being an ethicist. What I knew about the academic
study of ethics was exactly... *nothing*. I had never taken a formal course in
the field. I had done very little reading in this discipline on my own, and
what literature I had read seemed to be overly analytical, conceptually
abstract, dryly historical, and, frankly, very dull. Most of all, though, I
hadn't warmed up to ethics because the subject matter appeared to force
philosophers to become moralists, secular priests whose official function was,
through rigorous, technical argumentation, to push particular moral views
on people.

Because there was already an existing subject matter in moral and character education in the late 1960s, albeit rudimentary, and because its
potential applications were new, and still tenuous and evolving, I felt that
I could be a deliberate provocateur in the classroom. I could also be a neu-
tralist on behalf of balance and fair-mindedness, and a dialectician whose
main responsibility was to get all the conflicting views and programs aired
without special favor. Ethics was another story entirely, or so I thought.
Truth be told, I was scared to death of teaching this material. I had no idea
about the right thing to do in ethically challenged work settings, particularly those professional settings that were totally foreign to me. Moreover,
I certainly did not want to become a catechist in the classroom whose function was mainly to promote a set of dogmatic (and simplistic) moral
answers to complex ethical dilemmas. Most importantly, though, I did not
want to look stupid. I did not even know how to pronounce some of the
more technical terms in the discipline, words like *supererogatory* and *nonmaleficence* because in the 1960s, I was ashamed to say, I never heard them
spoken by anyone. What kind of philosopher was I anyway?

Then, in 1970, I read Hazel E. Barnes's *An Existentialist Ethics*

(1967), and it completely changed the way I thought about this material. Barnes, an existential philosopher and first translator of Jean-Paul Sartre's *Being and Nothingness* into English, attempted in this book to answer the following question: "If I accept the existentialist description of man [*sic*] and his relation to the universe, what sort of ethics naturally follows? If I am an existentialist, then what?" (p. vi). While Barnes was very interested in the traditional understandings of ethics as a series of duties or obligations, an "inner control" on immediate impulses, and as a set of "reference points" by which to adjudicate conflicts of interests, she also had strong existential interests as well. For her, ethics was always the result of a conscious choice that people made to "justify their lives" and to find them good. In her concise words: "The choice to be ethical embraces both the recognition that one is free and the acceptance of the responsibility which freedom entails" (p. 19).

Moreover, for Barnes, what she called the "choice to be ethical" is to some extent driven by feeling and intuition as well as reason, by needing to chart a coherent, long-range life plan as well as to fully experience life's momentary satisfactions, and by the necessity of respecting another's freedom as well as expressing one's own. The ethical choice entails that moral behavior encompasses both an *I* and a *they*. The most mature ethical expression is when individuals fully accept one another as subjectivities, all with the freedom to develop themselves in their own best ways, while assiduously avoiding causing harm to the other. In Barnes's (1967) own words: "An existential ethics recognizes the demands of both temporal and spontaneous self-realization in the person, so it balances the needs of the 'We' with the jealous preservation of each differentiated 'I'" (p. 463).

Now this was a perspective on ethics that I could live with. As the epigraph at the beginning of this chapter implies, thanks to Barnes, it would now be possible for me to think and teach about ethics without having to ground morality in some type of Grand Moral Theory. Moreover, I could talk about the place of individual freedom, self-interest, and the social construction of morality in ethical decision making without downplaying an individual's obligation to exercise social responsibility in making ethical choices. I could present ethics as the telling of a particular story about a person's continuing choice to be moral as well as simply following the moral commands of that person's church, temple, school, or family.

Barnes's approach to existential ethics gave me both a technical language and a philosophical framework for what I could do in the classroom. More importantly, though, it helped me to see that I could teach this material authentically—honestly and in a way that was consistent with my developing moral constructivism. The next step, and the hardest, of course, would be to construct an actual course offering for practitioners that would be practical, engaging, and intellectually demanding. Having read Hazel Barnes was all well and good, but if I could not convert my insights into a usable course offering, then I might very well be out on the street come tenure time.

Little did I realize in 1969 that although the necessity to keep my job was the mother of my inventing an applied ethics course, eventually this course would define me both to myself and to others more completely than anything else I had yet done up to that point in my professional life. In fact, at the present time, I teach four separate ethics courses, and, to this day, I am still considered to be my university's unofficial resident ethicist. Whenever I am referred to in this way, I beam with pride, even as I shudder at the burden such an appellation carries. I sometimes tell my friends that I probably know more secrets about colleagues at my university than anyone else there because so many have sought my advice on ethical issues throughout the years.

My friends in the outside world who are not professors frequently react with amazement at this delicious little tidbit of a disclosure. Outside of an illicit amorous liaison between a teacher and a student, and some occasional academic dishonesty to deal with, they cannot understand what might be so ethically nettlesome to professors. To many of my nonprofessorial friends, a professor's job is a cushy sinecure in every way, the only moral temptation being the enviable enticements of comely coeds. I can only hope that, for all those colleagues who have sought me out for over three decades, my ethical advice has been somehow wise and useful. I know that for my part I have tried to take their moral problems very seriously, by listening carefully and without prior prejudice. I have striven always to put the best construction on their efforts to resolve what can often be excruciatingly difficult ethical dilemmas. I must quickly add that very few of these dilemmas have had anything to do with sex or cheating.

The Lingering Doubts of a Pioneer

As far as I, or my colleagues in this field, can tell, I was probably the first person in a college of education in this country to create an applied ethics course for educators and other human service professionals. This was in 1969. I had no precedent for doing so in the late 1960s, except for a few nationwide courses I was able to track down (this was before the age of computer internet searches) in medical ethics, business ethics, and legal ethics. I tell this story of trial-and-error successes and failures in my 1996 book, *"Real World" Ethics*. Since that seminal period, I have had the wonderful privilege of teaching well over one hundred courses in applied ethics across four programs in my college, in addition to the dozens of courses in moral and character education like the one I describe in the previous chapter. My thousands of preprofessional and professional students have included teachers, counselors, allied health professionals, social workers and related clinicians, higher education administrators, among a variety of other social service professionals, including clergy, physicians, and lawyers. I have also offered countless numbers of consultancies, workshops, and lectures on applied ethics to these same groups throughout the New England region and the country.

Year after year, there is a common ethical ground that seems to bind together all of the preprofessionals and professionals who take my ethics courses. Despite their different settings and situations, all face similar ethical challenges in working with human beings. All need training in the specialized moral languages that will help them to grow in ethical discernment. All will eventually need to justify their ethical decisions to a number of constituencies. Moreover, many will themselves become ethics educators, either as trainers, consultants, advisers, workshop facilitators, or as full-fledged classroom teachers (as the example below will illustrate). Frequently, students will say to me that watching me trying valiantly to teach ethics, blunders and all, and listening to me talk openly about the ethics of teaching ethics while exposing myself to constructive criticism, was what encouraged them to take on the formidable task of teaching this material themselves.

A public school administrator in my state once remarked to me that I have probably been the sole source of ethics instruction for hundreds of educators in the public schools of Vermont. This is yet another of the bur-

dens of teaching courses in applied ethics at the only public university in my
state. To think that what many educators at all levels in my state might know
about ethical decision making is largely a consequence of their taking a course
with me is a realization that always brings me up short. It forces me to be
humble and tenative in my teaching, and to do everything that I can to stay
up-to-date on new initiatives in the discipline. Most importantly, such a realization is a reminder for me to take the responsibility of being considered
a virtuoso ethicist very, very seriously, even as I chuckle over such an attri-
bution. Starting out as I did, a bumbling amateur in the field, and even though
I later returned to graduate school during a sabbatical leave to earn a
degree in applied ethics, as well as having written a best-selling text in the
field, along with a number of well-received scholarly articles, there are still
more times than not when I feel like a virtuoso impostor.

The requisite ongoing intellectual retooling alone is daunting, as the
field is constantly undergoing change. The *theoretical* ethics literature is massive. Increasingly, philosophers, theologians, political scientists, historians,
and countless other academic specialists are getting into the act. They all
operate out of their own disciplinary perspectives. They carefully parse each
new ethical concept, explicate each new historical connection, and refute
or confirm theories that have come before. All of them do this from within
the intellectual frameworks of their highly specialized bodies of knowledge.
So too the *applied* content in ethics is expanding almost exponentially. Hardly
a month passes without a number of new ethics books coming to my attention, written by on-the-job professionals from a variety of fields, aimed especially at busy practitioners who have neither the time nor will to enjoy the
luxuries of theoretical navel-gazing.

Most of the original research in applied ethics occurs in such fields
as medicine, law, journalism, counseling, and business, among others. The
ethics scholarship in teacher education and related human services, however, is mainly derivative and secondhand. My biggest challenge is to
translate the findings of these other fields into a usable theory and practice of teaching and helping. Much of the time, I find that I am winging
it in my curriculum development and pedagogy. Original scholarly prece-
dents for the ethical work that I do in teacher education and related
human services are minimal, with a few excellent exceptions here and

there. I often wish that there were more human service ethicists writing about what they do so that I, and my students, could compare and contrast my efforts with others. At the very least, this exposure to alternative approaches would keep me honest and help me to develop a more critical and informed eye toward what I do.

One high school biology teacher recently wrote to let me know that, due to my influence, she was teaching an advanced placement senior biology course on ethics and the sciences she developed. What is more, she was using my book as her main text, and my problem-solving framework as her way of teaching students to analyze and resolve ethical dilemmas in the sciences. Immediately I began to question myself. Had I exposed her to a sufficiently diverse introduction to ethical approaches? Did too much of my own ethical philosophy and not enough of others' come out in class? Was she well enough prepared theoretically, as well as practically, to offer an ethics course to high school seniors? Did one graduate-level course with me qualify her to be an ethics instructor? What did she need vis-à-vis ethics content and pedagogy that she did not get from me? These *ex post facto* questions continue to linger long after students leave my classes. I believe that this is a good sign, not only because such second guessing keeps me modest and cautious, but it reminds me how close she and I could come to being litigated for malpractice. (I make the latter comment with only part of my tongue in cheek.)

A Shameless Ethics Bricoleur

My real world ethics approach is holistic. It is both personal and professional. It is a general way of thinking about, and resolving, ethical dilemmas of one kind or another. It grows out of the real-life stories that people actually believe, live, love, and tell. It is an all-inclusive approach to thinking personally and professionally about ethical problem solving and decision making that takes into consideration people's acts, intentions, circumstances, principles, background beliefs, spiritualities, consequences, virtues and vices, narratives, communities, and the relevant institutional and political structures. This approach doesn't tell us exactly what to do as much as it evokes important information in order to help us think more deeply and expansively about ethical issues.

I am, I suppose, what one friendly colleague-critic of mine once called a "shameless bricoleur," by which she meant that I am someone who patches together bits and pieces of a variety of ethical vocabularies, theories, and perspectives in order to help people think about, and resolve, real-life problems. She is right, if she means that I am less the dazzling, original theorist and more the applied, eclectic thinker. In fact, I am very proud to be a "bricoleur" (at least in the way that Jeffrey Stout 1988, the Princeton philosopher, uses the term), although the modifier "shameless" bothers me. I do not think that a sense of right and wrong is ever possible without a capacity for people to feel shame over some improper behavior. I agree with the philosopher David Hume (1902) that morality begins and ends with the human tendency to have feelings of remorse over deeds that are dishonorable or disgraceful.

Let me begin by laying out some moral assumptions that I make about people in general: We all live our lives in at least three overlapping moral worlds, and each world features its own special moral language. I call these worlds a *private, spiritual life-space, a concrete moral world of small communities, and a secular pluralist world of large organizations*, such as universities, hospitals, and managed-care offices. (I am indebted to such writers as Robert N. Bellah, et al. 1985, H. T. Engelhardt, Jr. 1986, James D. Hunter 1991, and Mary Midgley 1991, among others, for the notion of "moral worlds" and "moral languages.")

First Moral Language

The *private, spiritual life-space* is an interior world of meaning. It is what I call the "zero-level" of meaning, which I will describe in another section. I make the point for students that each of us constructs spiritual narratives which help us to make sense of an external material world that, for the most part, rejects any notion of moral and ethical certainty. What I mean by the word *spiritual* does not necessarily have anything to do with belief in god, or religious doctrines, institutions, rituals, or traditions, although, for many, it does, and this is fine. Instead, for me, spirituality is all about finding and creating meaning, either ultimate or proximate, religious or secular, spiritual or material, transcendent or imminent. Spirituality is our deepest sense of who we are, what we believe, and what life is all about. This is a world where many of us hold a set of what philosophers call "zero-level" convictions (a bottom-line morality), expressed in *a language of background beliefs*. I sometimes call this the *First Moral Language*.

It is one of my purposes as an ethics professor to help my students to access, and, when necessary, to articulate their languages of background beliefs, both to themselves and to others. Any conversation about ethical issues in the workplace, I contend, is bound to be influenced by the private, spiritual life spaces that professionals inhabit. When we can speak openly with each other in what I am calling the language of background beliefs, then I believe that we can begin to meet each other where we truly live: in our personal life spaces of faith, meaning, purpose, and hope. In my own experience, this kind of conversation is very rare in secular organizations. It is often perceived to be a threat to people's privacy, ethically irrelevant, too abstract, and idealistic. Yet, whenever I can help professionals to take a little time out to engage each other at this level, discussions of ethical behavior inevitably become richer and deeper. Hidden spiritual agendas tend to get surfaced openly and honestly. The pivotal set of questions that my first moral language asks is: What do I believe? Why? and How do these beliefs influence my thinking about particular ethical issues?

Second Moral Language

The *concrete world of small communities* is the space where we actually develop our language of background beliefs, both in the past and in the present, and, most likely, in the future as well. What we believe morally and spiritually has its roots in, and is always mediated by, those smaller concrete communities that have shaped, and will continue to shape, us as ethical beings. Some of these communites, such as our families and churches, may be more permanent in our lives; some, such as college alumni groups and professional associations, may be more transient. Of course, the reverse can also be true, depending on individual circumstances and temperaments. These groups, or what one of my students calls "nurturing moral nests," may be ideological, religious, ethnic, racial, political, recreational, instrumental, and/or familial. What all of these communities have in common, however, is that they send us powerful moral messages, and, what is more, they reinforce these messages in a variety of ways.

We often speak *a language of moral character* in this world, a content rich, ethically thick vocabulary that is concrete, sometimes colorful, and always particular. It is a psychological and sociological language. It is a language of personal narrative. It is a language of everyday morality, full of parables, down-home maxims, proverbs, and memorable moral bromides. This language is not afraid to speak of feelings, intuitions, personal and communal stories, concrete communities, and desirable virtues. Whenever I can get students to examine, and to talk openly about, the concrete worlds of their small communities, it does not take long for them to realize that the origins of many of their operative moral and ethical beliefs are pretty deep-seated, rooted in relationships and traditions, and often freighted with feelings. I sometimes call this the *Second Moral Language*.

A student affairs administrator in my university once asked me in class:

> Why does it seem necessary in the advising work that I do at the university for me to abstract out of my life all the truly important stuff, whenever my colleagues, student interns, and I discuss ethical dilemmas? Why do we force ourselves to talk about moral choices in a way that seems like we are using only nouns and verbs but no adverbs or adjectives? It all seems so lifeless and colorless. It makes ethical problem solving appear to be an automatic, by-the-numbers process. Check the professional code of ethics, grab onto a few catchphrases, and plug in the answers. Just be sure, though, that you can talk like a lawyer when you are defending your decision.

She really won me over when, for added emphasis, she quoted St. Anselm's assertion that "God does not save the world by logic alone." This administrator was saying to me and to her classmates that a formal set of ethical rules and principles, often codified in professional declarations of ethics, was not enough. Codes of ethics and formal statements of policy and practice can certainly serve as helpful guides to ethical analysis and decision making. However, the human service professionals I have worked with through the years rightfully require something more concrete in thinking about ethical issues. They appreciate an approach to ethical decision making that applies to real world events and people, and draws upon honest feelings and intuitions.

This student affairs administrator was declaring in her own eloquent way that who she is as a moral person is an embodiment of living her life in a variety of small communities, shaped by pivotal experiences in a number of organizations, and touched by influential others (real and fictional) who have come into her life at various points, and who continue to stay with her in lasting moral memories throughout her lifespan. The pivotal set of questions that my second moral language asks is: Who am I as a moral being? Where have I come from? Who do I want to become? Is it possible or realistic for me always to act in, rather than act out of, character in the workplace?

THIRD MORAL LANGUAGE

The *secular pluralist world of large organizations* is the world of the workplace, the professions, the public arena. It is the world where each of us will spend the majority of our adult professional lives. I myself have spent upwards of thirty-five years in the American university. It is a setting where individuals with different background beliefs, and memberships in different communities, often meet as "moral strangers," to use H. T. Engelhardt's (1986) poignant phrase—which, in my experience, is only a little bit of an exaggeration. It is the public space where professionals of diverse political and philosophical ideologies, personal and communal values, and who are each living out their defining moral narratives in particular ways, frequently find themselves face-to-face with the challenge of making collective ethical decisions together.

I often mention to my students that if they were ever to visit a faculty senate meeting at the University of Vermont, they would soon get a sense of the extent to which faculty are really moral strangers to one another, even though many of us have known one another for years. For example, during the year 2000–2001 on my campus, there was an explosive, yearlong debate about whether faculty members should form an AFT-AAUP collective-bargaining union. For an entire year and beyond, emotions ran high over this issue. Personal relationships grew more volatile, and administrators and faculty became bitterly polarized. Collegiality extended only so far as the side one was on. If one was on the so-called right side, then collegiality defined the relationship; if not, then the term was inapplicable.

Furthermore, the president of the university ended up facing a possible vote of no-confidence by the faculty. For three years, debates about the quality of her leadership, or the lack of it, brought out the best and the worst in us. Faculty either praised or blamed her for the way that she undertook a campus-wide strategic-planning initiative. Furthermore, she was either lauded or condemned by faculty and others for the way she handled a highly publicized, hockey-hazing scandal on campus. Personal political agendas surfaced throughout the university, and unwavering moral absolutes characterized the public rhetoric of both sides. The local newspaper, the largest in the state, did its best to add fuel to the fire with front-page stories and editorials castigating the out-of-touch, poorly managed "university on the hill."

During one heated senate meeting that I can vividly recall, some people whom I thought I knew well as moral friends turned out to be moral strangers, and vice versa. People rose to make their passionate public statements on presidential censure and unions by appealing to particular moral beliefs, principles, personal stories, and professional experiences that, at times, completely surprised me. Given the intensity of the fundamental principles and background beliefs that so many of us held, I honestly despaired over the prospect of our ever reaching any kind of agreement as a faculty over the issues that divided us. How, I wondered, could we ever transcend our deeply ingrained, first- and second-moral language differences in order to make a consensus-based decision on whether or not we should call for a vote of no-confidence and whether or not we should belong to a union?

As it turned out, the president resigned due to pressure from the Board of Trustees, and the faculty narrowly voted for a union to represent them. At the time of this writing, it is still too early to tell whether the vote in favor of forming a university-wide union has irreversibly divided or constructively united my campus. What I am sure of, however, is that I do not believe as a faculty we ever truly found the more neutral, therefore thin, third person moral language that recognized and respected genuine differences of moral opinion. Too often we were content to speak our first and second moral languages in order to promote our tenaciously held beliefs. Because these are largely private languages, we talked beyond each other. We had as yet discovered no multipurpose vocabulary to denote our common, collegial interests.

The secular pluralist world requires *an ethical language of codified rules and principles,* rooted primarily in an understanding that professionals and clients deserve respect and tolerance of their moral differences. Secular pluralist language is, of necessity, a bloodless, somewhat formal philosophical language that diverse professionals can employ in order to reach mutual understanding, tolerance, and possible agreement, regarding the resolution of ethical conflicts. It is a logical, procedurally rich discourse, well suited for rational, defensible ethical decision making in organizations that are secular, diverse, and complex. Tom Beauchamp's and James Childress's well-known principles of autonomy, nonmaleficence, beneficence, and justice, along with the theories of deontology and utilitarianism, have effectively served the needs of a generation of health-care professionals in analyzing and adjudicating their ethical dilemmas. For example, essays in *The Hastings Center Report*, a bimonthly journal for health-care professionals, are usually heavily weighted toward what Clouser and Gert (1990) call "principlism," or what I am calling secular-pluralist ethical language.

Ironically, despite its strengths, the majority of my students are critical of this language. They do not know what to do whenever moral principles like autonomy and beneficence are in conflict, or when moral theories like nonconsequentialism and consequentialism do not seem to exhaust the possibilities of ethical justification. Some feminists (both men and women) think of secular pluralist moral language as being uninspiring, masculine, linear, and much too impersonal and uncaring. One ethicist, Michael Davis at the Illinois Institute of Technology, claims that when ethical push-comes-to-shove, it is rare that professionals actually advert to rules, principles, and theories to think about, and to justify, their decisions. They prefer instead to use their ethical common sense, perhaps guided along by any problem-solving model that they find to be particularly useful at the time.

Also, from another perspective, one of my students, a Catholic priest, recently said to me: "I believe that simply being able to defend an ethical action for the right reasons is not enough to be a good human being. It is more important, in my estimation, to do the right action with the right attitude. In fact, I think that it is possible to be a good human being and even do the wrong action, with or without a principle-based, ethical rationale."

Curiously, however, even though some students are openly suspicious of a total reliance on secular-pluralist moral language, most students, I have discovered, gladly resort to it whenever they need to formulate their thinking about ethical issues in clear, mutually understandable terms. It seems to be a natural recourse for professionals to think through complex ethical dilemmas in this quasi-legal and lucid moral language. This language does the work that it is supposed to, even though it may be somewhat abstract and procedural, not as thick as first and second moral languages. The pivotal questions that this language answers are these: How can I best defend the ethical decision that I must make? What does my professional code of ethics offer me by way of specific legal and moral guidance? How can I ever secure agreement on controversial ethical decisions unless I use a moral *lingua franca* that transcends individual moral differences? I sometimes call this the *Third Moral Language*.

ETHICAL SILENCE

I believe that all three moral languages overlap and, in many ways, they are mutually interdependent. Any attempt to discuss ethical issues in a professional setting, and to resolve complicated ethical dilemmas, needs to take into account the existence, and persistence, of all three languages. I frequently encourage my students to speak these languages openly in their organizations whenever they talk about specific ethical dilemmas. Make no mistake, I remind them. These languages are always circulating in ethical discussions, but mostly undercover. Except for the third moral language of codified rules and principles, the other two are frequently repressed in professional conversations. I believe this happens because of a subtly induced, widely accepted ethical silence among professionals around thoughts and feelings that really matter. These exist far below the surface of the conventional moral clichés and the usual ethical problem-solving mechanisms.

In my opinion, this ethical silence is often a result of timidity, ignorance, and suspicion. For many professionals, first and second moral languages seem less practical and objective than the third. They do not appear to lend themselves to concrete problem solving. Thus, many professionals have no idea how to use them effectively when discussing ethical issues. Also, the first and second moral languages seem emotive, individualistic, and private, and potentially divisive to those who want their professions to present a united ethical front to the world. Finally, discussions among many professionals about ethical problems tend to focus mainly on right and wrong conduct, prohibitions and injunctions, and what is litigious and what is not. Although of vital importance, these ethical topics are more conventional, precedent-based, and amenable to a type of circle-the-wagons problem solving that often goes on in the helping professions.

In contrast, first and second moral languages open us up to what the older ethical traditions believed was most important regarding conversations about morality. More specifically, the most important element was talking openly with one another about such perennial moral questions as:

- What is the good life?
- What is good work?
- What are right relationships?
- What is the just community?
- What is it to be a moral professional?
- How can we construct moral communities that bring out the best, rather than the worst, in us?
- What am I willing to risk in my job by way of moral conviction?
- Just who is it I am striving to become as a moral being, and is this possible in the work that I do?
- If not, why not, and what can I do about it?
- How can I use my religious beliefs to inform my ethical decisions in a way that does not turn off my colleagues?
- At what point would the pressure to make moral compromises force me to leave my work?

The major purpose of these older types of axiological conversations was less to solve immediate problems and more to build communities of ethical understanding and moral commitment. They were meant to ennoble and edify individuals and groups. At this present stage of my career in teaching ethics, I want my students to engage in these kinds of conversations. I want them to construct professional communities of ethical understanding. I exhort them to talk with each other at their jobs about their controlling background beliefs, their taken-for-granted moral premises. I urge them to take a little time out from the daily rigors of serving students and clients to talk among themselves about what truly matters. These are the types of conversations that bind helping professionals into genuine communities. These are the discussions that give point, purpose, and rationale to the concrete ethical decisions that practitioners must make every day of their lives. It is too bad that so many professionals tend to do it alone.

Moral Philosophy Is Not Everybody's Cup of Tea

I made the decision early on, after reading Hazel Barnes, to go with both my strength and my passion in teaching applied ethics courses. I was interested in exploring the relationship of individual freedom and social responsibility in choosing to be ethical. Moreover, I wanted to see whether it was possible to make the ethical choice without believing in moral absolutes. Also, if moral choice is largely driven by self-interest, as Barnes contends, does it necessarily follow that social responsibility will suffer? I find in my teaching that I love the ethical questions that these sorts of problems entail almost as much as I do the answers. Socrates felt the same way. So too did David Hume. Today, Richard Rorty follows in the tradition of these famous ethics investigators.

Therefore, I try to keep these more difficult ethical questions front and center in my seminars. Some students challenge their practicality, of course, but, in time, most willingly enter into the spirit of philosophical and spiritual inquiry that these questions are bound to provoke. I work very hard to keep these inquiries close to my students' real world personal and professional experiences. I find that I am getting better at doing this the more I remain the philosopher rather than the consultant who poses as the all-purpose problem solver.

I am generally able to convince students that the solutions to ethical case-dilemmas are always tentative, continually subject to fresher interpretations and more creative redactions upon further examination. I know from years of experience that I am a good provocateur in ethics discussions, and that I can get students to think beyond what appears, at first blush, to be morally obvious. I know how to challenge them to take philosophical risks in their thinking through a possible solution to a thorny ethical problem. While I am fully aware of the necessity of organizing my three-language ethics framework around the resolution of actual case-dilemmas that my students themselves construct, based on their own professional experiences, I am always on the lookout for larger and deeper issues to confront.

It must also be said, however, that I am keenly on the lookout to avoid the philosopher's temptation to play the devil's advocate. This pedagogical ploy is just too easy for someone with philosophical training and too irritating to students. Neither do I want students to see me as an obsessed Socratic questioner, forever upping the ante by introducing more and more complex nuances to their ethical dilemmas. I have found from repeated experience that exotic complications like those I dream up in my seminars are unlikely ever to take place in the real world of human service practice. Finally, I do not want to become the academic know-it-all who travels the consultant's circuit, commands huge honoraria, and provides advice that is only half as clever as it is impractical. I hate to sound cynical, but I have met only a few ethics consultants who were able to avoid making practitioners feel ignorant and morally deficient. I have met even fewer whose advice outlasted their on-site visits by even a day. How many times have I heard in my own consultancies a variation of this complaint: "It all sounds good in theory, but it would never work in my field because...."

It is obvious that in many professional venues, including the classroom, the type of moral philosophy that excites *me* is not everybody's cup of tea. The technical language alone can be daunting. Such terms as deontology, utilitarianism, divine command theory, autonomy, supererogation, and nonmaleficence frequently intimidate and silence many students. The technical jargon can appear to some to be impenetrable. So too can many of the more specialized readings that I frequently assign. Moreover, there are always those students who never quite catch on to my three moral-language framework, thinking that it is an unnecessarily contorted way to think about ethical dilemmas. Why not, some contend, just consult codes of ethics or established practices to think through, and resolve, ethical dilemmas? What does jawbreaking philosophical language have to do with it anyway?

Having said this, however, I think it is important for ethics educators to remember that undergraduate and graduate students take courses outside their usual ken of knowledge all the time. These courses require at least a basic understanding of highly specialized vocabulary and difficult concepts. Whether it is a course of study dealing with the arcane argot of literary or linguistics theory, or the intimidating terminology of any number of science or economics courses, I contend that when students are motivated, they will learn the language and the ideas. In fact, many will master these. It has not escaped my notice how quickly and easily most students command what, to me, is the indecipherable speech and content of computer technology. The truth is that most students like being multilingual and multiknowledgeable, provided they can see the immediate and long-range practical payoff of these new acquisitions.

Many students tell me that at the end of my course they surprised themselves at how fluent they had become in understanding, and using, the three moral languages. I knew this all along, because, during the semester, I often point out to students how "language-smart" they are becoming. I also think it essential to distinguish for them the difference between being *fluent* in their use of ethics nomenclature and being *arrogant*. I do this on the principle that professional language, for better or worse, often defines reality for the people we serve. This understanding itself is a huge ethical responsibility for practitioners, and it must never be taken lightly.

IF I WERE TO BECOME THE DESIGNATED ETHICS CZAR

If I were suddenly to become the Designated Czar for teaching ethics in the American university, I would make the first required reading Kenneth A. Bruffee's (1993) *Collaborative Learning: Higher Education, Interdependence, and the Authority of Knowledge*. Bruffee's essential point is that if we want to "reacculturate" students into any new "professional knowledge community," then we must invite them to use the "characteristic language" of the "discourse community" from the very beginning of their training. What is more, we must encourage them to assist us in the continual reconstruction of such language. For Bruffee, learning a new discipline is to learn how to speak the language. This is best done, according to him, in a community of "collaborative learners" where the emphasis is less on lecturing and drilling, and more on conversing and inquiring.

Like Bruffee, I encourage my students to define, and to translate, trademark ethical jargon into their own words, while still trying to remain faithful to the basic meaning and intention of the original terms. This approach conveys the message that no single authority ever "owns" professional language, or has the final say as to how this language must be interpreted and applied. Applied ethical language is fluid. It is constantly changing and growing, adapting itself to new situations, to new professional and client demands.

The discipline of genetic engineering, for example, has changed so profoundly in the last decade that bioethicists are still trying to construct an ethical language that can speak realistically to the extremely complex and vexing moral issues that confront professionals in this field. So too, in the field of public education, with the widespread use of Individual Educational Plans, Ritalin, and Learning Portfolios, new ethical dilemmas (along with the need for an appropriate moral language to address them) arise to challenge teachers, counselors, and other school professionals. Bruffee and I are saying that, at times, we must encourage students to become research partners in developing a continually evolving and functional professional language.

The key for ethics educators, of course, is to take nothing for granted in teaching a new language. I repeatedly define all technical terminology many times during the semester. I put the words on the board, on an overhead, in a syllabus, or in handouts, whenever I can. I point out the appropriate Latin, Greek, French, or German etymological roots. I give a brief history of each term. I show how, despite its initial mysteriousness for the novice, technical ethics terminology serves a very useful purpose, in the same way that computer and medical parlance do. I insist that students use the language among themselves as often as possible, and that they define specialized ethical vocabulary in their own creative ways, whenever the problem-solving situation requires it.

The most convincing point that I make with students, however, is when I tell them that a knowledge of specialized language can enhance their competence in practice. In other words, the greater the amount of technical ethical language that professionals command, the more morally discerning they are likely to become. Consequently, the more probable it is that they will be able to avoid litigation, public embarrassment, and, most important, the inadvertent infliction of moral harm on their clientele (e.g., violating client autonomy, treating clients unfairly, lying to them, or neglecting to elicit informed consent). Technical ethical language empowers the practitioner (and the client) because it enlarges the range of professional vision. Practitioners, however, must always be vigilant about not using technical language in a paternalistic and controlling way, as this only ends up alienating and disempowering clients.

Many professionals who have taken my applied ethics courses through the years thank me for introducing them to the philosophical vocabulary, even though, as students, they might have cursed me when they were struggling to learn the meanings of difficult, polysyllabic words. This training, they now find, gives them just the words they need to analyze, and to work through, the challenging ethical dilemmas they must face in the workplace. Some of these students still keep their vocabulary journals (a course requirement some also disliked at the time) long after the semester has ended. Many even find a place for them on the bookshelves in their professional offices. Believe it or not, many of the required course readings end up there as well.

Moral philosophy, as I pointed out in the previous section, is obviously not to everybody's liking. Its immediate relevance to the professional needs of the kindergarten teacher, the high school basketball coach, the emergency room nurse, or the pediatric social worker might seem, at first sight, to be elusive. However, I do not see how it is possible to separate professional ethical problem solving from the deeper moral issues that underlie each and every ethical dilemma. Even a cursory understanding of the functions of first and third moral languages demonstrates the truth that no professional ever operates in a philosophical vacuum. To do the right thing in resolving an ethical problem presumes a right point of view. A right point of view calls for some kind of coherent, and defensible, philosophy of right and wrong.

This, for me, is where moral philosophy enters the picture. Ethical agents are thinking and feeling creatures, as well as practical agents. To teach only a real world problem-solving strategy without the philosophical scaffolding to accompany it is to do more than merely insult the intellectual abilities of students by dumbing down complicated ethical material. It is to leave them ultimately defenseless in the face of public challenges to their ethical decisions. Getting students down to what I like to call their "zero-level-beliefs" is what has posed the biggest challenge to me during the past decade. It has also given me, at this stage in my career, the greatest enjoyment and satisfaction as an ethics educator. The zero-level is where we all live. It is the habitus that serves as the location for our most unquestioned values and morals. It is the value system that seems perfectly natural to us, even though it sits there mostly unexamined. Each one of us is a fish, instinctively swimming in its waters. My job is to bring the moral habitus to the surface of understanding—to demystify it, so to speak—by exposing it to the light of day.

GETTING DOWN TO ZERO-LEVEL BELIEFS

Zero-level, first-language ethical questions are often the ones that stay in my students' memories, long after they leave my classroom. They are an outgrowth of the types of questions asked by the older ethical traditions. My use of zero level has little to do with whether or not there are "ultimate foundations" to our ethical assumptions. Neither do I believe, as I have said repeatedly, that any particular moral interpretation or perspective does indeed go all the way down to some rock-bottom zero level. Rather, I use the term "zero level" as a strategy to get students to work what I call their "downward verticals" in order to become conscious of their most fundamental control beliefs. For some reason, students seem to like both of these phrases.

I find that students are initially far more comfortable examining the "outward horizontals" that influence their ethical thinking. Their first inclination in responding to my zero-level, probe questions is to talk about *where* their background beliefs come from—i. e., the various people, stories, and communities that helped to shape them. Like all the rest of us, they are good individualists and contextualists, raised in a therapeutic culture, and they prefer to go inward, and occasionally outward for external validation, rather than downward. While this kind of horizontal conversation is important—it is the content of my second moral language—I also want students to grapple with some fundamental philosophical questions. I want them to plunge as deeply into the downward vertical as they can. Whether they know it or not, the downward vertical is the place where my students construct meaning.

To encourage this digging, I tend to ask them so many *why* questions about their guiding ethical premises that, frequently, my students will say "Enough!" "Stop sounding like my two-year old nephew who is always asking me 'Why this?' and 'Why that?'" It is never my intention to deliberately smuggle any of my own metaphysical presuppositions into my teaching of first moral language, although I know I do this at times. Who does not?

By temperament and training, as I explained in the previous chapter, I am just not an objectivist when it comes to teaching character education or applied ethics. I do respect those who are, though, particularly objectivists who have attempted to formulate a clear and defensible rationale for such a view. At this time in my life, however, John Dewey's *The Quest for Certainty* (1960) remains, for me, the single most effective critique of moral objectivism ever written by an American philosopher. Dewey's chapter, "The Construction of Good," is a challenge to the age-old belief that moral standards can only be "found in transcendent eternal values."

More importantly, Dewey's book is an invitation for all of us to consider the possibility that morality might be nothing more or less than the collective effort of intelligent human beings to solve their problems in a practical way. Ethics is everywhere a human activity, according to Dewey, partly a matter of taste, partly a matter of what works, partly a matter of sound rational judgment, and partly a matter of democratic planning. I am certain that Hazel E. Barnes (1997), whom I quote in this chapter's opening epigraph as saying that there is no need to "appeal to metaphysical certainties or any kind of absolute values" (p. 147) in teaching about ethics, would heartily agree.

"Zero-level" language represents my best attempt to prod students to think deeply about what really matters to them, and to apply these premises to their ethical decision making. Recently, I have assigned Annie Dillard's *For the Time Being* (1999) in order to confront my students with a series of first moral language questions about God, natural evil, individual existence, science, and morality. Dillard makes it impossible for students to avoid thinking deeply, even though they might not be philosophers, so relentlessly intense are her vertical musings about the meaning of life. I enthusiastically recommend Dillard's book to anyone who might be struggling to construct an articulable, zero-level moral language.

What follows below are some additional first-language probes that I use, including many religiously oriented ones. I find that during the last decade, students seem more willing to explore openly, as well as to acknowledge publicly, those religious and spiritual beliefs that exert a powerful influence on their ethical decision making. During the last decade of the twentieth century, and now into the twenty-first, there has been a great religious revival throughout the United States (see, for example, Roof 1999). Many students are becoming acutely aware of the moral and spiritual poverty that paradoxically exists amidst great material affluence.

As one of my students, who invested well during the dot.com stock boom, and then wisely got out of the market before his high-tech stocks lost their value, remarked:

> Let's face it. There's a worm in the apple of capitalism. It seems like I'm always being tempted to compromise my spiritual and moral beliefs, or else capitalism just won't work for me. Are wealth and security in America ever possible without lying, or cheating, or always having to be on the ready to wheel and deal on Wall Street? The more money I'm making, the more BMWs I'm buying, the more vacations I'm going on, the less I'm enjoying them. I know, why should you feel sorry for me with all my money? Worse, you probably think this sounds like some short-lived "I'm-about-to-find-Jesus" testimony you'd see in a Pat Robertson religious hour on television. Honestly, though, I'm out of touch with all the religious anchors I grew up with. I guess this is why I'm here in your course, knowing that you are going to hound the hell out of me to look deeply into myself.

The trick, I have discovered, is to ask first moral language questions in the classroom in such a way that students do not feel compelled to offer strictly religious responses to zero-level inquiries, although most do. There is simply no escape from students' first-language spiritual concerns. Some of my questions obviously overlap, but I find that getting to zero level in first-language, moral probing necessitates that I come at the classical metaphysical problems in a variety of ways that are not religiously loaded. Secularists too, I believe, need questions worded in such a manner that the language does not bias their responses in a religious direction.

- What gives your life meaning? What makes life worth living for you?

- Have you read any books (fiction or nonfiction) in the last several years which you can honestly say have changed the way you think about (or live) your life? Which ones? How so?

- What beliefs, morals, or ideals are most important in guiding your life at this time? What ones would you pass on to your children? Or to your clients or students, if they asked?

- Do you believe that your life should have a purpose? If yes, what is your purpose? If not, why not?

- Can you give some specific examples of how your important beliefs, morals, or ideals have found actual expression in your personal and/or professional life? If you cannot, why not?

- Whenever you must make an important personal/professional decision, what pivotal moral beliefs or ideals do you sometimes fall back on?

- Do you think that there is a plan for human lives? Is there one for your life? If yes, where does the plan come from?

- When your personal/professional life appears most discouraging, hopeless, or defeating, what holds you up or renews your hope?

- What does the concept of death mean to you? What does failure? What does success? What does happiness? What does justice? What does morality? What does evil? What does good?

- Why do you suppose some persons and groups suffer more than others? Why do some persons and groups experience more success and happiness? Why is it that some persons and groups act more ethically or unethically than others?

- Will human life go on indefinitely, do you think, or will it ultimately end? If you do not care for the question, why not?

- Some people believe that without religion morality breaks down. Do you agree or disagree? Why?

- What do you think of this statement? Ethically, we are all egoists, because, if we are completely honest with ourselves, we must admit that we act out of enlightened (or unenlightened) self-interest in everything we do.

- Or this statement? Egoism is ultimately a selfish philosophy. Without a commitment to altruism, people's actions would be unimaginably self-centered, cutthroat, and hopeless.

- Or this statement? There are no moral absolutes because morality is totally relative to a particular culture, group, belief system, or personal preference. We are all inescapably different.

- Or this statement? There are indeed moral absolutes because regardless of cultural or personal differences, people do, in fact, agree on a number of core moral principles. In some ways, we are all very much alike.

- If I were to ask you the following questions, how would you answer me? Why should I treat you fairly when it might be to my advantage to treat you unfairly? Why should I tell you the truth when it might be to my advantage to tell you a lie? Why should I keep a promise to you when it might be to my advantage to break the promise?

- Why should anyone bother about being moral at all? Why should you try to act ethically in an organization that seems inherently unethical? Why not just do what feels good, or what you can get away with, or what suits your fancy at the moment, or what gets you promoted?

- Under what conditions would you ever be willing to impose a moral judgment on anyone, or to hold anyone morally accountable in the work you do?

THE FUNCTION OF RELIGION IN ETHICAL DECISION MAKING

It sometimes seems to my more conventional religious students that my approach to teaching ethics is too secular, all my good intentions notwithstanding. They wonder how it is possible to resolve ethical dilemmas when the three moral languages appear to be so radically decoupled from their own deepest religious beliefs. I can only respond to these traditional religious believers that a nonreligious or nonsectarian language is the one that works best in a secular pluralist society whenever people come together to make ethical decisions in human-service organizations. We always do so as individuals and groups who represent a diversity of religious, political, and moral perspectives. We simply do not speak a monolithic first moral language. Therefore, of necessity, we need to learn to cobble together a kind of ethical *lingua franca,* a hybrid language of rules and principles that serves the very practical purpose of giving us a common moral vocabulary with which to work through our difficult ethical choices. From where I sit, both as a teacher and as an applied ethicist, this secular moral language is unavoidable in the real world, given the plethora of religious and moral views that professionals hold, many of them in perpetual conflict.

We do not live in a theocracy in the United States. We are not Iran, Iraq, Afghanistan, or Pakistan, four Islamic republics increasingly in the news during recent years. I suspect that educators and other human service professionals in these countries probably have an easier time than we in solving their ethical problems, because, as practicing Muslims, they are able to start with similar moral and religious premises. They have a priori reached a first moral language consensus, because their religious beliefs provide a common ethical foundation for their professional practices, at least in theory. I have had students in my courses from at least two of these countries inform me that while ethical decision making rarely takes on a perfect one-to-one correspondence with their religious convictions, no matter how devout they might be, there is, nevertheless, far more first-moral-language consensus in their part of the world than here.

Not long after I wrote the preceding paragraph, however, the myth of an Islamic religious and moral monism throughout the world dissolved with dramatic finality. Middle East terrorists bombed the Pentagon in Washington D.C. and the Twin Towers in New York City on September 11, 2001, leaving in excess of 3,000 people dead, including many Muslims. Americans soon came to understand through the ensuing media coverage that the Islamic world itself was actually as pluralistic in its theological interpretations of the Koran and the Sharia (the religious law of Islam) as the Judeo-Christian world was in its own diverse biblical exegeses. While some Muslim leaders in Afghanistan and Pakistan, for example, found textual justification in the Koran for an aggressive "holy war" against Western "infidels" bent on expansionism in the Middle East, others found exactly the opposite.

Some "Islamist" extremists, such as Osama bin Laden and leaders of the Taliban, declared a holy war against the "infidel" Soviet Union invaders in 1980, and against the United States and Israeli governments in the 1990s. However, other more moderate Islamic leaders, such as Imam Yahya Hendi, a Muslim chaplain at Georgetown University, claimed that suicide bombings, religious warfare, and deliberate aggression against innocents violated the very foundations of Islamic law. Bin Laden believed that the prophet Mohammed, on his deathbed, ordered Muslims to eject "heathens" from Arabic lands, even if this necessitated a massive slaughter of innocents. In contrast, Khalid Duran, a reformist Muslim scholar, called the terror attacks on United States soil the "mother of all perversities, an absolute distortion of Islam" (see Higgins 2001; Woodward, 2001). Moreover, Ishtiaq Ahmed, an Islamic political scientist at the University of Stockholm, said that "violence, terror, religious bigotry, sectarianism and narrow-minded and mean apologies for oppression within Muslim groups must be challenged uncompromisingly and with utmost honesty" (Higgins 2001, p. D8).

The religious situation in the United States is probably more pluralistic than in any other country in the world. In my opinion, this is our moral strength (as well as our weakness) as a nation. At any given time, we are a Babel of believers and disbelievers, Muslims and Jews, Buddhists and Christians, humanists and mystics, rationalists and emotivists, agnostics and pantheists, fundamentalists and neopagans. Even among Christian leaders in the fall of 2001, for example, there was considerable internal debate preceding the American bombing of the Taliban in Afghanistan as to what would constitute a religiously justifiable response to the catastrophic acts of terrorism on American soil.

Christian pacifists claimed that the "just war" theory of St. Augustine and Thomas Aquinas was an anachronism in the twenty-first century when wars of the future will likely be waged with weapons of mass destruction, including germ and other forms of biochemical warfare. Christian proponents of just war, in contrast, argued that nonterroristic countries had a moral responsibility to take up arms in order to establish justice and protect the innocent, as long as the principle of proportionality guided military decision making and the killing of noncombatants was strictly forbidden. Likewise, several Islamic scholars came down on either side of the just war question (Ostling 2001). Contrary to the title of a wonderful book by Jeffrey Stout (1988), I do not believe that in this country, or, indeed, in any country in the world, we will ever achieve a universal *Ethics After Babel*. We are just too diverse for that.

For example, in the United States, although the Gallup Polls continue to report year after year that upwards of 90% of Americans believe in a god, and a whopping 84% believe that Jesus is that god; and although Christians reportedly comprise 82% of the adult population, the polls also show something else. Sixty-four percent of these same people do not believe in moral absolutes, 44% believe that people can be religious totally independent of churches, mosques, and synagogues, 54% have little or no confidence in the clergy, and actual church attendance during the course of an entire year, in spite of claims to the contrary, is only 26.7% (all the data are reported in Reeves, 1996).

The fact is that a large majority of Americans, including professionals, "...go about their lives pretty much the same as those who have no faith at all" (Reeves, pp. 20–21). The moral is clear: The above data confirm that America is not a thoroughly religious society, and probably never will be. Americans can be both religious and irreligious, particularly when it suits them, and depending on the appropriate time and place. Even among the militant Christian Right and Christian Left, religious beliefs in the real, work-day world function more like tools to get things done than dogmas to be applied undiscriminatingly (see, for example, Alan Wolfe's *One Nation, After All*, 1998, and *Moral Freedom*, 2001).

I work with some colleagues at my university who represent both right and left Christian factions, and, although in private conversations I have heard them passionately express their first-moral-language religious views, in public it is different. Whenever we serve together on working committees of one kind or another, they wisely keep their background religious beliefs to themselves. How could it be otherwise, if they wish to avoid estranging potential political allies in the workplace who might think differently in the religious sphere but very similarly in the professional sphere? In work settings, political self-interest has a way of inducing us to make friends among the opposition, in spite of our significant first-moral-language differences. In my estimation, this is how it should be.

Irrespective of their theological differences, professionals who belong to the religious right or left are pragmatists, as are most Americans. Thus, whether we are atheists, agnostics, or theists, whenever we get together to solve ethical problems in our professional organizations, most of us know intuitively that we need to speak a moral language that is secular as well as religious, and practical as well as denominational. The main reason that I approach my ethics courses in the language and tone that I do is to appeal to the secular and pragmatic bent of human service professionals who sign up to take them. I want my students to construct an ethical discourse capacious enough to include professionals of all religious and philosophical stripes.

Notwithstanding any unintended, antireligious impression the above comments might leave, I am in no way antireligious. As I have been emphasizing throughout this book, I strongly believe that teaching is, at bottom, a spiritual activity. So too is ethical decision making. I am an avid interrogator of religion who is still in the midst of a career-long struggle to create a spiritual-pedagogical-moral narrative that makes sense to me. What I want to avoid is making some preferred version of religion normative for everyone. I am keenly aware of the folly of ignoring, or downplaying, the influence of religion and spirituality on an *individual's* ethical decision making. I readily admit that almost daily I could do a better job in the classroom to explore this influence in greater depth as a major component of first and second moral languages.

I remember clearly a high school principal saying something like the following to me after class one day several years ago:

> My professional ethic is actually the particular religious teaching I am trying to put into practice at any given moment. Without my religious convictions, and my church to support me, I've got no morality, period! Here I am ready to graduate with a master's degree, and even in this class on ethics I have not been encouraged to discuss the interplay of my morality, my professional practice, and my religious beliefs. For all you and my classmates know, I'm just a public school principal—another bureaucrat who takes courses, motivated mainly by the need to study the practical stuff that I need to become a superintendent some day. Even though you try hard to be open-minded, you insult me, and others like me, when you don't encourage me to talk openly about what really matters. I try to hear the voice of my God in all of my decisions, particularly my ethical decisions. Isn't this important?

Yes, this is very important. In fact, it is why, through the years, I have enlarged my approach to first moral language to include the expression of such powerful beliefs in my classes. Religion, for many, must play a key role in any examination of morality, ethics, and the formation of character. Despite claims to the contrary (e. g., Nielsen 1990), I believe that certain traditional religious virtues (e.g., faith, hope, love, piety, compassion, sacrifice, forgiveness, obedience, self-respect) still have considerable value in secular pluralist societies, even for disbelievers. Moreover, many students consider a purely secularized morality to be foundationless and arbitrary, hence relativistic. To intentionally omit religious considerations from applied ethical training is to deprive some students of the opportunity to use an important intellectual, spiritual, and emotional resource to become fully informed, first moral-language ethical decision makers.

Once again, however, in the interest of honest self-disclosure, I need to underscore Hazel Barnes's assertion that people can be moral without being religious or even spiritual. So too it is possible for people to be religious without being moral. I personally lean toward David Hume's thinking on this issue in his *Enquiry Concerning the Principles of Morals* (1902), first written in 1752. While religion per se can definitely be either a good or a bad influence on moral conduct, Hume believes that people are moral mainly because they are naturally "benevolent." They do not need religion. They are also motivated, in part, by "self-interest." Moreover, they wish to win the "good regard of others," just as they wish to achieve the "good regard of themselves." In addition, they fear the "threat of civil punishment." In my estimation, Hume provides a reasonable explanation for why someone can be a moral person with a keen sense of right and wrong without necessarily being a religious person.

However, Hume ought not to have the last word on this question. Ethics has never been a completely autonomous subject matter, and neither has religion. It is not possible, nor is it desirable, in my opinion, to completely bracket the theological infrastructure of ethics. Hume's reasons for acting morally are largely this-worldly and egoistic, grounded almost entirely in a narrow self-interest, as well as a need for winning the favor of others. I for one cannot say definitively—in fact, I seriously doubt it—that self-interest and social-impression management constitute the most enduring and functional rationale for morality in any society, and neither can Hume. I think it fair to say that at least as much evil has probably been done in the promotion of self-interest throughout history as in the name of religion. Of course, it is also true that self-interest and religion often crisscross, and the evil that results from this mix can be especially lethal.

Hume's reasons for separating morality and religion completely skirt the question of whether a secular morality without religious foundations is sufficient to address the overwhelming problem of terrible evil in the world. If we were to exclude religious considerations from ethical deliberation, as Hume would have us, then we run the very real risk of impoverishing our moral consciousness, or, at the very least, severely limiting its vision. How, for example, in the face of war, genetic deformity, the ravaging of the environment, the ever-constant threat of nuclear devastation, and genocide, can a morality entirely devoid of religious meaning make any difference at all in preventing, or at the very least, palliating the existence of these evils? This is a fundamental first-moral language question that I contend we need to discuss openly in applied ethics seminars.

Absent the height, depth, and breadth of a religious element to first moral language, how can we ever seriously evaluate the morality of the human condition? What standards would we use? How would we ever find spiritually satisfying answers to such difficult but persistent first-moral-language questions as "After all is said and done, why should I bother being moral anyway?" and "In the event that my self-interest and yours collide, why should I sacrifice my interests in order to do what might be right?" One of the major reasons why I think that religion is inseparable from the study of ethics is that it allows many students an alternative standard—one that represents a set of nonsecular criteria—with which to assess the value of various ethical frameworks. It is true that morality does not need to depend on religion for its validity, nor should it. However, without the possibility of a religious warrant for many students and professionals, ethical decision making becomes something purely arbitrary, hence vapid, unsatisfying, and simply inadequate.

As a thought experiment, whenever we undertake our work on first moral language, I often ask the disbelievers in my class to pretend that they are believers, and to think of some ways that religion might actually enhance ethical decision making. By the same token, I ask the believers to pretend that they are disbelievers, and to come up with some ways that religion might actually diminish ethical problem solving. This is an important exercise, I find, because it evokes from both sets of role players the best (and the worst) reasons that the opposing side has to offer. More to the point, it establishes empathy for a contrasting position, where before there was only suspicion and perhaps disdain.

Few people ever emerge from this exercise with their minds radically changed, but most develop a healthier respect for what they might have earlier experienced as moral anathema. Students also learn how to speak with each other about their background beliefs with far greater compassion and understanding. They become more open-minded in their views, and more cautious about proclaiming a final ethical truth. Best of all, in my opinion, they develop the virtues of humility and charity toward others, the indispensable qualities, by the way, for the majority of the world's greatest religions, including Judaism, Islam, Taoism, Buddhism, and Christianity. The ultimate purpose of such an exercise, in my mind, is not only to further a more harmonious communication process, or to construct a deeper and more expansive first moral language; it is to encourage a search for a common moral ground, one on which, we, as professionals, can all agree. In the end, as any serious study of comparative religions demonstrates, we benefit ourselves only to the extent that we are willing to live lives of generosity, truth, wisdom, kindness, affection, and justice in our interactions with others. The implications of this insight for ethical practice in the helping professions ought to be self-evident.

AM I SIMPLY DOING VALUES CLARIFICATION?

Every once in a while, some students claim that under the cover of ethics I am doing nothing more than values clarification. Worse, to them I appear to be hiding behind a postmodern perspective on ethics that is emotivist, to use Alasdair MacIntyre's word that I mentioned in the previous chapter. In this view, ethical decisions can never be rationally defended; they can only be exclaimed and felt. This is the philosophical stance of the noncognitivist (morality is mainly a matter of feeling rather than rational cognition), and in a secular pluralist democracy, I contend that it will always be found wanting. While it is true that feelings are an important, at times crucial, resource to tap in ethical problem solving, as I will argue in the next-to-last section of this chapter, I also believe that more is needed. Defending an ethical decision simply on the basis of how the practitioner feels about an issue is to invite from students and clients accusations of professional elitism, arbitrariness, and worse, malpractice.

In contrast to the strict emotivist, I hold that some ethical decisions in the professions are indeed better than others, in spite of the special circumstances, contexts, and individual tastes and preferences of practitioners. (I also argue, however, that, at times, all of these are important factors to consider in arriving at well-thought-out ethical solutions to complicated dilemmas.) I agree with the mainstream thinking in applied ethics that decisions are most valid when they are defensible. They must meet the test of publicity in the sense that the problem-solving process, along with its results, need to be communicated and shared, and, when necessary, tested and verified. Ethical decision making must frequently be done with others, both inside and outside the professions.

These decisions must also be guided (not predetermined) by both the codified ethical standards, and by the customary practices, of the professions. Moreover, they must be based on carefully constructed arguments that are intellectually convincing to reasonable people. Most importantly, however, they must be consistent with the professional's particular background beliefs, moral character, and guiding principles. If these last elements are missing, then the entire ethical decision making process is nothing more than an empty moral shell without a core.

How else, I ask, might we be able to achieve some kind of human solidarity across our many differences as a people; to find some way to stop inflicting pain and humiliation on each other whenever we display our different moral languages, our different background beliefs? What I have said above is not to be dismissed as mere values clarification or as encouraging only an insipid appreciation for moral difference. Neither is it meant to relieve us from the professional obligation to call others to account whenever they act immorally. When my system is working well, real-world ethical decision making is a rigorous exercise in engendering authentic moral discernment. Moreover, while it shows a healthy respect for the reality of moral pluralism, it also pushes us to take ethical positions and defend them, and it requires others to do the same.

Finally, I have thought a great deal about the extent of my professional responsibility to become a moral compass for my students. This, of course, is a variant of the same question I examined in the previous chapter regarding the best way to teach character education. I agree with many of my philosophical colleagues who contend that the study of applied ethics should extend no further than the teaching of appropriate problem-solving methodologies, along with a good dose of technical moral analysis when called for. They believe that applied instructors like me only get themselves into trouble whenever they add to their responsibilities the requirement to become living models for the moral behavior they would like to see in others. These philosophers argue that we are first and foremost formal ethical analysts. This is our expertise. Like everyone else, we are amateurs at trying to be good human beings. The fact that we have mastered a body of knowledge called moral philosophy or ethics does not guarantee that we are ethical exemplars. In fact, we could very well be nothing more than high-I.Q. moral scoundrels, able to justify any type of moral behavior because we are good arguers.

I have never had an intention to become anyone's moral mentor, if by this phrase is meant that I want to replicate my best moral self in the professional practice of others. I am too dense a mass of moral inconsistencies and compromises ever to want these things cloned. I ask only that my students read my words on the printed page and observe my behavior in the classroom with the following questions in mind: Is the professor working hard to translate his theory into his practice? Does he teach ethics ethically? If not, is he at least trying to do so, to the best of his ability, and how can he improve?

Admittedly, I am a pedagogical minimalist when it comes to teaching ethics, just as I am when teaching character education. I just do not believe that the art and craft of ethical decision making have much to do with instilling grand moral visions in students. I do not want to lose the individual in a grand moral or political scheme. Neither do I wish to run the risk of choosing inconsistent means (coercion, indoctrination, shame) in order to bring about laudable moral ends. Whenever I ask my students at the end of a semester what they might have learned about being better human beings as a result of taking my course, one type of response always remains a constant:

> Doing the right thing, and making the right decisions, takes work. They require enormous self-discipline, awesome powers of moral discernment, rigorous thinking, and, always, a spirit of generosity, fairness, and affection toward others. We actually learned more from watching you fail than seeing you succeed. Thank you for this.

To which I can only respond: "Yes, and thank you for that...I think."

REAL WORLD ETHICS IN A NUTSHELL

In this next-to-last section, I present a series of somewhat irreverent aphorisms that summarize, in a nutshell, what I have learned about teaching ethics for over three decades. As the student pointed out in the above quotation, I admit that I will probably be drawing as much from my failures as my successes in enumerating these learnings. Oliver Wendell Holmes once caustically remarked somewhere that, at best, science makes major contributions to minor needs. Like Holmes, I believe, with only slight exaggeration, that professional ethics courses probably only make minor contributions to major needs. Nevertheless, despite their shortcomings, applied ethics courses are all that we in the ethics "biz" have to prepare professionals to understand, and resolve, the disturbing moral dilemmas which they will face every day of their lives. My intention is not to make light of these conflicts in the aphorisms that follow. Instead, I find that a series of pithy, jargon-free assertions about ethics is what most of my students tend to remember long after the courses they take with me are over. A slight sense of humor seems to add just the right dash of pedagogical piquancy. I address these aphorisms directly to students in the constructions that follow:

Morality precedes legality. I look to my lawyer to protect me from litigation. I look to my ethics to protect others from me, and this includes my best intentions. When I mess up, the law does the work left over from my poor ethical decision making. If, therefore, I can do what is right, then I can avoid the legal consequences of advertently or inadvertently doing what is wrong. Thus, morality, of necessity, must come before the law. In fact, morality legitimizes the law in the sense that it provides the historical, religious, and philosophical basis for any culture's common law. The dilemma arises, though, when the right moral choice is not always the right legal choice, and vice versa. You need to understand both the differences and the similarities between the two domains, and when the two are in apparently unresolvable conflict, you need to know how and why to override one in favor of the other. This is no easy task, because so much is at stake. Good luck, and this, in the end, may be what it all comes down to.

Moral discernment is a skill one cultivates rather than a quality one is born with. I make it a point to read something like Randy Cohen's column each week in the Sunday *New York Times Magazine*, under the heading of "The Ethicist," to see whether I agree or disagree with his take on ethical issues. Cohen, and others like him, always remind me of how much more practice I need to become morally discerning, to be able to lift out of a situation those elements that are moral and those that are not. Go and do likewise. Get your ethical antennae out. Watch films and television with an ethical eye. Read everything, not just Ann Landers, for moral content. Observe your colleagues and friends as they wrestle with their own ethical dilemmas. Listen to call-in talk shows on the radio for the hidden moral agendas. Be an ethical fly on the wall. There is ethical grist for your discernment mill everywhere. Practice makes perfect when it comes to building ethical-discernment skills. It is no coincidence that Aristotle said something very similar about the best way to become a moral person.

Stop trying to make ethical mountains out of garden-variety, professional molehills. Not all case-conflicts are moral, however. Those that are keep folks like me in business. Settling some conflicts might require nothing more than simply collecting additional facts or privately ironing out some irksome interpersonal differences. Not all dilemmas that cause emotional upsets are ethical. Some are, of course, and these require well-thought-out ethical solutions. That's why I'm here. Other conflicts, however, require nothing more than a heavy dose of good common sense to unravel them. Regarding the latter commodity, professional ethicists may be the least qualified people to look to for help with this problem. So go ahead on your own and check out all your facts. Then list all your viable options. The Latin root of the word *viable* is "being able to live with." What solutions are you able to live with. It usually gets down to uncomplicated? basics like this. Whenever it does, however, you will need to know the difference between *viability* and *expediency*. Ah, another ethical dilemma! Sorry.

There is only one thing worse than getting caught in public with your proverbial pants down, and that is getting caught in public making your ethical decisions without considering all the major stakeholders to be affected by these decisions. Our hidden moral constituencies abound, everywhere. What we do ethically will always affect others. Sartre may have said somewhere that "hell is others." I am here to say unequivocally that "ethics is others." Existentialism breaks down precisely at the point where it depicts individuals as isolated voices making moral choices in a vacuum. The ripple effect of any and all moral decisions is huge. Short-visioned and cramped ethical decision making can be a disaster to forgotten stakeholders, and this means a disaster for you and me, especially if it gets into the newspapers. Because each of us moves within a circle of stakeholders that is continually expanding, we always need to know who else matters. What rights and interests do they have? What promises and commitments have we made to them? How can we evaluate the direct and indirect impact that our actions and policies might have on them? Along with lovers, beware of ethical stakeholders who feel scorned. Hell hath no fury quite like theirs.

Should I or shouldn't I? Is it more important to consider consequences or principles when trying to do the right thing? Should I be a consequentialist or a nonconsequentialist, a utilitarian or a deontologist? In the end, does it really matter to anyone other than some academic ethicist writing a textbook? Of course it matters. The simple answer to these timeworn, in-house academic questions is that good ethical decision making calls for serious, balanced consideration of both outcomes and principles, costs and benefits, beliefs and actions, means and ends. Immanuel Kant once said somewhere that a fanatic is someone who dreams according to principle. I will raise Kant one: I say that a fanatic is someone who dreams according to black-or-white, either-or principles. Every principle, in principle, can be countermanded by other principles, whenever conflicts arise. The trick is to know how to override principles and still remain a principled ethical decision maker. Back to moral discernment again.

Good moral decision making leaves no ethical stone unturned. Textbook dualisms and absolutes are simply untenable in constructing a real world ethics. Be warned, though: Regardless of whether we emphasize deontology or utilitarianism, egoism or divine command theory, social contract or social justice, or even all of these in our decision making, we will sometimes live to regret, or at least second-guess, ourselves. Just around the corner, waiting like some big beast to devour us, is a thing called "unintended outcomes." No decision is ever completely comprehensive, safe, or final. Inevitably, something will come back to gnaw us you know where, and it is bound to hurt.

Ignore at your peril those personal beliefs that sit below the surface feeling like dead weights. They are really living things, and they can give your ethical decision making purpose, meaning, and direction, not to mention a little peace of mind.

The Old English etymology of the word *belief* is to desire or to love. Therefore, without our first-moral-language, background beliefs, we are unable to love. We are bereft of convictions. Nothing is real or true anymore. We have nothing to give to others, and they have nothing to give to us. We can neither love nor be loved. We are empty, and so is our professional practice. If, however, we do have beliefs, we are able to desire. We can help others because we believe that this is both possible and desirable. We can help ourselves because we believe that we have selves worth helping. We know that our lives have meaning, because we believe they do. Not only is it impossible to be an effective helping professional without guiding ethical beliefs, it is inconceivable that one can be an effective human being without a story to give life a sense of value, to foster community, to inspire moral action, and to explain the unknown. This, in fact, is the primary function of religious stories, to help us to become effective human beings, and it is one of the excellent reasons that they have hung around so long.

Did you honestly think that a philosopher could mention the word *belief* without delivering at least a one-paragraph homily on the meaning of such a signature word? But wait, there is more. Think of your *general* background beliefs as those behavior-guiding stories that you tell yourself about the world in order to make sense of it, and in order to function in it with some degree of integrity and sanity. Then think of your *moral* background beliefs as those stories that you tell yourself about your relationships with close others, including your confidantes, intimates, friends, and neighbors, in order to do what is right by them and to avoid doing what is wrong to them. Then think of your *ethical* background beliefs as stories you tell yourself about your professional relationships with your colleagues, clients, patients, or students, in order to benefit them and to avoid harming them. So there. These types of distinctions are what people like me get paid to make.

Trust your feelings and intuitions. Horace Walpole once said somewhere that the world is a comedy to those who think, and a tragedy to those who feel. I say that any ethical decision made without consulting your intuitions and feelings somewhere along the way will end up being far more of a tragedy than a comedy. The tragedy is that, in spite of your best rational intentions, you and your clients will most likely get hurt, and I don't mean just your feelings.

Intuitive flashes of insight, and emotional stirrings, can often be powerful guides to moral deliberation, if you learn to trust them, and if you learn to treat them with caution. Does this mean that you should let your feelings be your only guide in ethical decision making? Am I advocating a dangerous anti-intellectualism when I urge you to trust your noncognitive faculties? Am I finally coming out of the closet as an emotivist, dressed in fancy, postmodern clothing? Am I merely another devotee of Oprah Winfrey, getting in touch with my inner emotional bliss? The answers to these questions are in order: no, no, no, and no, although I have to admit that I like Oprah very much. She is smart, and her heart is in the right place. I would welcome her in any course that I teach, only in part because she might choose one of my own books for her famous, on-the-air, book-of-the-month chats. Apart from foolishly dreaming about an Oprah-backed best-seller, though, what I am saying is that the best approach to ethical deliberation is one that fully integrates feelings, intuition, reason, logic, facts, context, socialization, and professional norms and codes.

To feel or to intuit does not mean that you must always surrender to irrationality. In a sense, feeling and intuiting can be understood as alternative ways of thinking, and, thus, surviving. Think of fight-or-flight responses to presentiments of imminent danger, long before the intellect kicks in, both in the wilderness of the forest and in the jungle of the university. Think of feelings and intuitions as also necessary for ethical survival in the professions. I would argue that morality itself is impossible without feelings of empathy, compassion, caring, and love. Without these qualities, is there really any ethic worth practicing? At times, our feelings can educate us, push us in the right moral direction, signal a right or wrong turn. So, too, can our intuitions. I have often had second thoughts about an impending ethical decision, provoked by a strong emotional or intuitive moment of unease. In several instances, I have wisely changed my mind at the last minute. I suspect that Oprah would approve. It is time for the academy to catch up with all the Oprahs in the real world. Nonacademics like her think and feel, reason and intuit, and, gasp...so do we.

Who you are often speaks louder than what you know, say, and do. In the words of Amitai Etzioni: "Moral character is the psychological muscle that moral conduct requires" (cited in Goleman 1995, p. 285).

Better still, in the words of a wise octogenarian who once took my ethics course:

I came to your course on ethics to watch you with my eyes more than to listen to you with my ears. At my age, I have become an excellent moral crap detector. What I saw week after week was full of the usual contradictions, but at least you were trying, often heroically I will add. I didn't need to read your book on ethics. I only needed to watch you write your real book week after week by the way you related to all your students, including me, particularly when things were not going well. Let me only say this, and I mean it as a compliment: I'd be willing to come back for more, although not right away. I'm old, and I need some rest.

This student was saying that acting in character means being consistent: knowing who you are, where you came from, and who you would like to become. It means being acutely aware of the ethical story about your life that you would like to write in the best of all possible worlds. It also means being aware of your past and present communities that have been so central in defining you as a moral being. Finally, it means being true to those dispositions, qualities, motives, and intentions that define you to yourself as an ethical professional. To act out of character is to betray everything that is precious to you. It is to compromise, to turn away from your best moral self, to abandon those defining communities, stories, and qualities of character that nourish and sustain you. Whether or not I did all of these things in the course she took with me is doubtful, but I tried to.

Ask yourself the following types of character questions as you work your way through your ethical dilemmas. The octogenarian I quoted above inspired many of these inquiries. I believe, as she does, that they can serve as a wake-up call to challenge our moral self-deceptions. They can help us to become our own best moral crap detectors.

- Could I live with myself after I make my decision, even if I can rationally defend it?

- Could my professional community support me enthusiastically and without equivocation?

- If my decision were to receive heavy media coverage, would I blush in shame or beam with pride?

- Could I explain my ethical decision clearly and honorably to those I love?

- Would my personal integrity remain intact? If not, am I willing to compromise it for the sake of doing the expedient thing, or merely pleasing others?

- Could I defend my decision before a legal jury of my peers, or better, before the church community to which I belong?
- Could I defend my decision before my professional organization's ethics committee in a language that they would understand?
- Would I be happy and supportive if my colleagues, friends, or family members were to make the same decision if they were in my shoes?

Official codes of ethics are capable of being so much more than just window dressing or quick fixes for beleaguered professions looking for moral credibility. Codes can do the work they were intended to do provided that you avoid the temptation to invest them with biblical authority. They are not infallible papal encyclicals. They are often the work of harried committees, and, unfortunately, the writing can take on a quasi-legal tone that is, in all honesty, deadening. Learn to look for the moral meaning between the lines and beyond the colorless language. Codes of ethics are essentially declarations of professional manners with a tough job to do. They need to secure from practitioners what John Fletcher Moulton once called "obedience to the unenforceable." What an impossible and thankless task. How would you like to do it?

Codes, it is important to remember, are not legal statutes. They are creative stories about good and evil rather than infallible doctrines. They simply point the way to the good; they do not stipulate the good. They remind professionals of the rights and wrongs of practice; they do not (and cannot) by themselves regulate that practice. Most importantly, they rely on the goodwill and integrity of professionals to observe the moral spirit of the code, because not only is the letter of the code subject to multiple interpretations; but the code itself is virtually unenforceable unless the profession unanimously agrees on the precise meaning and application of its prescriptions and proscriptions. Has this unanimity of agreement ever happened in any profession? I doubt it. Moreover, no set of ethical regulations imposed from above will ever do the work that individual practitioners should be doing from below.

My advice to you is this: Approach your ethical code as an inspiring story that your profession is trying to tell to itself and to outsiders. This story is your profession's ideal construction of what ought to matter morally, both to itself and to you. Thus, your profession's official code of ethics is more of a profession of moral ideals than a precise blueprint of specific ethical behaviors that you must display in each and every circumstance. Look to your code for information, inspiration, guidance, and support in thinking about your case-dilemmas, but not for the final word. Look for the angel in the moral aggregate, and you will be less likely to be overwhelmed (or underwhelmed) by the devil in the moral details. Of course, there will always be times when a conflict will arise between your personal code of ethics and your professional code. Then you will have an additional moral dilemma, itself demanding resolution. Alas, nothing will ever be easy.

Cherish your second guesses and afterthoughts. These are where the real learnings reside in ethics. In truth, no solution to an ethical dilemma will ever be fully adequate or fully self-satisfying. You will soon discover that you could have gone in another direction, made another decision, second-guessed yourself yet one more time, gathered more data, consulted another authority, and re-parsed another codified ethical principle. Everything is interpretable, again and again and again. The upshot is that you need to continue to do the best you can, let the ethical chips fall where they may, and explain and defend your final decisions only with "tenuous tenacity." What is more, you need to do all of this with dignity, style, and grace. The latter might very well be the most difficult act of all to pull off, though.

Be grateful for your nagging afterthoughts. You are bound to have them, regardless of how airtight a case-resolution you think you have constructed. Afterthoughts are an important check on ethical arrogance. They continually remind us of how arbitrary and fragile moral decision making really is. The doubts you have about the ethical roads not taken are exactly what you need to remember when you face the next ethical dilemma in your life. Afterthoughts allow you to revisit your cases many times, sometimes step-by-tedious-step. Best of all, they keep you humble and open to alternative views.

Isn't it true in ethical decision making that the best way to avoid tedious second-guessing and annoying afterthoughts is to fall back upon the Christian

*version of the Golden Rule? Doesn't the Golden Rule answer all the really impor-
tant moral questions?* In a word, yes, no, and maybe. "Do as you would
be done by," Jesus said. Nice. Simple. To the point. Unarguable. Right?
Um.... As historians of religions have pointed out many times, there is some
version of the Golden Rule in most theological systems. For example,
Confucius said "What you do not want done to yourself, do not do to others." Hillel came up with the rule: "Do not do unto your neighbor what
you would not have him do unto you." The Golden Rule is actually one
of my favorite moral precepts, guiding me in almost everything that I do
with others. As a teacher, I work very hard to find ways to restate the Rule
in a twenty-first-century, King James Version. However, the basic meaning is still there, and, frankly, I don't know how to say it any better: How
would I like it if you treated me the way that I'm treating you?

Invariably, people will agree with the nugget of common sense that
the Golden Rule manages to convey to everyone, relativists, absolutists, and
skeptics alike. Generally, you can't go wrong in keeping the Golden Rule
front and center in your personal code of ethics. It is not without its dif-
ficulties, however. That old killjoy, George Bernard Shaw, once said that
we should be careful about doing unto others as we would have them do
unto us because their tastes may be different. Sadomasochism is still a popular sexual preference, not for everyone, of course, but for some.

Simple ethical maxims, whether religious or secular, can be very helpful as general action guides, but morality and ethics, like religion, will always
have their subjective elements. These subjective elements guarantee that
obstinate ethical and religious disagreements will persist. This is the nature
of the beast. This is also the hell of taste and temperament. The lesson for
all of us is to lower our moral sights a little bit, particularly during open
ethical conflict. Look for places to compromise without feeling that you
are acting like a moral sellout. Be forever willing to unpack and stretch the
meanings that you attach to maxims like the Golden Rule. Realize, too, that
others attach their own unique meanings to maxims, no matter how universalizable or generalizable some of these might appear to be on the surface.

Despite what I have just said, though, I still like the Golden Rule. I
enjoy discussing its multiple meanings with all those whose tastes are different from mine. These discussions are, for me, the vital center of ethics.

David Hume may have been right when he said that matters of taste are not to be disputed. However, they must certainly be discussed, particularly when *your* matters of taste threaten *my* welfare, and mine yours. This, after all, is why there are peanut-free zones in some public school cafeterias and airplanes. Right?

A VINDICATING TELEPHONE CALL

To conclude this chapter, I want to talk briefly about a very satisfying conference telephone call that I recently had with a former ethics student of mine. He was teaching an honors course in applied ethics to juniors and seniors at a major southern university, and my book, *"Real World" Ethics* (1996), was the main reading assignment. To surprise his students, on the last day of class he set up a conference call between me and the class. Here was their chance, probably for the first time in their college lives, to talk to an author of the course text which they were all required to purchase and to study. Like them, I had never talked on a telephone before with a group of students who did not know me, so I approached the experience with more than a little caution and trepidation. In all honesty, I was reluctant to sit in *their* hot seat on *their* terms.

I had written my book more for faculty members than I did for students, and more for practicing professionals than I did for preprofessionals. Therefore, I anticipated that there would be a number of angry complaints about its formal, academic language. I also expected the usual concerns over my refusal to tell readers outright what money-back-guaranteed ethical choices they should make. Most of all, though, I worried that even honors undergraduate students would completely miss the point of my three-language approach to applied ethics. I imagined them ready to scold me for refusing to give them a step-by-step, easy-to-use formula for ethical decision making.

My anxieties were totally misplaced. A scheduled hour-long conversation expanded to well over two hours. I heard many words of praise along with some excellent criticisms, delivered always in a sensitive manner. Over twenty-five students, some confident, some not, some articulate, some not, volunteered to come to the speaker phone that afternoon.

The *academic* questions were always thoughtful and honest; some were even penetrating.

- "Why did you choose a three-language approach to ethical decision making instead of a more practical code-of-ethics approach?"

- "Why did you limit the moral languages to three? Why didn't you construct a political language? Or a language of caring? Or a language of encounter?"

- "What if there isn't enough time to go through all the languages in making decisions? Then what do professionals do?"

- "What moral language is *your* favorite, and why?"

- "What moral language would you improve upon now that you know its strengths and weaknesses after teaching it?"

The *personal* comments were remarkably insightful; some were truly illuminating.

- "I find it easier when thinking about ethics to fall back on the little moral proverbs that my mother taught me when she used to read me children's books. I didn't realize how powerful these stories were in my learning how to be a good human being."

- What I find most upsetting about your ethics system is that now I'm going to be out of step with a lot of my friends who don't have the training that I have. What if they speak a totally different moral language from the ones that I learned this semester? In some ways, isn't ethical insight going to alienate me from others who might think that I am holier-than-thou?"

- "How can anyone be ethical without being religious? What's the point? I try to be a person who lives her life in a way that is consistent with her religious beliefs. I learned all three of your languages in my religious community when I was growing up. What you say about moral languages makes sense only within the context of my religious understandings. This may shock you, but I found your book to be really spiritual, even though you probably didn't intend it to be. I shared it with my minister, and she loved it. My mother wondered, though, why you didn't put God front and center in your writing."

The *concrete recommendations* that students made for changes in my text helped me immeasurably with my preparation for a second edition.

- "I wish that you had included a glossary of technical words at the end of the book."

- "Would you consider adding an applied chapter at the end of the book that integrates all three of your moral languages around resolving a particular case-dilemma, in order to show us how it's done?"

- "How about two separate chapters at the end, one that speaks mainly to preprofessionals like us, and one that speaks to professionals and to professors?"

- "Is it possible that you tried to speak to too many audiences in your book? Would you do this again in a second edition?"

- "Have you ever considered dropping the language approach and using instead a narrative approach? Then you could talk about first moral narrative, second moral narrative, and third moral narrative. In a sense, isn't every language actually a story that people concoct to deal with ethical challenges?"

- "Next time, would you write a chapter on how somebody like me could use his religious beliefs to solve ethical dilemmas without turning off people who believe differently? How can I make my case on religious and spiritual grounds to secular folks in such a way that I could get them to take me seriously, without thinking of me as some Christian fanatic?"

What I took away from that bracing and warm telephone conversation was a personal vindication that, no matter the age or extent of professional experience, most students are fascinated with ethical content. They want to make the right ethical choices. They want to live lives of moral probity. They want to live the examined moral life. They want to be happy and successful in their careers, it is true, but not at someone else's expense, and not as an all-consuming obsession. They want to live their lives as ethically coherent stories, with continuity, verve, and purpose. They do not want their moral stories to be a mass of contradictions. What was reinforced for me once again was the fact that most college students today are not amoral, Generation-X slackers; they are really moral pluralists who ask only that we, their teachers and authority figures, try to *convince,* rather than *compel,* them to live their moral lives in a particular way.

Most surprising, though, is that all the students who talked with me that day seemed genuinely sensitive to the wisdom of Ludwig Wittgenstein's assertion that "in philosophy, the winner of the race is the one who gets there last" (quoted in Halberstam 1993, p. 201). They understood with a wisdom beyond their years that ethical dilemmas can be incredibly complex, and there are no ready-made, simple answers. Moral discernment is the outcome of sustained philosophical reflection, no-holds-barred questions, and deep personal introspection. It is also the outgrowth of spirited and honest conversations with others.

All of this takes time and tenacity. Ethical decision making is not a quick sprint to win, but a long marathon to endure. The prize is for all of us to finish the run with our personal integrity and spiritual beliefs left intact. In another sense, of course, the biggest prize of all is to leave intact the integrity and spirituality of the people we serve, or in Kant's terms, to treat them always as ends in themselves rather than as mere means to our ends. Ethical decision making is to arrive at a moral truth that we can all live with instead of a Moral Truth that we think we must die with. If I had been physically present in the same room with those students during our telephone conference, I would have hugged each and every one. They made me proud to be an ethics bricoleur.

CHAPTER FIVE

A Spirituality of Teaching

The Passion for Meaning

> There is a place where we are always alone with our own mortality, where we must simply have something greater than ourselves to hold onto—God or history or politics or literature or a belief in the healing power of love, or even righteous anger. Sometimes I think they are all the same. A reason to believe, a way to take the world by the throat and insist that there is more to this life than we have ever imagined.
>
> —Dorothy Allison, *Skin: Talking About Sex, Class, and Literature,* 1994

> Not being religious myself, yet believing that most of reality is likely to be permanently unknowable to human beings, I see a compelling need for the demystification of the unknowable. It seems to me that most people tend either to believe that all reality is in principle knowable or to believe that there is a religious dimension to things. A third alternative—that we can know very little but have equally little ground for religious belief—receives scant consideration, and yet seems to me to be where the truth lies.
>
> —Bryan Magee, *Confessions of a Philosopher,* 1997

THE SEMINARY AND HUBRIS

I have never told a single one of my students that, when I graduated from high school in 1956, I entered the seminary for two years to study for the Roman Catholic priesthood. There are times in my ethics and religion courses when I almost mention this, but something always seems to hold me back. Perhaps it is because, to this day, I am still a little embarrassed to reveal this morsel about my private life. Maybe I fear that I will lose my intellectual credibility if I make this disclosure. After all, my students know me as

a self-professed, albeit deeply curious, postmodern skeptic when it comes
to matters of religion and the spirit. Regardless of what might appear to
be a contradiction, however, I did spend two of the most important years
of my late teenage life in a Catholic novitiate, listening to the Jesuits
(Society of Jesus) talk about what is worth living and dying for. I have never
forgotten their religious and moral influence. It remains with me to this
very day, as integral a shaper of who I am as the genes and chromosomes
I was born with. In the early 1980s, during a sabbatical year, I made a midlife choice to return to a Jesuit education, this time at Georgetown
University in Washington, D.C., where I earned a graduate degree in liberal studies and applied ethics. Once a product of Jesuit training, always a
product, some Jesuits say. I am living proof of the truth of this bromide.

My own formal religious upbringing during my childhood was highly
unorthodox—particularly for an Irish family, living in an ethnic urban
neighborhood in Boston, in the middle of the twentieth century. My
mother and father, both of whom were orphans with no extended family,
with no traditional religious affiliations, and with very little formal education, were never conventionally religious people. Both were proud, self-
proclaimed theological skeptics who considered "people of the cloth" to be
"hypocrites who had no right telling anyone else how to live their lives." I
have no memory of ever being in a church with them, except recently
when they celebrated their sixty-fifth wedding anniversary. For some reason, they decided to renew their marriage vows for all the world to see in
a large Catholic Church in Phoenix, Arizona. My brothers and I, along with
our families, felt strangely out of place with them in that setting. Although
slightly embarrassed, my parents glowed over all the public attention the priest
gave them for remaining together for such a long time. He remarked with
sweet irony (because he did not know) that they must be "good Catholics."

Despite my parents' natural suspicion of organized religion, they made
the decision to send their five sons to Catholic elementary schools so that
"they could learn basic values which they would not get in the public
schools." In order for me, their oldest son, to attend St. Gregory's grammar school in Dorchester, Massachusetts, I needed first to become a
Catholic, however. At the age of five, on the day that I was to enter the
first grade, I have a clear memory of undergoing a makeshift baptismal ceremony in the church rectory. Because he was the only Catholic available

at the time, the church janitor became the chief witness, along with the pastor, to my being received into Holy Mother Church of Rome.

For the next eight years, the Sisters of Notre Dame at St. Gregory's took charge of both my religious formation and my academic education. Thanks to them, I learned how to read, write, and pray—the latter not very well. Thanks to them, also, I learned to think critically. Contrary to the popular stereotype of "recovering Catholics" who hated their authoritarian, guilt-inducing, parochial school training, the nuns taught me to accept very little on faith alone. The Sisters, although devout believers and staunch defenders of the church, were also tough-minded pragmatists. Moreover, they were feminists in their own right, long before such a term had even been invented. The nuns taught me never to be ashamed to ask questions about the things that I did not understand or that did not work for me. I took them at their word, and I still do, to this day. I think that, along the way, I also inherited a little bit of their not-so-subtle anti-clericalism, rooted in their barely concealed skepticism toward celibate male church hierarchies. I try very hard today not to let this unconscious bias get the best of me whenever clergy show up for my courses and workshops.

I entered the seminary after graduating from a public high school (my family had no money for a Catholic secondary education), mainly because I wanted to experience further Catholic education. In my mind, the seminary was the only avenue to higher education open for me. My parents could ill afford to send me to college, and so I took the next best route, or so I thought at the time: I entered the Glenmary minor seminary in Connecticut in order to study with the Jesuits at Fairfield University. This, I reasoned, would be my ticket to a college degree. I could decide later whether to go on to pursue further theological study for eventual ordination. I never reached this point, however, as I lost my already slender faith in God during my time with the Jesuits. Ironically, I read my way *out of* the church while studying to become an *advocate for* the church.

I recall a particularly troubling conversation that I had in my second year with a well-known Jesuit theologian about the hoary subject of good and evil. I could never understand why innocent people had to suffer so much, given the claim that the Christian God was all-loving and all-powerful. After going back and forth with me for a while, and getting nowhere, the theologian's patience began to wear thin. His words to me were direct:

You sound so bitter and proud. Why do you talk only about pain and evil? Why don't you talk more about God's overflowing love, kindness, and forgiveness? None of us is God, and so we'll never understand why he permits what looks to us like unnecessary suffering. Life is not fair, and if you expect it to be, you are dictating the rules of *your* game of life to a God who is bigger than any man-made rules. Go read Job in the Christian Bible. God tells Job that he has no right to question God because he is not God, and he can never be God. For now, you need to be quiet, like Job was in the end. Trust in God's almighty Providence. After all, like Job, neither of us was around when God started the whole thing, were we? And it's unlikely that we'll be here when it's all over. Your hubris is getting the best of you. Stop your questioning, and get down on your knees. If you truly have a religious vocation, then you'll start showing a little humility.

Hubris, it was the first time that I had ever heard the word, even though I had attended Boston Latin School and studied Greek and Latin during my early teen years. I looked it up, and I immediately felt ashamed. I did not want to be a "wantonly insolent or proud" person. For the Catholic Church, pride and arrogance, along with sexual libertinism, were the cardinal sins. They led ineluctably to theological questioning and disobedience, resulting eventually in heresy, dissidence, and excommunication from the Church. Why then, I wondered, did the nuns encourage questioning? This disconnect between what the nuns had taught me to do and what the Jesuits had made no sense to me.

Several heated conversations in the seminary, like the one I had with the famous theologian, on a number of philosophical and religious topics, eventually forced my hand. All these conversations usually ended up in the same place: My confusion was a result of a personal defect, my willful arrogance. As I was told time and time again: The answers to my questions would only be found in frequent confession, prayer, and, if necessary, in extensive pastoral counseling. I slowly came to realize that a college degree under these conditions just did not seem to be worth the effort. I was fated to be an inveterate questioner, thanks to the lifelong example of my skeptical parents, reinforced by the canny nuns at St. Gregory's elementary school. I walked away for good from the seminary, from Christianity, and from what had been, at best, a tepid and expedient Catholic faith. Except for a few short-lived, nugatory flirtations with the Church, I have remained for forty years what I would call an existential agnostic regarding conventional religion's truth claims. Some Jesuits today would undoubtedly think that I am still suffering from the sin of hubris; in fact, I am sure that they would claim it has gotten the best of me, and, therefore, I am lost. It gives me no satisfaction to say that there are times when I would agree, except that, now, I feel no pangs of guilt or remorse.

THE INTOLERABLE PROBLEM OF EVIL

Among other reasons, I lost my faith during my early adulthood over what philosophers and theologians call the "problem of evil," or theodicy. More to the point, I lost my belief in a merciful and compassionate being, because I feared his ineptness, or, to be more honest, his cruelty, in the face of human suffering and dying. Why, for example, did God continue to look away through the centuries as mothers killed their children and fathers abandoned and/or raped them? Why, I wondered, did God tolerate blindness, epilepsy, malignant tumors, or fiery bus crashes full of children returning from Sunday school? Why did he step aside and watch as lightning bolts killed church workers during an electrical storm, or as a tornado swept through a Christian summer camp and destroyed everything in its path, including hundreds of children at prayer?

Where was God during the Black Death when bubonic plague decimated Europe and Asia in the fourteenth century, or during the twentieth century Jewish Holocaust? Why were 27,000 innocent people killed by a seismic ocean wave in Japan on June 15, 1896? For what reason did typhoon waves drown 138,000 children and adults in Bangladesh on April 30, 1991? Why does the omnipotent, beneficent, merciful Creator-God of Christianity and Judaism, or the 250 million deities of Hinduism, or the Great and Almighty Allah of Islam allow a Mao Tse-tung, former chairman of the People's Republic of China, to destroy thirty million people? Or a Hitler to incinerate six million Jews? Or a Stalin to starve to death seven million Ukrainians? Or a Pol Pot to kill two million Cambodians? Or the flu epidemic of 1917–1918 to obliterate twenty-two million people worldwide? Or the millions of black people of all ages throughout the centuries to be disenfranchised, beaten, oppressed, humiliated, raped, and killed by exploitative slaveowners in Africa, America, and in other countries? Or the hundreds of thousands of AIDS victims worldwide to die excruciatingly painful deaths, often reviled by some spiteful religious believers as "getting what they [homosexuals] deserve," even though, today, most AIDS victims are heterosexuals, women, and children (See Dillard 1999; Easterbrook 1998).

Or another thirty million, blameless children under the age of five to die each year throughout the world? To put a human face on this last statistic: These are thirty million defenseless children of all ages, dying, for no valid supernatural reason, some screaming out in vain, others suffering and whimpering inaudibly in the darkness, still others wasting slowly away over interminably long periods of time from neglect, hunger, oppressive weather and living conditions, brutal physical and psychological cruelty—meeting death painfully, day after day, month after month, year after year, decade after decade. I grow more numb than despairing whenever I contemplate these senseless horrors.

Is this numbness a necessary survival adaptation? Is it the reason why I am able to set aside the hideousness of these statistics as I go about the pleasurable and comforting routines of my sheltered and privileged day-to-day life? Was David Hume (1902) right when he said that most self-declared religious people, if forced to make such a gruesome choice, would stoically countenance the destruction of millions of people in a country far away than suffer, without an anesthetic, the surgical excision of the tips of their fingers and toes? Why have I and those I love been spared terrible misfortunes? What makes me and them so special? In the end, is life just an evolutionary crapshoot? Is human survival merely a matter of developing the right gene pool and the right natural adaptations?

Not long ago I came across the devastating words of Eli Wiesel (quoted in Armstrong 1993), the Nobel Prize winner and Holocaust survivor, remembering the time he watched the "black smoke of the crematorium coiling to the sky" at Auschwitz. This is after his mother and sister were gassed to death and later incinerated. He says, "Never should I forget that nocturnal silence which deprived me, for all eternity, of the desire to live. Never shall I forget these moments which murdered my God and my soul and turned my dreams to dust." And, later, when the Gestapo hanged a small child in front of thousands of people, Wiesel could only blurt out the following words to a fellow prisoner: "Where is God now? Where is He? Here He is—hanging here on this gallows" (p. 375).

Wiesel causes me, to this day, to seriously question the existence of a personal God who refuses to lift a hand to prevent the deaths of millions;

the same God who looks on helplessly (or delightedly? Who knows for sure?) at the suffering of a single, guiltless child, gasping for breath, choking to death in the chilled, morning air, taking almost an hour to die because of his very light weight. Why? For no other reason than that he is a Jew. Who, I sometimes ask, needs this silent, disappeared God? He is not worth the bother. I continue in the sixth decade of my life to ask these kinds of unanswerable questions. Do these hideous events, and millions of others like them, render the idea of a God, or some other protective transcendent force, totally implausible? If God's existence has not been invalidated once and for all by unspeakable human and natural evil, perhaps it is time for all of us to ask another question: Why is the Christian/Jewish/Islamic God so malevolent? To paraphrase David Hume once again, if God genuinely wants to stop the escalating cycle of pointless suffering and death in the world but cannot, then he is impotent. If he can, but chooses not to, then he is immoral. Which is he?

To this very day, nothing seems to work for me in trying to reconcile the abundance of goodness in the world with the crushing and intolerable presence of evil. On a personal level, I often experience my own successes as failures and my failures as fearsome reminders of my finitude. I struggle constantly to find some transcendent rationale for human suffering—yes, and also for human joy. I strive for a meaning beyond the traditional meanings offered by churches, holy books, sacred doctrines, and authoritative, papal magisteria. I want to make sense of war, cruelty, natural disasters, injustice, grinding poverty, slavery, suffering, and the very real personal death—most likely the extinction—that awaits me and all those I love.

I also want to know why even the most exquisite moments of happiness and contentment in my life are usually so short-lived, and, in the end, so unsatisfying. I want to unravel the impossible dilemma of why upwards of 120 billion people have been born, lived, and died since the beginning of human life on earth. I can only ask: to what supernatural end? At whose pleasure or will? Or is it all a matter of blind, evolutionary chance, a cosmic roll of the dice, a monumental, anthropic coincidence? Is the total meaning of my life contained in the fact that I am but one of those 120 billion souls who never asked to be born, who arrived unbidden and who departed either mourned or unmourned; who, while alive, wondered and hoped, cried and laughed, worked and played, taught and learned, procreated and died?

I mention all of the above—my early religious training, my loss of faith, and the endless litany of pain, suffering, and death that has plagued humanity since the beginning of history—because many of the questions that I asked when I was a seminarian and a college student still torment me today. I also find, at the present time, that several of my students raise these types of questions, each in their own way. I remember, just before I left the seminary, reading Bertrand Russell's (1957) famous essay *Why I Am Not a Christian*. I began to consider seriously, for the first time, the possibility that when all is said and done, when my life comes to an end, I shall, in Russell's stark word, "rot." Nothing more awaits me. Everything else is fantasy, mere wishful thinking, a consoling illusion to make sense of the terrifying void, the utter, desperate meaninglessness of it all. Later on, my studies in existentialism seemed to confirm these dark and despairing realizations.

At this time in my life, however, Russell's insights, along with the existentialists', simply provoke further questions. Neither Russell, Rorty, Barnes, nor anyone else have offered even remotely satisfying answers to stay my doubts over the problem of theodicy, or any other religio-spiritual dilemma that I have. Today, I want to know why these somber ruminations about theodicy continue to haunt me. I have a highly successful career, a wonderful family and friends, and excellent health to show for my life. Why is it so difficult for me to take to heart my own advice to students that all we can ever know for certain is the moment we are presently living. Thus, we need to cherish the moment with *joie de vivre,* letting the metaphysical chips fall where they may (if there are any chips at all). As a postmodernist, I claim to believe that the past is gone and the future is yet to be shaped. I teach that conceptions of past, present, and future are, at best, culturally constructed devices that function to keep us sane and satisfy our peculiar needs for narrative order. However, the more I read and write, teach and think, the less I seem to know about anything with any degree of certainty, and the more restless I become. At this stage in my life, I take little comfort in Socrates' observation that the more he knew the more he realized he really knew nothing at all.

Don Cupitt, Postmodernism, Spirituality, and Theodicy

During the 1980s, my metaphysical restlessness led me to the works of Don Cupitt (see, for example, a later work, *After God: The Future of Religion*, 1997), an ordained Anglican priest in the Church of England, a fellow of Emmanuel College, Cambridge University, and the author of over twenty books. Cupitt, even though a priest in good standing, is an acknowledged postmodernist, aetheist, and mystic. Having heard about Cupitt from a religious studies colleague who knew him personally, I hungrily devoured his writings. I found a kindred spirit almost immediately, although Cupitt and I come from very different social classes and academic backgrounds. He is a British, upper-class gentleman who is Oxbridge educated, a priest, a post-Christian/Zen Buddhist, and a scholar who delights mostly in tweaking the noses of what he calls "pre-Enlightenment" Christian hierarchs.

Despite his enormous ego, his overzealous attempts to settle old scores with his enemies, and his deliberate, inflammatory writing style, I find Cupitt's thinking to be as important to my own intellectual understanding of religion and spirituality as any other writer I know, living or dead. In fact, I can think of only three other thinkers, Friedrich Nietzsche, Paul Tillich, the Harvard existential theologian, and the Episcopalian bishop, John Shelby Spong (1998), who have had a similar impact on my thinking and writing about religion and spirituality. I must quickly add, however, that as provocative as all these thinkers have been for me in my intellectual development, they have made me even more restive spiritually. They speak to my intellect, and, certainly, to my contrarian temperament, but they completely miss my unsettled heart. I am grateful to all of them, nonetheless, particularly to Cupitt.

Cupitt believes in no ultimates. For him, everything is "proximate" and "relative." What we might conceive to be absolute or timeless regarding spiritual matters is simply a product of our finite languages. We can never get outside the languages we have created in order to define our lingering need for some meaning greater than worldly meaning. *God, the supernatural, the transcendent, and ultimacy* are linguistic inventions of particular people at particular times. The particular construct of an omnipotent God that survives to this day is really a leftover from an era that lived under absolute monarchy. Thus, God becomes the divine monarch in the sky, the absolute patriarch who controls his creation, and who we must appease for worldly favors and eternal rewards. In Cupitt's mind, God is the heavenly king, and we are his weak, earthly subjects. Unfortunately, this theology is an antiquated one, Cupitt believes, developed during the Iron Age, somewhere between 800 B.C.E. and 200 C.E. This was a time when there was a need for rulers, subjects, obedience, reparation, and sacrifice.

According to Cupitt, a postmodern world requires a postmodern construction of God, one far less dualistic, authoritarian, judgmental, and totally other. Human beings are no longer weak, vulnerable, and dependent on Divine favors to survive. They now possess an advanced politics, science, technology, art, philosophy, theology, and economic system. They have, in effect, become like Gods with the potential to create a better world for everyone, here and now, in the Already instead of waiting for the Not Yet. We are all there is; there is nothing else. Religion is something we made up, a crude, perhaps genetic, adaptation necessary for early evolutionary survival. However, now that human-made substitutes are readily available to answer our cries for consolation and contentment, justification and validation, the whole formal apparatus of religion is unneccesary, a useless throwback, that serves only to keep us perpetually at war with each other over which one is right.

Cupitt offers what he considers to be a satisfying postmodern answer. The age-old needs for purpose, meaning, love, hope, and trust can best be met by a commitment to "radical humanism," the only spirituality that will save us as a species. This is a requirement of the post-Enlightenment realization that there is no supernatural world out there, no reality that is more real than the ordinary reality that envelops all of us. The two worlds that really matter are the material world that swirls outside us, and the psychological world that lies within us. The internal world of the psyche, however, is the only one that we can fully control. It is also the one that all human beings have in common. We own this interiorized world. We narrativize, theorize, historicize, and interpret it. We put it into the languages we speak. It is up to us to continue to develop, enrich, and understand it. No other power outside us can do this for us, because there is no other power but us. There is no life after death. In fact, authentic "Christian life is life after life after death." This is to say that when each of us begins to live our lives as "risen" lives, only then can we liberate ourselves from fear, greed, attachment, and the need to live forever as gods.

In order to live this way, however, Cupitt believes that we need to understand the true meaning of life. It is all about contingency and transience. Nothing is permanent. There are no indubitable, otherworldly foundations, only those meanings that we have created and that belong to this world. Everything "pours out and passes away." Rather than being a depressing realization, this understanding motivates us to live our interior and exterior lives by being fully absorbed in them. The paradox is this: We must learn to get *out of* ourselves in order to live lovingly with others, but we must also learn to get *inside of* ourselves in order to reach for a more profound understanding of what makes us tick.

The only Christianity that makes sense in a postmodern world is one that has abandoned the "old, cruel, authoritarian" church. The new Christianity must be here-and-now, democratic, and humanistic. For Cupitt, the Quakers are a good early model of an unchurched Christianity. Theravadin Buddhism is an even better model, a religion that is religionless, a spirituality that is godless, a series of practices that are noninstitutional and nondogmatic. Theravadin Buddhism is based, instead, on a compassionate commitment to help others reach enlightenment for its own sake, rather than as a precondition to gain entrance to some imaginary hereafter.

Cupitt's take on the problem of evil is thoroughly post-Christian, even post-organized religion. Thus far in my own thinking about theodicy, Cupitt's approach seems closest to my own. To the question *unde malum: whence the evil?* Cupitt tells us that we are looking in the wrong places for an answer. Because we were raised to think of God as a watchful, fair yet demanding parent, we expect virtue to be rewarded and vice to be punished. We expect perfect justice. The truth is that this patriarchal God narrative no longer works for a postpatriarchal people. The cosmos, rather than being determinate and predestined, is indeterminate and random. The world is neither benevolent nor malevolent; it is dumb, in the sense that it is "unformed and innocent."

There is no divine protection against evolution's unpredictablity. The proper conclusion to draw from the fact of life's "sheer contingency," according to Cupitt, is to accept the reality of our own "vulnerability and mortality." We have no immortal souls. What we possess is what we inhabit right now: our minds, bodies, relationships, and natural habitats. Life is only flux and chance; it is not a predetermined path leading to a world more real, permanent, and satisfying than this one. Cupitt (2000) offers this advice: "Learn to live in a way that is fully absorbed all the time, and you will be learning solar living, a way of living that forgets the past and the future and which simply burns, now" (p. 64).

The Professor as Restless Spiritual Seeker

It is within this paradoxical context of acknowledging and accepting my postmodern restlessness, but also of refusing to berate myself for needing something more than Cupitt can give me, that I bring a perpetual, spiritual unease to my classroom and to my scholarship. This spiritual disquiet affects virtually everything that I do with character education, moral education, and applied ethics. It is the dominant feature of the narrative I am writing about myself as a teacher and scholar, and, yes, as a parent, husband, and friend. As I mentioned earlier, in the 1980s, during a long-awaited sabbatical, I, a tenured full professor, returned to graduate school to earn a degree in applied ethics and religious studies. I also took additional time off to earn still another graduate degree, this one in moral theology.

Why, I asked myself, would a person who for so long claimed publicly to be temperamentally indisposed to matters of the spirit spend so much money and energy pursuing further studies in religiously oriented disciplines, and at Catholic universities to boot? Was this my way, as in Dorothy Allison's epigraph, of having something greater than myself to hold onto, of seizing the world by the throat in order to find more to life than I ever could have imagined? At least on the face of it, these mid-career degrees had no official payoff for my work as a professor. In fact, to this day, I do not even bother to mention them on my Curriculum Vitae for fear of appearing impractical, or worse, intellectually self-indulgent, to colleagues in my professional school.

In retrospect, I now understand that while I may never have been comfortable as a conventional religious practitioner, or even as a believer, I have always been an eager observer of religion and spirituality. I now accept the fact that in all the professional courses I teach I am actually a spiritual seeker and proud of it. I am a spiritual seeker because, although the world of material phenomena (e.g., science and technology) is important to me (after all, I do work in a professional school that is concerned with the prosaic, but no less real, problems of human service practitioners) the world of the intangible is important to me as well. This world of the intangible evokes questions of being, first principles, my particular *bête noire*—good and evil, intuition, the origin and validity of knowledge and morality, and, most importantly, the meaning and purpose of my and others' existence.

As a spiritual seeker, I love to ponder the imponderable. Maddeningly, I invite my students to ponder these imponderables right along with me. I nag them to wonder, to speculate, to ask the truly difficult, often unanswerable questions, the questions that end up exasperating most of us, because they threaten our deep-down, secure, and certain places. Examples of these types of first-moral-language questions are:

- In the larger scheme of things, if there is one, why does what I do really matter?

- Why, as a professional, do I experience those sudden, uninvited moments when I regret the vanishing of a past I have barely lived and can only faintly recall; a present that continues to slip away from me until it, too, becomes a rueful reminder of possibilities forever lost; and a future that looms as being more ominous than hopeful?

- Is there something more to life, to *my* life, that gives it purpose and rationale?

- Why is it so difficult for me to believe in the existence of something greater than the here-and-now, particularly when there is so much inexplicable pain and suffering everywhere?

- Why do I find myself, at the most inopportune times, looking for something more in my life?

- Why am I so restless?

- Why do I cling to the elusive hope that wisdom is ultimately attainable, that it is possible to live a life with genuine dignity and integrity, that somewhere, somehow, I can find a sustaining meaning in it all?

■ Why am I alive anyway?

Seekers like me tend to ask *why* rather than *how* or *what*. Staying at the how and what levels of everyday existence in teaching a professional seminar is a significant piece of my job, I readily admit. However, after many years, it has become the least satisfying piece for me, and, I am convinced, for many of my students as well. You see, my heart, and theirs, does not reside in the sphere of hows and whats. I resist their understandable attempts to push me into the role of an expert, a know-it-all problem solver, in spite of the fact that I have virtually no empirical experience myself in most of the professions that students in my classes represent. As a teacher, I want to lead with my strength. As a philosopher, I would rather entice students to ask the above types of questions because these are the inquiries that I believe deliver a much-needed sense of proportion to their professional existence. They add a sense of depth, perspective, and distance. They have the potential of profoundly touching, and changing, practitioners' inner and outer lives. When asked authentically and engaged honestly, these questions run the risk of surfacing professional frustrations and doubts, it is true. However, more importantly, they possess the power to revive buried hopes and activate faded dreams.

A SPIRITUAL PERSPECTIVE

In a word, this is a spiritual perspective. It is unsettling in the academy, because it refuses to be silenced or contained by the quotidian routines and practical demands of teaching. It enlarges; it does not constrict. It strives to disturb professionals' everyday work worlds, rather than simply conform them to their jobs. It encourages them to formulate a vision, to nurture a passion, to forge a commitment. I, for one, refuse to spend my days being dishonest by supplying facile answers to technical professional questions that, in truth, I rarely ask myself. Despite their importance, these questions too often seem trivial and beside the point. In my experience with students, what often starts out as a simple question about professional methodology or technical content frequently ends up in a vivifying conversation about the questions that truly matter to them, and to me as well. During those rare and precious moments when we manage, however feebly, to shelve our many ideological differences and to meet each other in genuine *why* dialogue, something inexpressible happens that transforms our lives, if only for the moment. We listen carefully, respectfully, nondefensively to each other, and we find that we reside in the land of the holy.

I must confess something, though. This asking of *why* questions does not always thrill my students. At least initially, many do not want to live in the land of the holy, especially *my* holy. Why should they? Most of them rightfully come to my courses seeking practical answers to clear-cut professional questions about moral and character education, philosophy and history of education, and ethical decision making. What they frequently end up getting is spiritual tribulation. Here I am, urging them to consider the influence of their early religious upbringing on their subsequent ethical development; nagging them to think about the differences and the similarities between objectivism and constructivism; insisting that they reflect for a time on the roles that faith, mystery, and doubt might possibly play in the work they do as professionals; and occasionally forcing them to delve into complex cosmological and ontological questions like the astonishing one that the philosophers Leibniz, Schelling, Schopenhauer, and Heidegger continually imposed on their own students: "Why is there something rather than nothing?"

At first, many of my students react with extreme dismay that a professional course of study would emphasize such apparent irrelevancies. A few wonder whom they might see with their complaints, someone in charge (a dean or chairperson perhaps?) who might be able to admonish this professorial impostor. Gradually, however, most come around to my spiritual goading, even if somewhat reluctantly. Similar to Moliere's character, the *Bourgeois Gentilhomme,* who suddenly wakes up and realizes one morning that he has actually been speaking prose his whole life, most students, in their own manner, become aware that, like it or not, they have actually been grappling with philosophical and religious issues without really identifying them in that way. They understand, for example, that the *profession* (the duty to profess a belief in something) of teaching, in addition to its etymological, religious connotations, cries out for a way of tying together the tag-ends of their often chaotic professional practices.

As one student, trying to put the best spin on our activities in a philosophy of education seminar, blurted out in class: "The quest for an educational vision, for something passionate in the work I do, is really a quest for God, isn't it?" To which another student promptly confessed: "But why is it the deeper I go, the further away I get? In the end, doesn't it seem like an exercise in futility attempting to explain the inexplicable?" Perhaps. However, what I do know for sure is that, after a while, most students are unable to resist the invitation to spend some time digging into the deeper things of life, into the larger spiritual reality that some of them believe encompasses us all.

I intentionally combine the two words, *religion* and *spirituality,* in my teaching. In spite of students' widespread popular disdain for the former and their near unanimous approval of the latter, I believe the two terms actually represent two closely related perspectives—the institutional and the personal—on the same phenomenon, *transcendence.* In my usage, religion is what we do with others, spirituality is what we do within our selves; the former is public faith, the latter is private faith. Religion is head; spirituality is heart. Religio-spiritual language is my awkward way of attempting to reunite what too many students have torn apart, what they too glibly discard as an irreconcilable dualism.

For me, a belief in transcendence assumes that there is always something more, something larger and greater, in our lives than what we can directly experience or perceive, something that will forever remain a mystery, an object of awe, something that will always manage to surpass our human understanding. In the face of this mystery, and in the pursuit of transcendent meaning, most students are willing to place their trust only in a private spirituality rather than in a publicly professed religious faith. Few are willing even to consider the truth that the fullest experience of transcendence will sometimes require both self and others, the individual and the community, the private life and the public life, head and heart, religion and spirituality.

FINDING FAITH IN HONEST DOUBT: A SPIRITUALITY OF TEACHING

Some skeptics in my classes, of course, get no further than to agree with Freud that religion is nothing more than a universal obsessional neurosis; or with Marx that religion is an opiate; or with Feuerbach that religion is simply a projection of human qualities onto an object of worship. Others less cynical come to appreciate the opportunity in a professional course to search for ultimate meaning on the chance that they might discover some irrefutable, all-embracing value underlying everything. Only a few students, I find, are content to ponder the words of Alfred Lord Tennyson, words that have long guided my own interior life and directed much of my teaching in recent years: "There is more faith in honest doubt than in all the religious creeds of the world" (quoted in Haught 1996, p. 188). Sadly, more students, rather than less, agree with Augustine when he said: "I would not have faith...if the authority of the Church did not compel me" (quoted in Mendelsohn 1995, p. 53).

In this late stage of my career, I have been trying to create a pedagogy I call a "spirituality of teaching." In all the classroom work that I do as a college professor, I am driven by Tennyson's aphorism, by the unwavering conviction that, for me, a genuine faith must somehow find a way to wrestle with the demons of honest doubt. The objective is not to overcome the doubt, because this is neither possible nor desirable, but to fully incorporate it into any final declaration of belief and call to action. For me, honest doubt is a believer's intuitive sense that no ecclesiastical leader, or dogma, or doctrine, or sacred book, or teaching, or ritual can ever capture the fullness of life's ultimate mysteries. It is the humble understanding that, when everything is said and done, one's frail and wavering faith is all that is left to fill the interval between saying too much and saying too little about what is essentially incommunicable.

Here is Peter L. Berger (1992) on the perils of dogmatic certainty:

> It may well be that the quest for certainty is a deeply rooted trait of human nature. If, in the course of a lifetime, we attain this or that certitude, we should gratefully accept it as a gift of grace. But we should not feign to certainties that are, in fact, the result of strenuous and never-ending efforts at faith. By and large, the modern quest for certainty has had both intellectually and morally deleterious consequences. They are all, to use again Erich Fromm's apt phrase, "escapes from freedom." (pp. 136–137)

Spirituality, as I conceive it, has little to do with dogma, certainty, or escapes from freedom. Neither is it directly related to Christian or Jewish understandings of such terms as ruach, pneuma, and spirit. Nor is my notion of spirituality something that is God-bestowed, incarnational, or even coming to a vivid awareness of some supernatural presence. It most definitely has nothing in common with New Age occultism. Instead, for me, a spirituality of teaching simply calls for the student, and the teacher, to undertake, in trust, an inward journey together whose ultimate destination is to fashion a deeper personal response to the mystery of existence. Spirituality is all about fashioning meaning, establishing high moral purpose, cultivating hope, and putting faith in one another in the creation of mutually supportive communities.

A spirituality of teaching, regardless of the subject matter, puts the central emphasis on the student's (and the teacher's) continuing quest for a richly textured interior life. It recognizes the pivotal communal nature of this activity whenever it is undertaken in an educational setting. It encourages, at all times, the development of a richer, more complete spirituality on the part of individuals, one that reaches for a meaning far beyond the mere professional mastery of the newest data, the freshest techniques, and the latest technology. Most of all, a spirituality of teaching recognizes, in Fenton Johnson's (1998) words, that

> Faith is first among the cardinal virtues because everything proceeds from it including and especially love. Faith is the leap into the unknown—the entering into an action or a person knowing only that you will emerge changed, with no preconceptions of what that change will be. Its antonym is fear. (p. 54)

A spirituality of teaching, among other things, attempts to elicit candid first-person accounts of the larger meaning of students' lived experience, whenever these meanings are appropriate to the subject matter at hand. It attempts always to exemplify such qualities as truthfulness, courage, and integrity. I consider these to be the cardinal spiritual virtues not only of teaching and learning, but of living an excellent life as well. I predicate my spirituality of teaching on the well-tested assumption that, given an ethos of mutual support and caring in the classroom, my students will not hesitate to talk with one another about how their deepest beliefs, ideals, hopes, fears, doubts, and, yes, religious faith (or lack of it) influence the work they do as educators.

They are eager to do this, I believe, because they live during a time when it seems that more and more people are talking about topics which seem less and less important. So much talk in America today is wasted in vapid chitchat (e.g., e-mail and on-line chat rooms), in angry name-calling (radio and television talk shows), in academic one-upsmanship and textual nit-picking (many college seminars), and in an endless cycle of media-generated, self-serving political spin. Sadly, the kind of religio-spiritual talk I am encouraging in the college classroom rarely occurs anywhere else in America—not in the family, not on the therapist's couch or even in the priest's confessional, and certainly not in the teacher's room, superintendent's office, or college president's suite.

At times in the classroom, this type of talk will take me and my students on a trip through the great monotheistic religions of the world. At other times, it will take an Eastern direction. Often it will settle for nontheistic forms of religio-spiritual commitment as found in nature, loving relationships, philosophy, literature, art, and music. I am growing more and more convinced that the subject matter in a professional course that deals with spiritual meaning can surprisingly make students better professionals, even if they never overtly mention the words *religion* or *God* in their own classrooms and other educational venues. I have a strong belief that without the opportunity to travel this inward journey—without the challenge of creating a personal spirituality of teaching—the outward life of the educator threatens to become repetitive and sterile.

COMING OUT OF THE SPIRITUAL CLOSET: RELIGION AS NARRATIVE

One day it was bound to happen. Thirty years into my university teaching career, I enthusiastically, but cautiously, accepted the challenge of a very wise former student who remarked: "Robert, when are you going to come out of the spiritual closet? Why don't you offer a special course to educators and other human service professionals that deals exclusively with religious content, instead of sneaking this stuff in through the back door of all your other courses?" So I did. I created a course—"Religion and Spirituality in Education"—that I now offer twice a year, with long waiting lists. I describe this course in some detail in a book that I wrote called *Faith, Hype, and Clarity: Teaching About Religion in American Schools and Colleges* (1999).

While the book has received much critical acclaim (named a Critic's Choice Final Selection by the American Educational Studies Association, a *Choice Magazine* book of the year, and a nominee for the 1999 Grawemeyer Prize), I am most pleased with the fact that it touched a responsive chord among many audiences *outside* the religious studies field, including teacher education, public schools, and higher education administration. While I cannot truthfully say that because of the course or the book my own inner life (or anyone else's) has been radically changed, I can say this: I am learning that, as a professional, my work as a teacher educator is, in large part, framing how I think and feel about religious and spiritual issues.

That is, my own spirituality of teaching is a variation of the postmodern assertion that, at some level, all theory is autobiography. I believe that teaching, like religion, is really autobiography, a highly personal narrative that the believer creates in order to elicit, and to answer, the most confounding existential questions, the ones that defy easy scientific, political, or technological answers. Whenever I read Andrew M. Greeley (1990), I realize why my own childhood Catholicism continues to have such a strong hold on me even today, long after I have formally abandoned it. When I was a child, it totally captured my imagination, not with its authoritative dogmas and doctrines, its magisterium and moral teachings, but with its compelling and memorable stories. These include stories about Mary and Jesus, life, death, and resurrection, the saints and the popes, martyrs and heretics, the local church pastor and the ladies' sodality, the Jesuits and the Sisters of Mercy, the Catholic elementary school and Notre Dame University, and, of course, the Catholics and the Protestants, the Irish and the English.

These stories inspired and edified me. The official church teachings only served to induce guilt, boredom, and rebellion. For religion to work well, as least in my case, and, I suspect, for the majority of my students, it must first be born in narrative before it grows into creed, rite, and institution. It must be profoundly autobiographical and appeal to the narrative imagination, long before it can convince the discursive intellect.

The most captivating religious narratives—e.g., Buddhism, Hinduism, Christianity, Islam—feature unforgettable characters, momentous events, and luminous ideals. In addition, their languages are often sonorous and seductive. At its best, religion as narrative, as a powerful storytelling device, reaches out and captures our imaginations, because the vitality of its message and the vividness of its language are potentially life-transforming. We are moved to fresher understandings of the deeper, previously concealed, meaning of our lives. The lesson here for teachers and related helping professionals is surely not an original one, but of the utmost importance, nevertheless. A spirituality of teaching ought to recognize that good teaching, like good religion, is all about storytelling, and that the best pedagogy aims first at the heart and soul before it can ever find its way to the mind.

During a recent sabbatical leave, I developed this notion of teaching as storytelling into a book called *Religious Pluralism in the Academy: Opening the Dialogue* (2001). In this book, I make the case that we are more likely to get college students from a variety of religio-spiritual backgrounds to open up publicly about their guiding beliefs when we de-emphasize the revelational, doctrinal, and corporate elements of religion in the classroom in favor of the aesthetic and the poetic, the philosophical and the literary. I argue that we ought to approach discussions of religion as a series of compelling and useful narratives that people have constructed for thousands of years in order to explain life's tragic anomalies as well as its unexpected gifts of grace. I acknowledge in this book that, as a teacher, I know of no better way to mine the richness of an escalating religio-spiritual pluralism on secular college campuses throughout the United States than to get students to exchange their religious stories with each other in a nondoctrinal, mutually respectful manner.

In fact, I would argue that the brilliance of all the religions and spiritualities the world has ever known lies in their peculiar narrative power. If, as I contend, religion is basically a story devised by people to give meaning to their lives in a particular place and time, then one must continually ask whether the narrative still speaks to people's needs today. In Neil Postman's (1996) words: "Does it provide [them] with a sense of personal identity, a sense of community life, a basis for moral conduct, explanations of that which cannot be known" (p. 7)? This question, in my opinion, ought to be the engine that fuels to-and-fro, robust, campus-wide discussions about religion and spirituality.

As each week passes during the term in which I offer my new course, I come to realize that, for me, my own teaching narrative is deeply spiritual. It is about helping students to name their doubts about themselves and their work with honesty and integrity. At the same time it encourages them to create and nurture a faith in themselves, their students, and their work that is honest and integral. Whether we are talking about religion or education, my students and I struggle throughout the semester to create individual professional narratives that combine the qualities of faith, doubt, honesty, and integrity in such a way as to deepen our understandings of our-selves and our teaching. We are trying to create a sense of vocation—see-ing our professional work as a calling, as a leap of faith without guarantee, as a risky response to the summons deep within us to minister to others wisely and compassionately.

Breaking Stereotypes

Thus far, my new course has attracted a richly diverse group of stu-dents. It has included several African-Americans, Native Americans, and Asians; students ranging in age from their late teens to their early eighties; gays, lesbians, and bisexuals; Jews, Hindus, Buddhists, Christian Fundamentalists, Evangelicals, and Pentecostals; atheists and agnostics; and professionals representing at least twenty fields, from classroom teachers, to principals, to social service workers, to allied health caregivers, to higher education administrators. Most of the students in these classes appear to fit the profile that Wade Clark Roof characterizes as baby-boomer seekers, although their dramatic departures from this stereotype are instructive and what finally make them and the course such a vital experience.

Roof's deservedly acclaimed studies, *A Generation of Seekers* (1993), and *Spiritual Marketplace* (1999), focus mainly on conventional and post-conventional Christian believers, New Agers, and what he calls "seekers." These are people who have questioned, and even, in some cases, abandoned their parents' religions, ethnic heritages, politics, and nationalities in order to discover for themselves a more compelling religio-spiritual basis on which to build their lives. My own experiences with those students who rep-resent pre-boomer, boomer, Generation-X, and millennialist time periods confirm some of Roof's findings, to be sure, but also go far beyond his depic-tions. Roof, at times, oversimplifies the complexity and richness of individuals' religio-spiritual journeys by collapsing all of his respondents into one huge, unnuanced designation he continually refers to as "seekers."

In thirty-five years of teaching college students of all ages, I can assert confidently that there are simply no prototypal seekers. In fact, there are many different types of seekers, including myself, because nobody ever pur-sues religio-spiritual meaning outside of a particular perspective or personal narrative. Each of us, I submit, is an intellectually situated (as well as a culturally situated) being. Our search for meaning in a fractured American culture will always originate in a set of distinct preconceptions that we hold about religion and spirituality. Unlike Roof (1993), I am wary of generalizing about all seekers that they "value experience over beliefs, distrust institutions and leaders, stress personal fulfillment yet yearn for community, and are fluid in their allegiances" (p. 8). To this I can only say—"Well, yes, some do, but some don't."

Another highly respected sociologist, Alan Wolfe (1998), makes similar kinds of generalizations in his well-received study of middle-class Americans, *One Nation After All*. He claims that a "capacious individualism" characterizes the religious faith of the middle class. According to Wolfe, middle-class Americans are not deeply devout, they have lost a sense of the tragic (Wolfe is writing before the acts of terrorism on American soil that took place on September 11, 2001), they experience no wonder, and they mourn the erosion of "necessary constraints on hedonism" (p. 82). Wolfe believes that middle-class Americans operate from a "rational-choice" theory. They are free-agent churchgoers who calculatingly choose and switch their denominational allegiances according to what they believe will make them happiest. Wolfe concludes that, among the middle class, personal religious belief will always be more important than institutional affiliation.

While it is definitely true that some of my own middle-class students express a strong commitment to Wolfe's brand of religious individualism, many do not. Some, wary of privatizing their faith and hoping to influence public policy, organize social-justice groups in their churches and temples, and even in their schools. Others, tired of their spiritual isolation, join Bible-study and mutual support groups in order to create richer, more intimate forms of community life. Some students are deeply devout believers, others are deeply devout churchgoing skeptics, some are proud nonbelievers, and others mostly keep their beliefs to themselves. Unlike Wolfe, I can not honestly identify one student in my courses who is without a sense of wonder, or who fails to recognize the tragic and comic elements in human life. For all his remarkable sociological insight, Wolfe utterly fails to realize that a growing percentage of middle-class Americans is becoming intensely involved with Eastern and New Age religious teachings.

Many of these religions, such as Buddhism and Hinduism, understand all too well the significance of wonder and the omnipresence of tragedy in human affairs, and the need for compassion in the face of suffering. In order to get a sense of the allure of alternative religions for some middle-class Americans, Wolfe might consider reading the popular Vietnamese Buddhist and pacifist, Thich Nhat Hanh, whose *Living Buddha, Living Christ* (1995) has become a runaway best-seller in this country. One student in a recent religion and education course of mine, "Jonathan"—a self-designated "recovering Christian"—continually pointed to this book throughout the semester as having transformed him from being a "dead Christian" to a "live Buddhist-post-denominational Christian." Jonathan, a high school English teacher, has begun to use Hanh's book in his Advanced Placement class. He claims that, after reading the book, many of his high school students are able to find new ways to revitalize their Christian and Jewish faiths.

Hanh speaks vividly to people of all religious faiths, particularly disgruntled Christians like Jonathan, about the importance of understanding God, not as an abstract concept, but as a living reality. So too does the Dalai Lama, author of an immensely popular book—*Ethics for the New Millennium* (1997)—that I have used with my students during the last two years. Hundreds of thousands of middle-class readers appear to respond to both authors' observations that, in the past, Christian triumphalism has frequently prevented authentic interfaith dialogue and fostered a disrespect for religious pluralism of all kinds.

What Hanh and the Dalai Lama do for American middle-class believers like Jonathan and other students like him is to remind them of the significance of the deeply reflective life, and what they call the practice of "mindfulness"—the capacity to attend to everything that happens in the present moment. This is the beginning of enlightenment, and something that contemporary Western faith stories either ignore or dismiss, even though Christianity and Judaism have a rich and lengthy tradition of contemplative spiritual practices (Cupitt 1998; Gordis 1995). Many teachers, counselors, social workers, and administrators in my small, rural state have become devoted followers of Hanh. They are learning to become mindful meditators who seek refuge in the Buddha (the one who shows the way), the Dharma (the way of understanding and love), and the Sangha (the community that lives in harmony and awareness). During a recent public appearance in my state, Hanh drew thousands of his followers to a college lecture and subsequent series of workshops on such spiritual topics as mindfulness, pacifism, meditation, and holiness. Several of my students attended these events.

Eight Types of Religious Stories That College Students Tell

Not all of my students find Buddhism to be an attractive spiritual alternative, however, although many do. In this section, I will sketch eight miniature portraits of the dominant spiritual narratives that I find in classes at my university, and throughout the country, whenever I visit other places to speak. I have constructed eight religious stories that I hope are capacious, diverse, and fluid, in order to avoid the stereotyping that bothers me in the work of such authors as Roof and Wolfe, whom I mentioned earlier.

I have found these religio-spiritual narratives to be represented among every age-, gender-, racial-, ethnic-, and socioeconomic group in my work with students. No single narrative exists as a pure type, of course, and, at least in theory, none need be mutually exclusive. I personally find something appealing in all of them, although a few obviously speak to me, an honest doubter, in a very special way. I also find that most students only need a little encouragement, the right questions, and a supportive dialogue space to tell their stories to each other and to me. Because I have developed them in far greater depth in my two aforementioned books (Nash 1999, 2001), I will only outline these stories briefly in the sketches that follow.

The *Orthodox Believers* come in all religious and philosophical stripes. With only a few disturbing exceptions, they usually remain humble but unyielding in their claims to be in possession of an absolute, revealed truth that most of their classmates and I obviously lack. Their confident, sometimes gentle, sense of certainty attracts, more than repels, many of us throughout the semester. In class, a small coterie of anti-orthodox skeptics, however, always manages to remain unconvinced, and they often have great difficulty concealing their disdain for any expression of uncompromising orthodox belief. The core leitmotif for the Orthodoxy story is this: There is a Truth that is unimpeachable, immutable, and final, and it can only be found in a particular book, institution, prophet, or movement. The mission of the Orthodox Believer is to deliver this Truth to others as an act of love and generosity.

The *Mainline Believers* constitute a very large group of college students. These students are neither excessively conservative or avant-garde. They dislike authoritarianism in religion as much as they dislike faddism. They prefer a life of traditional worship that balances traditions, standards, self-discipline, and moral conscience with a degree of personal freedom, biblical latitude, and the *joie de vivre* of close community life. Often they remain in the Catholic and Protestant churches (and temples) of their parents and grandparents. They are the proud holdouts against postmodernity and the religious experimentation and deconstruction that so often accompany it. The controlling theme in the Mainline narrative is this: People need an organized, sacred space, one that provides clear boundaries between the sacred and the profane, a stable support community, a sense of order, and a moral bulwark against the excesses of secularism. Although Mainline religion appears to be alive and well in America, some of us, nevertheless, ask Mainliners two complementary questions: When does the need for religious stability and rootedness turn into a denial of those changes that any denomination needs in order to remain vital, responsive, and pastoral? However, also, is it possible for the mainline denominations to make reasoned compromises with the world without the co-optations and dilutions that too often accompany those compromises?

The *Wounded Believers* include those students who define their religious experience mainly as a reaction to the physical and mental abuse (often perpetuated in the *name* of religion) that they have suffered at the hands of hypocritical, over-zealous clergy, lovers, parents, relatives, and friends. Their self-disclosing narratives of suffering, denial, reconciliation in some cases, and eventual healing always win our attention, believer and nonbeliever alike. Sometimes Wounded Believers embarrass us, sometimes they inspire us, but they never fail to captivate us. The thematic thread that winds throughout all Wounded Belief narratives is this question: If there is a good, all-loving God, why has there been so much unbearable pain in my life?

The *Mystics* remind us continually that more often than not a genuine faith requires a discerning silence on the part of the believer, instead of a learned, theological disquisition. Some turn to the East; some to alternative American religions; some to folk religions; and some to private forms of spirituality. Most express a love for mystery, stillness, and attunement that eludes those of us who too easily fit the stereotype of the fitful, ambitious, hard-driving Westerner. At the heart of the mysticism narrative is this motif: The transcendent is best experienced, not through idle chatter or abstract concepts, but by way of meditation, mindfulness, and, above all, a pervasive calmness. The rest of us listen, learn, and wonder how on earth we can ever find the mystical stillness that is said to inhabit the center of all our frenetic activity. Some students, however, reject the mysticism narrative outright as too quiescent and self-absorbed.

The *Social Justice Activists* urge us throughout the semester to consider the possibility that believers must be responsible for building the Kingdom of God in the here-and-now, rather than waiting for some distant paradise to come. They advocate an activist faith dedicated to the liberation of oppressed peoples, equal rights, and social justice for all, and radical social transformation marked by full democratic participation in decision making. For them, religious leaders are judged to be effective only according to their commitment to bring about massive social reform on behalf of the least among us. The common theme in the activism narrative is this: Religion makes the most sense whenever it tells a story of human rights and social transformation, whenever it invites believers to criticize existing structures of power and privilege such as the wealthy, white, male hierarchies in the churches, universities, businesses, media, and government. While many students are drawn to the transformative elements of the activism narrative, others dismiss it as merely partisan liberal politics with a religious gloss.

The *Existential Humanists* help us to understand that all too often believers turn to the supernatural in order to escape from the difficult responsibilities of individual freedom. For them, a humanistic, self-centered ethic can stand on its own as a defensible way of a person's being in the world and living an authentic human life. What is necessary is that all of us confront the inescapable fact of our human finitude, and make a conscious choice to create ourselves through our daily projects, that is, through our courageous strivings to make meaning in an absurd universe. The recurring idea in the Existential Humanism story is this: The stark truth is that God has forever disappeared—if he ever existed in the first place—and now it is up to us to get on with our lives. After listening to the Existential Humanists, some of us begin to understand, for the first time, the significance of Jean Paul Sartre's assertion that we are all unique selves "condemned to freedom," and Paul Tillich's postulation of a "Ground of Being" as a viable substitute for a personal God, the traditional God of theism. We proceed to look for constructive, alternative ways to cope with the loss of absolutes. Others find the story too bleak and individualistic.

The *Postmodern Skeptics* are also deeply suspicious of any and all religious claims to absolute truth. However, in contrast to the existential humanists, they reject the existence of an unsituated, context-free self or soul. As committed moral relativists, they openly challenge our religious and moral certitudes, our ethical universals, and our grand spiritual narratives. They frequently encourage the rest of us to accentuate rather than integrate our many differences, to recognize our cultural situatedness as a critical fact of life, and to put our faith, not in metaphysical doctrines or dogmas, but in the awareness that we are all social constructors of our own religio-spiritual realities. The leading theme in the postmodern skepticism narrative is this: An informed sense of contingency, irony, and doubt, and a willingness to repudiate religiously grounded, patriarchal systems of social domination, are what make us truly human and our lives truly worth living. In reaction to the Skeptics, some of us confess a gnawing pessimism over life's ultimate prospects. A few, fearing the onset of a corrosive cynicism and nihilism, refuse to take these people seriously.

The *Scientific Empiricists,* while genuinely open to the possible existence of a cosmological God who created the universe, nevertheless argue that the evidence of astrophysics, organic evolution, biology, and the brain sciences effectively contravenes this hypothesis. No empirical evidence is able to establish incontrovertible proof of a supernatural power greater than nature or ourselves. However, neither can the alleged existence of a transcendental power be controverted scientifically. The core of the scientific empiricism story is this: We are utterly alone in the universe, beyond final Divine revelations and interventions, and left to our own human devices, accompanied by the findings of science, to create a better world for everyone. In response, some of us express the hope that religion and science can indeed be compatible. Others, however, can never get beyond what they think is the fundamental irreconcilability of faith and reason.

Individual representatives of each of these types always have a powerful religio-spiritual story to tell throughout the term. I try to honor their narratives as respectfully as I can in every class that I teach. I feel privileged that I am able to spend fifteen intense weeks each semester with such stimulating people. Each of these seekers demonstrates in every class meeting that the search for a spirituality of teaching and living is never-ending and persistent, even though at times it might exist just below the surface. This search for meaning also shows that it is virtually impossible for any analyst, whether Roof, Wolfe, or myself, to capture adequately the complexities and nuances of the distinct religio-spiritual narratives in any easy, catchall way. Thus, it is my double intention in offering my course to try to maintain the wonderful distinctiveness of educators' religio-spiritual views (and to encourage them to recognize the uniqueness of religious views of their own students), while at the same time to provide them (and, by implication, their own students) with accurate and helpful narrative classifications by which to investigate the rich variety of religious experiences among a number of middle-class and working-class Americans today.

LETTERS OF THE SPIRIT

During the semester that I teach my religion, spirituality, and education course, I make it a point at four different intervals to write lengthy, personal letters to each and every one of my students. I call these "letters of the spirit." Most of these students are articulate representatives of one or another of the eight spiritual narratives that I outlined in the previous section. I find that when I write a carefully crafted, reflective letter to each student, I am able to say things to them that I cannot usually express in the rapid give-and-take of seminar discussion. Because I try to keep each letter informal and reader-friendly, somewhat like a well-edited e-mail, I am able to engage students in a format most are used to and enjoy. Everyone, I find, likes to receive a personal letter, particularly from an instructor.

No problem my students confront in the course material is ever too large or too small for me to discount or ignore in my letters. No response of theirs is insignificant. No personal account regarding their peculiar religious struggles and successes is irrelevant. Everything is important because the subject matter is religion and spirituality, content that deals with the very meaning of life. It resides in the bone marrow of each student's lived existence. I take very seriously the immovable, religious promontories on which each of my orthodox and mainstream students stand, just as I do the fluid, spiritual journeys which my mystical and humanistic students travel throughout the course. I also listen carefully to the impassioned critiques of organized religion and New Age spirituality which social justice activists, scientific humanists, and postmodern skeptics raise.

In these letters, I carry on a type of rolling, back-and-forth conversation with students. There is much candid self-revelation on my part, as I frequently make myself vulnerable to their more personal religious inquiries, just as many of them do to mine. I find that I am still able to deal effectively with the intellectual issues that students raise about the course content, even while I engage in semi-autobiographical writing. What I end up doing in my letters is to construct a number of very subjective reflections on topics as diverse as education, the meaning of life, suffering, love, commitment, and ultimate concern. I am also able to comment on such pertinent topics in the news, for example, as the Bush Presidency's faith-based initiatives, the morality of stem-cell research, public school violence, even the NATO bombing of Serbia and Kosovo during the late spring of 1999. My reflections are always triggered by what my students have written in their papers and in their impromptu e-mails to me. I also use this exchange of letters as an opportunity to respond to what students might have shared publicly in class, and privately in my office or over a breakfast or lunch in a local coffee shop. They serve as great feedback devices.

I think of these letters as a series of religio-pedagogical narratives that I write to individuals in order to expose and to examine thoughtfully my own views (and theirs) in the continuing conversation we are having about religion and spirituality. Thus far, at least according to student evaluations, my letters have been nothing short of a resounding success. They have encouraged the majority of my students to express their own religious narratives more courageously, both in writing and in seminar discussions. More importantly, they have helped students to enter the narratives of one another with greater empathy. As one student put it in an anonymous, semester-end evaluation:

The letters that the professor wrote to us helped us to become part of *his* religious story just as he became part of *ours*. We, in turn, wrote letters to other students in the seminar. In this way, we became part of one another, students and teacher, students and students. Isn't this what religion ought to be about, binding us together, forging a connection with one another, pursuing the mystery of it all communally?

Although the letters I write consume many hours of my time, the personal rewards are abundant. My letters to my students are really letters to myself. They are an ongoing account of my *epektasis*, my own straining toward meaning, toward "god," both in and out of the classroom. In fact, in a very real sense, my letters to my students are really letters to a god I do not yet know or cannot even begin to fathom. At this time in my life, therefore, I can say that, notwithstanding their feedback value to students, I write my letters primarily in order to *find*, or, for that matter, to *lose*, a god…once and for all.

Maybe, in truth, what I am really looking for in my letters is a god beyond the god of religions, a god of inexpressible depth, a god that is not "once-and-for-all" but "once-and-for-always-a-mystery." A la Cupitt, and other postmodern theologians, maybe the most that we can ever know are concepts, constructs, and stories about god. A la Cupitt again, Jesus himself used stories to preach about the Kingdom to come; unfortunately for Cupitt, it was the Church that came. In the place of a wise and prophetic humanism, we got a professional caste of priests, accompanied by canon laws, written scriptures, temples, churches, and dogmatic theologies.

In challenging Cupitt's Zen-like atheism, and Richard Rorty's postmodern disbelief, however, I would assert that I cannot call myself an absolute atheist unless I am willing to declare for all the world to hear that life is utterly without depth, mystery, or otherness. As an unbeliever, I must be bold and stark enough to declare to anyone who will listen that my life and theirs is shallow, without meaning, something lived entirely on the surface, something that is totally devoid of a single truth that I take seriously and without reservation. Even though I am a convinced postmodernist, and a teacher entirely sympathetic to Cupitt's Zen-like, spiritual-atheistic project, I am simply unwilling to deny the infinite and inexhaustible depth that somehow gives shape and substance to my life. I do not think that Cupitt himself is willing to do this, of course, but his particular "solar" approach to the spiritual meaning in his life does not fully resonate with me at this time. Nor should it, I will add, in order for it to be valuable.

In some as yet inscrutable way, I stand with that troubled nineteenth-century genius, Friedrich Nietzsche, who said, "The world is deep, and deeper than the day could read. Deep is woe. Joy deeper still than grief can be. Woe says: Hence, go! But joys want all eternity, want deep, profound eternity" (quoted in Tillich 1948, p. 63). I, too, in spite of my postmodern bravado, want the deep, profound eternity that makes all the world's grief and woe endurable. In contrast to most conventional religious believers and spiritual practitioners, however, I want this eternity on my own terms, in my own way, and I want it here and now. I fully accept that this may be a grievous contradiction in terms, but I am more than ready to live with the fallout.

I find myself, at this time in my life, poised precariously somewhere between Dorothy Allison's (1994) need to "take the world by the throat and insist that there is more to this life than we have ever imagined," and Bryan Magee's (1997) conviction, in this chapter's opening epigraph, that "we can actually know very little [about life's mysteries]," and still not need "a religious dimension to things" (p. 564). In fact, I have already begun to make my peace with a paradox that includes both embracing and demystifying the unknowable. Actually, it is this type of paradox that ignites my passion for teaching about religion and spirituality, as well as about ethics and morality. I am convinced that, without the challenge of puzzling, often tormenting paradoxes like this one, there would be no fire in my pedagogy.

EXCERPTS FROM AN EXCHANGE OF LETTERS

What follows is a series of excerpts from several letter exchanges during my religion and education course that have taken place over the last few years between myself and the student types I mention above. I offer these abbreviated paragraphs in order to convey the flavor of these exchanges. All of the paragraphs are fictional composites of the type of actual student-professor exchanges that occur in my seminars. It is this kind of student material which has stimulated so much personal reflection on my part. In fact, I could not have written this book—requiring such intense self-reflection and analysis—without the intellectual and spiritual provocations featured in passages like the following. In a very special way, then, every single student in my religion, spirituality, and education classes during the past four years has been a co-author of this book. Each has been the *sine qua non* for all that I am able to say in this chapter in particular, because without them I am silent. They have helped me to find, and to express, my own developing, religio-spiritual voice.

Excerpt from the letter of an Existential Humanist: "…I have a very strong love of nature, and feel a strong connection to it, yet I have seen nothing that has convinced me that there is a creator. I try not to figure everything out, as you attempt to do, Robert, because there is really nothing to figure out. The point is that there is no point. There is meaning in my life, but it has nothing to do with a God or a religious doctrine. A character in the movie *American Beauty* makes the remark, 'Sometimes there is so much beauty in the world, I don't know if I can stand it.' This statement exemplifies my belief that perhaps it is not *why* these moments exist, but *that they do* exist that is so important. This is all that I really need or care to know. I am the maker and breaker of my own life, and I am the one who chooses whether or not to find meaning there. I'm not convinced, though, that *finding* meaning is as important as you say. I think that *living* it is more important…."

My response: "…I envy you your love of the glories of nature. At this point in my life, my own spiritual narrative has little room in it for nature, mainly because I am physically allergic to almost everything in it. In contrast to your comment that there is no point, I believe that there is always a point, even if it's the point you make that there is no point. When you talk about what gives your life meaning, you are actually constructing what I would call 'mini-narratives' which make their own point—in your words, 'visiting an old and familiar farmhouse, golden memories from your distant past such as fishing, being comforted by [your] sister, lying over the heating vent after a cold shower in the morning, being with [your] high school friend as he lay dying, and learning how to live and love from respected educators and smart peers.' As I understand it, the point to your religious narrative is this: You do indeed find meaning, and this is in life's ordinariness. These events are profoundly spiritual for you, because they represent the true breath of life. I love your words: 'They are palpable.' I am sympathetic to your suspicion of an institutionalized god who exists mainly as an abstract, manipulable construct, a mere tool in some group's particular toolbox...."

From a *Postmodern Skeptic:* "...In my opinion, religion and spirituality have value only as subject matter to be studied, not as truths to be lived. I don't bother to demonize religion and spirituality, as some of my friends do. You see, I am a pluralist who is willing to set aside my innate skepticism, particularly toward the religious right, in order to see if I can begin to understand even a little bit of their intensity about possessing a final Truth. So far, I haven't been able to. But during this semester, I have been saying to my colleagues in the high school where we teach that we need to foster what you call a 'robust religious pluralism' in our classes, if only for the sake of pursuing the free discussion of religious ideas in a thriving democracy. If we are going to insist on multicultural education, then we must add an understanding of religious difference to the agenda. It certainly won't hurt any of us to take our minds off our concerns about race, gender, and sexual orientation, and refocus them on issues of religious pluralism from time to time...."

My response: "...You yourself are the best evidence of the value of a semester-long study of religion and education. You now refuse to demonize conservative worldviews and religious narratives, preferring instead to extract some truth from the core of their teachings. You are willing to set aside, at least for academic reasons, your own skepticism toward the religious right, for example. You do this in order to act in a way that is consistent with your belief that a genuine pluralistic attitude toward difference is good. You believe that with proper training and perspective, teachers can learn how to teach about religion with impartiality, or at least with a disciplined pedagogical agnosticism. I call this 'structured empathy,' borrowing a phrase from Ninian Smart (2000). I have learned from your willingness to consider seriously what you refer to as the 'free discussion of religious ideas in our schools.' I have learned from you, because I suspect that you were a thousand miles away from this belief when you first signed up for my course. You have enlarged your skepticism to include a genuine openness to religious diversity. I like this, and I think your students will too...."

From a *Mystic:* "...I am a seeker, always searching for something more. What is over that next mountain ridge? What will happen during my next life, and the one after that, and the one after that…? How is it possible for me ever to find eternal salvation or the 'true' meaning of life outside of myself, my meditation, and my mindfulness of the moment? The conclusion that I have reached at the end of this course, Robert, is that I am better off not simply for asking these types of questions, but for resisting the temptation to look for answers to them. I float between and among all of your spiritual narratives, questioning all, landing on none, admiring each and every one. The joy that I have found in searching for a meaning in my life has been in letting go of some internal need to find an absolute truth. I have no hunger for quick fixes and magic bullets. I only want what you and the Taoists call the true 'stillness in the center of it all.' This is my good life, and, once again in your words, I am willing to 'keep my mouth shut and open myself to the wonders and mysteries of my multifarious existence.…'"

My response: "…Your language is eloquent and inspiring. All of your words lead to the wise conclusion that the 'good life' for you is one wherein you 'disappear from your accomplishments with dignity, style, and grace.' You came to my course a very different person from the young man I knew three years ago, the one trying so hard to be a leader. You have learned, if I may say so, that sometimes the best way to arrive at the sustainable truth that will set you free is to stop looking so desperately for it. I thought at one time that you were too self-conscious about doing what marketers call 'impression management.' You were trying much too hard to create a particular image of yourself as the wise administrator, trying to be the quintessential politician, trying desperately to be respected and accepted, and then becoming the angry outcast when he wasn't.

"How far you've come since then. You have discovered what, in my mind, is a magnificent truth: The good life is a life lived in not consciously seeking the good life. The good life mostly happens when we are unaware of its happening. You have learned that impression management leads mostly to the unhappy life, one that is phony, self-compromising, empty at the center, and overly dependent on others for a sense of worth and purpose. My wish for you is that you experience the good life throughout your life, but a good life in lower-, not upper-case letters.…"

From a *Scientific Empiricist:* "…I was a social science major in a fancy, ivy league college. What was real to me was what could be directly experienced, measured, interviewed, and/or tabulated. I was what you've called a 'scientific realist,' someone who believed like a missionary that there were real features in the world, and the responsibility of both the natural and social scientist was to document these in a rigorous, empirical manner. My father's death threw all my scientific certainties into turmoil, however. I spent his last night alive holding his hand. I talked to him about the Boston Red Sox, about my new house, and my graduate studies. I talked to him about love and letting go. Then a piece of me did. I left at five in the morning for my trip to Vermont and graduate school, after kissing and holding my dad for a very long while, the last time as it turned out.

"On the way to Vermont and the beautiful, green mountains, I suddenly experienced what you've referred to as an 'existential moment': Here I was, I and nature, the road and the car, the sun and the clouds, and the weeping daughter. I felt a strange sense of calm and was conscious of a message: Somehow, life is bigger than now, and bigger than this, and bigger than us. Maybe this is the meaning of it all. My miracle of a father dying this torture of a death, and here I am feeling a greater spirit. I have always been suspicious of your notion of 'numinous moments' and 'loss of rational boundaries.' I'm a scientist after all. But for that one powerful, brief moment on the long drive up to Vermont, I let go. I was taken out of myself for a flickering instant. I was utterly alone, yet reborn by feelings of sorrow, of loneliness, and of a strange joy. I realized that I and you and others live in a compassionate world, one that somehow manages to deliver us some sweet comforts to mitigate our miserable grief...."

My response: "...This is the incredibly sensitive person who I was certain resided within the tough-minded scientist you presented to the rest of us early on in the course. I remember your saying in class once that you 'did not have a personality suited for faith,' that you were 'afraid to let go, to experience a numinous moment, to live on a boundary.' Well, guess what. Nobody's lived on a boundary better than you in this class. Your powerful experience with your dying father which you call 'deeply transformative' sounds very spiritual and numinous to me. The words you used to describe your father's dying, as well as your existential moment while driving to Vermont, moved me like no other writing you've done this semester.

"You say that you want your writing to reflect a 'brilliant and rigorous intellectual discourse,' and you seem apologetic that your language this semester has been so personal. Why can't personal narrative writing be brilliant and rigorous in its own way? Whenever you spoke in class, you didn't speak as a research scientist. You spoke as a person struggling to understand her faith journey, to put the experience into language that your classmates might understand. I watched your cohorts warm to you a little more each week, listen with rapt attention to your insights, and learn from your courage in disclosing some very personal doubts about your spirituality.

"I would heartily agree with you that your need to control everything is not likely to get you closer to the numinous that you say you want so much. My advice to you, which, remember, you asked for, is both simple and well-intentioned: Keep a journal. Let your daily entries be very personal and reflective. Write about the ordinary moments, the experiences that evoke wonder, anxiety, joy, and love in your day-to-day life. Reflect on the mystery of your finitude. Don't worry so much about achieving 'brilliant intellectual discourse.' The kind of writing that you have done for me this term is both intellectual and brilliant in that it expresses what's in your heart and soul as well as what's in your intellect. What a crowning achievement...."

From a *Wounded Believer*: "...My upbringing in Catholicism has poisoned my feelings about organized religion. The church was far too masculine and patriarchal for me as a child and teenager. Whenever I entered the confessional, I left only with a huge guilt. Where was the sense of purgation that some of my friends felt after confessing their sins? All I got were lectures about sex from celibate, uptight, male priests. If God is indeed everywhere and all-knowing, why did I have to confess my innermost thoughts and secrets to some condescending white male? What right did he have to make me do penance?

"I never met a priest I could like and respect. Priests always told me to get on my knees to pray for forgiveness whenever I was having what they called 'impure thoughts.' As far as I was concerned, my sexual development was perfectly normal for a very hormonal adolescent. I remember one priest telling me that 'because you are a girl, it is even more important for you to stay pure until you marry. Boys will go only so far as girls let them. Your responsibility is great, young woman, to make sure that boys respect girls!' I haven't had a healthy sexual relationship with a man (or a woman) since the time I got that stupid advice. I know that I should grow up, stop whining, and get a life, but I still directly blame the church for my dysfunction...."

My response: "...Thank you for talking so honestly about how your evolving feminism stemmed from your disillusionment with your childhood Catholicism. I think I now understand why the construct of what you call an 'androgynous god' has such great appeal to you. It is obvious that you have been left with much residual guilt from your early Catholic training. I have some of this guilt as well, but I have worked hard to transform it into a healthy skepticism and a well deserved sense of pride over my rebellion. You might check out a wonderful, readable book by Scotty McLennan (1999) called *Finding your Religion: When the Faith You Grew Up With Has Lost Its Meaning.* Also, a rereading of a book we studied in class, Jack Mendelsohn's *Being Liberal in an Illiberal Age* (1995), would be very rewarding for you. One of the latent messages of both books, and perhaps the main message of my course, is that one is able to construct a genuine religious faith only by going through the trials of honest doubt. It is through continual questioning and doubting that one can arrive at a belief strong enough to encounter challenge, difference, and critique, without withering in the face of such opposition.

"I agree with you that teaching about religion in public schools like the one where you work will be challenging. You ask me what types of studies you ought to pursue to prepare yourself for this formidable task. I would recommend that you consider doing a major or a minor in religious studies. I would also recommend some work in communications theory, psychology, group dynamics, and pedagogy. Moreover, I would strongly urge that you and others, who might want to teach religion in public schools, get some pastoral/psychological counseling in order to become clearer about your religious and antireligious biases, projections, and distortions. We all have these, you know. Finally I hope that your newly developing feminist-theological narrative helps you to find the peace and reconciliation that I sense from your writing is one of your spiritual goals in the years ahead...."

From an *Orthodox Believer:* "...I come from an extensive background of conservative Protestantism. I studied for the Lutheran ministry for several years, before being weeded out by the authorities for being more conservative than even they would like. I then joined the Coalition for Christian Outreach and the Southern Baptist Church, where I am now a campus minister and a private school teacher. This course of yours was the first religion class that I had attended in twenty years, and, frankly, it rocked my comfortable little world. Here there was dialogue. Here there was a respect for pluralism. Here there was an opportunity for me to reflect on my personal religious narrative in a way that was always respected by my classmates, even when I came on a little strong.

"I realized that, compared to others in this class, I was an exclusivist when it came to religion. I did not like this in myself, and I worked hard to become a little more inclusivist. I probably will never be a true pluralist, though, because I think that conservative Christianity is the home where the full truth lives. I am not prepared to give up over four decades of living in Christian righteousness. I need something very substantive and very certain to build my faith upon.

"For me, God is very much alive, very real, not a human construction but a superhuman constructor. My dilemma, however, is a big one: How can I maintain my conservative religious beliefs, which I call reformed evangelical, and at the same time embrace a pluralistic belief system? I loved it when you said in your book that every educator at every level has a responsibility to encourage students to share their religio-spiritual narratives. How did you word it? 'All students need to tell their stories, not because their stories are right, but because they have a right to tell those stories.' Is it possible for me as a conservative evangelical Christian to find a way to assure that everyone's story is voiced without abandoning my exclusivist views? I need to be able to do this in my teaching, or I will never truly reach my students...."

My response: "...You ask whether you can be a genuine pluralist, yet still hold onto your conservative, Christian faith as the exclusive source of absolute truth. Diana Eck, the comparative religions scholar whom we read in class, would say no. Therefore, she would exclude you from the pluralistic dialogue because she would consider your mind to be closed. She would also exclude me because I am on the near side of atheism, and she would consider me to be closed. Despite her many wonderful insights and strengths as a religion scholar, I think that where Eck is vulnerable in her views is when she arbitrarily excludes others from her pluralistic club. Ironically, she becomes an exclusivist, who reserves a place at her table of interreligious dialogue only for those who meet her narrow specifications for being pluralistic: firmly grounded in some kind of religious tradition, but always open to the truth in other traditions. Fundamentalists and atheists need not apply to be members of her club.

"I wish you could have attended a colloquium I sponsored and hosted a few weeks ago. On a beautiful, sunny Friday afternoon, over fifty students, staff, and faculty came together to talk about the role of religion and spirituality on a secular campus. All types of believers and disbelievers sat together. One undergraduate student, an agnostic, said publicly that he was 'lost,' and had turned to drugs for meaning. Another undergraduate spoke of his deep 'ambivalence' about his Judaism. A graduate student talked inspiringly about finding a faith-filled Christian group that helped her to overcome her terrible sex addiction. Another student complained about the 'total lack of interest in religion' in her philosophy classes. Still another student spoke passionately about how religion has been both victim and victimizer throughout history, and maybe, in the long run, 'humankind would be better off without it.'

"The conversation was personal, authentic, and genuinely inquiring. Many students asked probing, unanswerable questions about faith, meaning, evil, and dogma. Some just listened and did not want the colloquium to end. Some believed in no truth; some wanted desperately to believe in some truth; some struggled to articulate their truths to the rest of us; and the campus ministers who came mainly to observe, in spite of themselves, frequently became animated and partisan participants in the conversation. They managed both to pacify and to provoke us. They were great coconspirators in stimulating the conversation!

"In my opinion, you could have led this conversation at least as effectively as I and they did. You would have engaged each of the students with empathy, generosity, and intelligence because of your strong faith convictions, not in spite of them. This is, in fact, how you comported yourself throughout the semester in our class. You were perhaps the most conventional believer in the group, but you were also, in my opinion, the most unthreatening and supportive presence week after week. As far as I can tell, you have come a long way in your quest to resolve the disparity between what you see as exclusivism and inclusivism in your life and in your teaching. I deeply appreciate your willingness this semester to enlarge your narrative to include folks like me. You are a fine, pluralistic role model for all of us. I think that, in her best pluralistic mood, even Diana Eck would agree and enthusiastically invite you to her table for dialogue...."

From a *Mainline Believer:* "...I am basically a person who is very happy being a reformed Jew. I have a great fondness for my temple, my rabbi, and my community. I identify myself as both a religious and a cultural Jew. In fact, I would say that being a Jew is all about being a believer in Judaism. Judaism forms my Jewish culture rather than the other way around. I was concerned throughout the semester, however, that mainline believers like me got very little notice, comparatively speaking. To be a mainliner isn't sexy, I guess. I have no complaints about my faith community. I am not in the throes of any great religious identity crisis. While I liked the readings, I really couldn't see what all the fuss was about. Isn't religion really a simple matter? You grow up in a religious community, you make friends, you attend services, sometimes you lapse, sometimes you don't, but you've always got something to fall back on. You pick and choose what to believe.

"If you feel that you don't belong in a particular religious group, just leave and find another one. If you are not comfortable as a believer, then don't believe. Nobody is forcing you to be religious or spiritual. For myself, I can only say that my religious community provides a safe and secure place for me to be, both ethnically and spiritually, especially nowadays when so many people in America seem to take pride in being what you call 'postethnic' and 'postreligious.' Shouldn't we be communicating positive things to students whenever we talk about religion in the classroom? Why do we make it all sound so complex and threatening? Religion is delightful. It's the major source of meaning for all of us, whether or not we recognize it, and, if we don't, we soon will as we get older. Don't people eventually return to the religions of their youth anyway?..."

My response: "...In my opinion, mainline or institutionalized religion has been unfairly criticized as an unnecessary atavism in today's experimental, neognostic, spiritual society. There is much to admire in your religious narrative, and, as you probably noticed, the majority of our course books were written by mainline authors, some happy with their affiliations, some not. I understand your frustration with the lack of airtime that your narrative received during the semester. I understand even better your concern that the mainline faiths, like Judaism, appear to be easy targets today, given the growing interest in New Age spiritualities, social justice churches, Eastern religions, and agnosticism and atheism.

"I am here to agree with you that without the mainline faith traditions, America would lack a center that means a great deal to tens of millions of believers. I would add, with only slight irony, that without this center, it is unlikely that much of the religious or spiritual experimentation we see all around us would be taking place today. So much of the new in any social movement is a reaction to the old. I would like to see the various religio-spiritual innovators and deconstructors in this country be considerably more respectful of the older, established mainline communions than they are. Why is it that some people need to denounce and renounce, before they are able to announce the coming of something they believe to be worthwhile?

"I must also add, however, that religious belief and religious affiliation aren't always as easy as you suggest. To you, a Jew, religion means so much more than simple church attendance and undeviating allegiance. To you, Judaism provides a stable cultural identity, a bulwark against centuries of oppression and persecution. To many more people today, however, religion is not a stabilizing influence. Neither is it an identity-enhancing force. Institutionalized religion has been mainly destructive. In some cases, it has been provincial, racist, sexist, and homophobic, and too cozy with entrenched, capitalistic economic structures. In my opinion, these issues need to be discussed and addressed in educational settings, always, of course, in an age-appropriate, respectful way.

"The two overall questions that I would ask you are these: Is it possible for the mainline denominations to make reasoned compromises with the world without the co-optations and dilutions that often accompany those compromises? How does any religious community balance the need for eclecticism and transformation in order to stay timely and relevant with the need to maintain the integrity of stable religious heritages? I wish that you had been more willing to help us understand why you are so happy with your mainline Jewish community, and how your temple is coming to terms with such challenges...."

From a *Social Justice Activist:* "... I really got involved with the content in our course when we read James Cone's *God of the Oppressed* about halfway through the term. I honestly did not think that there were any black theologians in Christianity. As an African-American man who long ago became disillusioned with a Baptist Church whose members seemed to spend more time weeping, wailing, and wallowing than doing anything constructive in the inner city where I lived, I always thought of Christianity as a kind of distracting happy pill meant to blunt the pain of racism and injustice. When Cone mentioned 'doing theology from the standpoint of those who are enslaved, lynched, and ghettoized in the name of God and country,' I sat up and took notice. I even e-mailed him at Union Theological Seminary to tell him how much his book meant to me.

"Cone is right, you know, even if most of the white students in our class were pissed off at him for saying that Jesus came to redeem black people, not whites, and that Jesus was really a black messiah come to deliver blacks from the white oppressors. Cone helped me to see that the central question of all Christian teachings should be this one: How effectively does a theology and a church speak to oppressed peoples and their fight for liberation? If Christian theologians and other church leaders ignore this question, then Christianity is simply irrelevant. Worse, it is evil. I know that this was never your intention, but, since taking your course, I have decided to join a progressive, black Christian fellowship in my city. We spend most of our time together reading the Bible from the standpoint of those who suffer injustice. We also work together in the neighborhood to make life better for those who have been exploited and left to die alone in silence and despair. This is the kind of religion that excites and inspires me...."

My Response: "...Yes, the class got angry over some of Cone's reactions to white theologians. I think that many white students reacted mainly to Cone's scare words, and, unfortunately, missed the real sentiments and meanings behind them. As you point out, Cone is saying that black liberation theology puts Christianity back where it rightfully belongs: as being partial to the weak, the neglected, and the disenfranchised. Cone is also saying that, in addition to the Bible, there are other testimonies at least as relevant for black people. These include black spirituals, diary entries of slaves, speeches by black leaders, literary writings, and the music of the blues, jazz, and rap. Cone's central argument is that theology must begin with the struggle for justice. If whites do not agree, then they are not black people's allies in the fight for liberation. Blacks will then need to bypass whites entirely in the struggle for social justice. In fact, Cone points out, 'white people have been the most violent people on the planet.' He wonders, therefore, what they have to offer black people.

"Some of the white students in our seminar took everything that Cone was saying in a very personal way. His deliberately provocative language spoke louder to them than did the extraordinary insights in his black liberation theology. I want you to know that I deeply appreciated the manner with which you dealt with your cohort's confusion and guilt. You calmly explained where you thought, in your words, 'Cone was coming from.' You redacted Cone's angrier rhetoric in such a way as to help our group genuinely understand his justifiable frustrations with Eurocentric, Christian theology. I admired your sensitivity, courage, and eloquence in strenuously defending Cone. I also valued your efforts to reach out to build bridges with those in our class who either totally misunderstood or, worse, rejected outright what he had to say because they felt so alienated from him.

"By the way, last year I had dinner with James Cone at the downtown Unitarian Universalist Church in Burlington, and I told him about our class's response to his book. I also mentioned you. Cone is a very gentle and modest person when talking one-on-one, and he listened carefully and nondefensively to what I was saying. He said: 'Thank you for telling me about your class. I'll continue to think about some of their comments. I do hope that they learned some good things from my book.' He reminded me that he tried to address many of the more current critiques of black liberation theology in the preface to the 1997 edition of *God of the Oppressed*. I read his preface later, and indeed he did. I hope you too have a chance to check out his preface, and, if you do, please let me know what you think...."

TAKING WARM, NOT COLD, BATHS

In the next, and final, chapter, I attempt to tie together some pedagogical and personal loose ends that I know I have left dangling. I do not want the following chapter to be read as the usual *coda* at the end of a book, however, something independent of what has preceded it, something simply tacked on to remind the reader that a book has reached its final (possibly merciful) conclusion. In my mind, any successful final chapter must present, in addition to a useful summary of sorts, a fresh and vigorous reinterpretation of many of the significant issues that an author has raised throughout a book. I will try to do this in a series of aphorisms, much like the format I used to end chapter 4, but without the humor.

While, obviously, there is much for which to fault Friedrich Nietzsche regarding his *Übermensch* (superman) politics, and his sometimes irrational, anti-Christian bigotry, what he does have to say about the art of writing is, to me, nearly faultless. Nietzsche was the master of the aphorism. He once remarked that some problems were so complex and profound, that the best any writer could do was "to draw a cold bath," in order to allow the reader to do a "quick in, quick out." For Nietzsche, an aphorism was like a cold bath, but because it was quick in and quick out for the reader, a good aphorism also needed an author's willingness to do some "brief deciphering." Moreover, an aphorism required a reader's willingness to do some "rumination." Nietzsche also contended that "the worst readers are those who behave like plundering troops: they take away a few things they can use, dirty and confound the remainder, and revile the whole." In contrast, the "best reader" was a "monster of courage and curiosity, also something supple, cunning, cautious, a born adventurer and discoverer" (Hollingdale 1977, pp. 15, 20, 24).

What follows in the final chapter, I hope, is more of a warm bath than a cold one. I want the reader to step gingerly into the text and choose to stay just a while longer. I need a little more time to work some things out in my own mind. My aphorisms about teaching and learning are aimed primarily at eliciting some rumination on the reader's part. I enjoy, as does Nietzsche, the presence of readers in my courses who are the supple adventurers and discoverers. These are the folks who love the commentary as much as the catchy *bon mot*.

Passionate Teaching— Spiritual Learning

The Power of Narratives

As for the cosmic meanings of human life, I am content with a deep and abiding modesty. I simply do not know. But as for the finite meaning of human life, experienced in dazzlement and deliverance, in rights and repression, in surprise and struggle, in living and dying, I have no uncertainties. These meanings are real. They matter. I cannot and will not abdicate the quest for finite fulfillment. If, cosmically speaking, human life is a trip to nowhere, so be it. I will not live my life, precious gift that it is, according to that rubric.
—Jack Mendelsohn, *Being Liberal in an Illiberal Age: Why I Am a Unitarian Universalist,* 1995

The great end in religious instruction...is not to stamp our minds irresistibly on the young, but to stir up their own; not to make them see with our eyes, but to look inquiringly and steadily with their own; not to give them a definite amount of knowledge, but to inspire a fervent love of truth; not to form an outward regularity, but to quicken and strengthen the power of thought; not to bind them by ineradicable prejudices to our particular sect or peculiar notions, but to prepare them for impartial, conscientious judging of whatever subjects may, in the course of Providence, be offered to their decision; not to impose religion upon them in the form of arbitrary rules which rest on no foundation but our own word and will, but to awaken the consciousness, the moral discernment, so that they may discern and approve for themselves what is everlastingly right and good.
—William Ellery Channing, *The Sunday School Discourse,* 1841

Teaching is storytelling. It is the place where lives can meet.... Stories create intimate conversations across boundaries. Stories disturb and challenge.... They are able to incite humor or passion or even irrationality.... I use stories to create deeper connections with my students, to reveal the universal human themes that we share, and to bridge the realms of thinking and

feeling.... In those moments of personal revelation students experience my vulnerability, my trust, and my respect.... As their teacher, I offer them my "dreams," and I ask them to "tread softly."
—Sara Lawrence-Lightfoot, *Respect: An Exploration,* 2000

MY PURSUIT OF COMPLEMENTARITY

My overall assumption about what constitutes successful teaching and learning is this: Passionate teaching leads to spiritual learning, both for the teacher and the taught. However, the opposite is also true—spiritual teaching leads to passionate learning, both for the teacher and the taught. I am saying that there can be no genuine spirituality without passion, just as there can be no productive passion without spirituality, especially where effective teaching and learning are concerned. This is the meaning of complementarity: The state of completing something or bringing it to perfection, combining separate parts to complete a whole. The two Unitarian Universalist ministers whom I quote in this chapter's opening epigraphs, even though a century and a half removed from one another, are religious educators, who, in my opinion, are fully aware of the importance of the interdependence of passion and spirituality. Their own spirituality, passion, and teaching form what for me is a wonderful complementarity.

Jack Mendelsohn (1995) was the former senior minister of historic Arlington Street First Unitarian Church in Boston. Mendelsohn's particular attempt to find a functional correspondence between his passion and his spirituality resonates with me. He realized that his ministerial work with parishioners must, of necessity, deal with the cosmic meanings of human life. However, even though he honestly had no idea what this meaning might have been, he still found his passion to exist in the finite surprises and struggles of everyday human living. His *spirituality* was based on a conviction that the quest for finite fulfillment was real, even though it might have ended up being a trip to nowhere. His *passion,* therefore, was to live his life as a precious gift, to experience it fully as dazzlement and deliverance, with no divine assurances that it would lead anywhere beyond the present, concrete moment. His spirituality and his passion formed an ideal complementarity. Some years ago, I heard Mendelsohn preach, and I found his eloquence from the pulpit to be an extraordinary blend of gentle reverence for all forms of life and an aggressive commitment to the cause of social justice.

William Ellery Channing (1986), an early nineteenth-century prophet of religious liberalism, lived a spirituality based on a profound love for the quest for truth, a nondogmatic belief in a divine Providence, and an enduring faith that human reason would enable people to fathom the meaning of God's word in the scriptures, which Channing revered. Channing's deep, somewhat unconventional, nineteenth-century spirituality ignited his passion as an educator to stir up the minds of the young. Throughout his life, he eschewed religious indoctrination in favor of fostering a taste for independent discernment and judgment. He strove to awaken the spiritual consciousness rather than imposing religion upon the young. Channing was able to combine a spirituality grounded in thoughtful, scholarly exegeses of the Bible with a fiery zeal for reforming such doctrinaire, and what he considered to be fallacious, Christian teachings like the Trinity and the atonement.

My goal as an educator is to come close to the kind of complementarity and wholeness in my own teaching and writing, spirituality and passion that I find in such extraordinary exemplars as Mendelsohn and Channing. In addition to their lucid insights, the personal stories that they lived can be potentially life altering in their impact on readers. I have likewise found varying degrees of complementarity and wholeness in the lives of other thinkers whom I have referenced throughout this book, chief of whom are Theodore Brameld, Richard Rorty, Hazel Barnes, and Don Cupitt. Most of all, though, I have witnessed remarkable integrity and complementarity in the lives of many students and loved ones whom I have met in my journey to become a more authentic and responsive educator, lover, and friend. While it is true that I am not a minister, and I have no interest whatever in preaching the word of God from any pulpit, ecclesiastical or otherwise, I do find the gist of what Mendelsohn and Channing are saying about spirituality and truth to be highly compatible with my own views.

Here, in the paragraphs and sections to follow, is where I stand today. This is where my long journey to spiritual understanding has taken me...so far. I fully expect to make continual refinements in the years ahead. Like Mendelsohn (1995), I strive for an abiding modesty regarding what I do and do not know. I, too, delight in the surprise and struggle which are prominent features of my everyday life. I am utterly convinced, along with him, that there is meaning to my life, even if it is finite. I also try to live each day of my life as if it is a precious gift, even though this gift might more than likely be the product of sheer, evolutionary chance.

Like Channing (cited in Mendelsohn 1995), I want to be an educator who stirs up the passions of his students to find and live their own truths. I also want to increase the capacity of their heads and hearts to overcome prejudice, ignorance, and fear. If they are believers, I want their beliefs to be a consequence of their own carefully informed choices, absent the arbitrary impositions of authoritarian others. Finally, I want to awaken their consciousness so that one day my students might become discerning enough to approve for themselves what is everlastingly right and good. I will, nevertheless, reserve the right to quibble over the objectivist meaning that Channing assigns to the word *everlastingly.*

Aphorisms and Narrative Understandings

In the next section, I will present a number of aphorisms about making meaning through the use of narrative. These aphorisms will take the form of a series of personal credo statements. Each one will be accompanied by a brief commentary. These credo statements, taken as a whole, become, at once, my pedagogical narrative, my spiritual manifesto, and my overall declaration of what gives my life meaning at the present time. I hope that these observations will adequately sum up what I have learned about my profession of faith in the power of education to transform lives, particularly my own—during the several decades I have spent in a college classroom. I do not mean for my creed to be doctrinal, dogmatic, or final. It is not, nor could it ever be. Once again, in Diana Eck's terms, I want it to be perceived as a tractable, yet passionate, statement of those beliefs I am enthusiastically "willing to give my heart to," at least for now.

I choose to emphasize the centrality of *narrative meaning* in my teaching because, in the words of Sara Lawrence-Lightfoot (2000), whose epigraph leads off this chapter, I believe that "teaching is really storytelling. It is the place where lives can meet. Stories create deeper connections with students, and they reveal universal human themes" (p. 107). I love the narrative construal of meaning because I believe strongly that our stories are the only devices left to us to get us closer to some guiding truths. At their best, our stories are symbols for God, ethics, morality, justice, wisdom, truth, love, hope, trust, suffering, and meaning. Our stories give us the courage to confront the incredibly complex, joyful, and dreadful dimensions of our lives.

Our stories help us to understand our histories, shape our destinies, develop a moral imagination, and give us something truly worth living and dying for. Those childhood stories that define us as adults, occasionally to our dismay, will continue to have a strong hold on all of us, right up to the day we die. What grasps my students in each of the classes that I teach are not the fancy, intellectual *algorithms* that I invent but the simple *allegories* that I tell, particularly when I am at my best. What they remember most of all, however, are the stories that I am able to evoke from them, particularly those stories that enable them to craft coherent selves out of the dizzying commotion that occupies their lives. I find that I can evoke these stories, only when I am most compassionate, and only when I allow myself to become most vulnerable to students. Just as everyone else, though, I have my good days and my bad days.

Let the reader be forewarned, therefore, that I am still a very long way from achieving that striking complementarity between what I profess and what I do that I find so appealing in Mendelsohn and Channing, as well as in so many other scholar-activists whom I have repeatedly mentioned throughout this book. Even so, in spite of my frustrating setbacks (becoming fewer, I hope, as I age), I continue to forge ahead with the unassailable faith that, somehow, I will manage to meet each new challenge to improve my theory and practice as a teacher. In honor of another intellectual mentor of mine, John Dewey (1897), who also denounced dualisms and advocated an educational philosophy based on discovering the complementarity of apparent opposites, I call the next section "My Pedagogic Creed."

This is the title of what, for me, is the most powerful discourse on education that Dewey ever wrote, in part because of its uncharacteristic brevity and clarity, but mainly because of its palpable passion. Immediately below, then, is a truncated list of postmodern assumptions that I make about life and teaching. Following this list, there is a more developed commentary on these assumptions in the form of personal belief statements. Somewhat out of character, I will deliver the latter as a series of universalizable teaching-learning beliefs. I can only say that all of these beliefs, no matter how homiletic they might sound, are, to me, infinitely arguable and always provisional. I enthusiastically invite spirited, and, I hope, friendly, rejoinders from readers. This is how I grow as a teacher, by learning both where I am strong and where I am weak in my thought and in my practice.

"MY PEDAGOGIC CREED"

ASSUMPTIONS

- We do not live in reality itself. We live in stories about reality. Stories are true or false according to aesthetic and psychological criteria, in addition to theological, political, philosophical, and educational criteria. What makes a story true is not simply whether it is revealed, rational, relational, or refined. Truth is also a function of what works for the narrator and/or the reader/listener in the never-ending quest to find and construct self-defining narratives of meaning.

- Each religious and spiritual narrative, like all narratives, is as much a story *about* the believer and disbeliever as it is *by* the believer and disbeliever. Each of us is both constructivist and constructed. The stories we construct then turn around and construct us, and we them…forever. This is the constructivist circle, and there is no escape. We are condemned to construct and to be constructed; that is, to make, and to be made by, meaning.

- The trouble with trying to discover objective truths in our worlds is that we are constantly distorting them with our narrative truths. No objective truth ever exists outside of a constructivist narrative, including, of course, this opinion about the narrativizing of objective truth.

- No master story will ever again dominate the world's local stories. Henceforth, teachers and students will need to approach all stories that claim absolute validity with charitable incredulity. The problem, of course, is that master stories can deliver hope, while charitable incredulity can deliver despair. The reverse is also true.

- In order to see the world, we first need to believe what we see. Too often, many of us continue to believe, even when what we see is no longer there. Our beliefs continue to hold us in their iron grip. A postmodern approach to teaching tries to break the iron grip of those deeply buried beliefs that are no longer serviceable. Sometimes, of course, critical scrutiny serves to confirm these beliefs.

- There will always be a vast distance between word and world. Our words mediate our views of the world. They do not mirror our views of the world. We describe the world in vocabulary that others have created. Thus, we create the world, in large part, by the vocabulary we bring to it, by the same vocabulary that creates us. This is to say that there are times when our languages speak us as much as we speak them.

- Our whys to live depend on our hows, whens, and wheres. These, in turn, depend on the ways we were raised. Our whys are a product of our peculiar tastes, temperaments, talents, timing, tribes, and training. Personal transformation is possible and even desirable, of course, but it will always be bounded by the impact on us of our particular genetics, psychologies, histories, sociologies, and nests and hives of influence. Despite their boundedness, our whys, religious or otherwise, provide our ultimate reasons to live, to love, to learn, and, above all, to accept, even celebrate, our finiteness. Without our whys, life is severely impoverished. A good education helps students to understand, appreciate, and, when appropriate, to modify their whys.

- Human agency is not unlimited. It is always restricted. We construct the reality that, in turn, constructs us, *ad infinitum*. There is no construction *de novo*.

- The only perspective worth having is the perspective that all perspectives, including the postmodern one, are at one and the same time true and false, whole and partial, strong and weak, each in their own ways. We need contending narratives and perspectives to bump against each other, so that our own narratives can be kept honest and respectful.

- There is no Truth all the way down. There are only interpretation, perspective, point of view, and preference. There is no Down down there, no Unimpeachable Foundation upon which to rest, once and for all. Interpretation and perspective do indeed go all the way down. Truth and Reality are infinitely interpretable. Everything is up for grabs. There is no final word on anything, including, and especially, this assertion.

- There are no opposites. There are only differences of degree and transitions. The opposite of absolutism is not subjectivism or relativism. Neither is it nihilism nor despair. Rather, it is perspectivism. It is hard work, persuasiveness, responsiveness, energy, building a case in behalf of a cherished perspective, generosity, open-mindedness, and working with, and learning from, others. Absolutism and relativism, certitude and fallibilism, share at least one quality in common: They are all fragile, sometimes desperate, attempts to construct meaning.

COMMENTARIES

I believe that all people, including preprofessionals and professionals, construct a series of life-sustaining stories that help them to make sense of who they are, how they live, and what they do for a living. It is these stories, many of them spiritual, that get them up in the morning and off to work, particularly during those burnout times when the prospect of facing one more client, patient, or student seems dismal at best. It is these stories that provide a context for accepting the awesome responsibility and privilege that come with being professionals.

We are storied people. We do not live in a world where there are actual spiritual, moral, or ethical certainties. Rather, we live in a world where we actually construct stories that may or may not include all of these certainties. In spite of, perhaps because of, this loss of religious and moral certainty, each of us still strives to make, and to find, meaning. In fact, consciously or unconsciously, we are each living out a series of stories that confer meaning on our lives. This is, in part, what I mean by the word "spiritual": those narrative constructions that help us to invest our lives and values with both ultimate and proximate meanings. These stories clarify our deepest sense of who we are and what our lives are all about. Thus, at some level, we are all spiritual beings. In this sense, spirituality may or may not have anything to do with belief in god, attendance at churches, synagogues, or mosques, membership in organized religious groups, or adherence to a set of traditional practices, doctrines, or dogmas.

Our spiritual stories express our humanity. They tell the rest of the world who we are. We spend the greatest part of our lives trying to live out our stories with consistency and integrity. We are both author and reader of our stories. This is to say that we create the stories that we live, but we also live the stories that we create. The stories that we tell to others, and the life stories that we are trying to live, speak volumes about the moral and spiritual meaning of our practices. I often say to my students: Tell me the stories that you love and hate, and I will tell you what you value and what you do not, and who you are striving to become both personally and professionally and who you are not. For example, tell me the story of your atheism, and I will tell you a counter-story of theism that you might find to be attractive, and vice versa.

I believe that good teachers everywhere, not coincidentally, are themselves fine storytellers. More important, though, they are even better story-evokers. Good teachers are able to elicit these stories in a classroom. They are adept at encouraging students to exchange them publicly with one another. Moreover, they can gently challenge students to transform their stories whenever they might appear to be spiritually, morally, or professionally dysfunctional.

I am learning through the years how to tell my own story to students in a way that, I hope, is becoming less intrusive. I try very hard not to invade the sacred spaces of their attentiveness to course content and to one another—and to the meaning which this material might convey for their own evolving life-narratives—with my personal issues. I am working to become more clear and consistent about the line of personal privacy and professional decorum I will not cross with my students.

Whenever my classes become more about me than about them, then I deliberately back off. I return the spotlight to where it belongs in all classrooms at all levels, to the students who have stories of their own to narrate, and, when necessary, to reconstruct. I am less interested in the deconstruction of students' narratives, however, than I am in the construction of more purposeful and useful narratives of meaning that might help all of my students to get from one day to the next with integrity, compassion, and enthusiasm. My primary aim in telling my own story to students is always to do it in such a way that it evokes stories from them. At times, of course, every effective teacher must provoke in order to evoke. However, I want to learn how to do this with the kind of sensitivity and grace that is less about my cleverness and more about my students' struggles to create meaning.

Stanley Hauerwas (1977), the theologian, observes that "a story is a narrative account that binds events and agents together in an intelligible pattern.... To tell a story often involves our attempt to make intelligible the muddle of things we have done in order to have a self" (p. 76). Like Hauerwas, I want to have a self amidst the muddle of things. My own narrative is the particular account I construe in order to structure the chaos of my life into some kind of order and purpose. I refuse to accept my life as nothing more than what William James once called a "whirligig of blooming, buzzing confusion." I prefer to think of my own narrative of meaning as one that, while confusing and contradictory at times, also tells a coherent tale of an exciting, often unpredictable pilgrimage that I am on.

My own journey, or story, is to create some lasting meaning for my life in those personal relationships with family, friends, and former students that continually renew me; in the teaching, advising, and service that occupy so much of my professional time; in the scholarship that helps me to enlarge, deepen, and challenge the convictions that I hold; and in the generative contact that I have with students and colleagues to build a mutually nurturing, living-learning community at my university. It is true that in my efforts to get from here to there on my journey and, perhaps, back again, I experience many fits and starts, some productive, some merely distracting. However, I am convinced that my life has meaning, because I can put it into the framework of an ongoing story of discovery, one that features many unique characters, ordinary and extraordinary events, intriguing plotlines, stubborn obstacles to overcome, many anticipated and unanticipated outcomes, and a series of comic and tragic, sometimes wonderfully clarifying, denouements. All of this, in a phrase, is the spritual narrative that I am living.

Moreover, my narrative is residually Christian in the sense that Christianity's three cardinal virtues are prominent throughout. My story is full of hope, because I trust that something good will come from my efforts to help others, if not sooner, then later. I try valiantly to live my story with love, in that I have no need to remake my students in my image. I attribute the best motive to them by affirming their rights to live their lives in their own best ways. The biggest challenge for me, though, is to try to live my story with the faith that somehow, somewhere, there might be a meaning that transcends my particular time and place, both in the longer evolutionary scheme of which I am a natural part and in the shorter historical period in which I am presently living.

Finally, I am trying to construct an overall narrative that will help me to get to the sources of my anxiety, despair, and frustration. Occasionally, these feelings flare up in the work that I do, particularly in regard to the bleak future that, in my darker moments, I occasionally foresee for myself and others. I have an old-country, Irish tendency to "wait for the other shoe to drop," according to my wife. I cause her pain with my attitude that no joy or success can ever be satisfying enough, as these must always teeter dangerously on the razor-thin edge of catastrophe and ruin. This pessimism about life's prospects, sadly, I count as one of the more deleterious holdovers from my childhood Catholicism. I am thinking here of its antiquated and cruel, pre-Vatican II eschatology of heaven and hell, of the threat of everlasting punishment, of always having to be on guard against the lures of sin, because a soul, no matter how pure, can be lost in an instant with one bad choice. I am convinced that this harsh teaching has led to my continuing torment over the problem of good and evil. I am happy that, according to recent reports, more progressive members of the Catholic clergy today have renounced a belief in hell and purgatory. Some have even questioned the existence of a heaven. I believe this to be a healthy and enlightened approach to eschatology. Don Cupitt would agree.

I believe that ethical practice in teaching, and in other forms of human service, begins in a mutual willingness to encounter, and to understand, the narratives of meaning that professionals and clients, teachers and students, bring to their relationships with each other. I am talking particularly about those spiritual stories that help us to recognize the full humanity of all those persons who come to us for instruction, advice, and help. I am also interested in those stories that help us to understand, and to put into compassionate perspective, the strengths and weaknesses in our own lives as a way to understand, and to celebrate and forgive, the strengths and weaknesses in others' lives.

I am interested in helping students construct stories that bring all of us a little closer to the moral ideals that we pursue, to the virtues that we want to exemplify, to the ethical principles that help us to make the right decisions, and to the existential challenges that force us to grow and to stretch as professionals. I am especially interested as a seeker myself in getting all of my students to listen carefully and sensitively to the spiritual stories of others, and to look for ways to get inside of these stories in order to discern just where they might be taking themselves as well as others. One strategy I use to achieve this kind of discernment is to instigate talk about narratives of moral meaning, and how these types of stories always play a role in getting many of us through the worrisome perplexities of ethical dilemmas.

It is important to note that just as we professionals construct narratives that confer meaning on our private and public lives, so also do our clients and students. They, too, profess a belief in some very basic values, and whenever we fail to detect these organizing beliefs, these recurring meaning-motifs, in our conversations with them, then we miss a wonderful opportunity to discern what is truly important to them. Worse, we talk past them with all of our professional know-how, because we have no context for understanding what they cherish, and, hence, what is ultimately important to them.

I am convinced that what makes genuine dialogue possible between two people is not for the professional to strive for a textbook kind of *empathy* as commonly taught by the helping professions. Because the other is, at some level, insuperably and intrinsically unknowable, we can never really think another person's thoughts or feel another person's feelings. Rather, the most empathy that we can ever achieve is to listen to the other's stories in such a way that we acknowledge the person as a unique meaning-maker, unlike any other meaning-maker. The trick is to locate the core of meaning, of spirituality, that resides in the center of each story that a student tells.

I myself prefer the word *compassion* to empathy. Empathy is a teachable skill, highly prized by the helping professions. It is a truly worthwhile strategy in knowing how to express sympathy for another's plight without becoming emotionally involved. The Greek root, *empatheia,* means to project one's own passion and feeling *onto* the other, not to take the other's suffering *into onself.* Compassion, by contrast, is an all-encompassing quality of character. It includes affection, sympathy, sorrow, and a deep urge to help.

Etymologically, *compassio* means to suffer with the other, to reach out, to feel deeply, to absorb the pain. It has nothing to do with projection. Instead, it has everything to do with the unconditional acceptance of another's narrative of suffering on its own terms. It means allowing oneself to be touched by it. Tibetan Buddhism teaches that compassion grows out of a profound understanding that all people wish to be happy and to avoid suffering. The teacher who wants to show compassion is the one who cultivates qualities such as love, patience, tolerance, and forgiveness. Happiness consists both in giving and receiving these qualities. For the Tibetan Buddhist, compassion is a comprehensive way of constructing a life's narrative. It is far more than merely a therapeutic technique.

To talk openly and compassionately about narratives of meaning, of spirituality, and of morality is hardly a popular undertaking in the academy that I have worked in for lo these many years. It is risky, for example, to talk about religion and spirituality in any public forum, unless, of course, somebody is running for political office or speaking from a pulpit. I have been struggling for several years now with how to engage secular academic communities, including faculty, students, and staff, in a respectful, cross-campus dialogue about the influence of spirituality in our students' quests for meaning. For a variety of very understandable reasons, faculty find this type of dialogue very threatening, except when it takes place in the religious studies classroom or in the campus minister's office (and I have been told by many students that they do not get it even in these places).

Some of this difficulty is due, no doubt, to a stubborn religiophobia on the part of many professors on college campuses. Some of it is a consequence of simply not knowing how to have these kinds of conversations without violating what is seen as the First Amendment separation of church and state. Also, some of it is the result of wanting to contain spirituality to the private spaces on a college campus where it won't cause any trouble. I am convinced, however, that if we academicians continue to ignore or to marginalize students' narratives of spiritual meaning, we will be sending them the all-too-clear message that this type of story is irrelevant to either a liberal or a professional education. The result will be that what should be talked about openly, if the quest for meaning is to be taken seriously in the academy, will remain forever buried beneath the surface. I would argue, however, that despite its calculated removal from the public educational space, it will continue to lurk in the background of any encounter between professor and student in the classroom.

I believe that teachers everywhere, at every level of schooling, have an ethical obligation to acknowledge, and to understand, their colleagues and students as narrative-bearing, narrative-telling, and narrative-interpreting persons. How, for example, can a teacher truly understand how a student will respond to a challenging reading or writing assignment, a piece of difficult advice, or a well-intentioned criticism or recommendation, without first understanding the narrative of meaning that the student brings to a particular educational encounter? While I think it is safe to say that every student wants competent educators who are knowledgeable, respectful, and personally accessible, they also want something more: They want to be understood from within the matrix of narrative meaning with which they frame and negotiate the world.

Certainly, students want compassion; and obviously they want fairness, intellectual stimulation, and enthusiasm from educators. However, above all, they want to be understood, and to be heard, from the nucleus of the stories that they are living. I am not talking here only about respecting students' rights to ask us questions, or to give us their informed consent whenever we make our risky educational interventions, or to expect us to be well prepared and nonexploitative in our dealings with them. I am talking about a right that is far more difficult and challenging: the justifiable claim on the student's part for some unchartered time to engage in honest, heartfelt narrative interchanges with us and with one another.

At the very least, teachers' willingness to engage in narrative dialogue with students underscores the ethical principle that, as professionals, we can only begin to make contact with them if we are willing to let them tell us their stories, and if we are willing to listen. Equally as important, whenever it is educationally prudent, teachers need to be willing to tell students a little bit about their own stories, particularly when these might overlap with theirs in such a way as to lead to mutually beneficial learnings.

I will be personal here. Sometimes the stories we tell ourselves about ourselves are inaccurate and self-defeating. Good teachers are able and willing to correct our narrative misimpressions. My memory is vivid of a dear colleague and friend of mine, a veteran professor of education at my university, who helped me to overcome a severe writing paralysis during my most recent sabbatical year. I was mentally blocked for over a month when I first attempted to write this current book as an in-depth, autobiographical memoir. It seemed that I was just not able to do a tell-all, deeply probing, psychological account of my life as a teacher, seeker, and lapsed Catholic. My colleague helped me to see that I was mistakenly thinking about a memoir in either-or, all-or-nothing terms: as either a navel-gazing, let-it-all-hang-out, personal confession, or as a dispassionate scholarly account of what does and does not work in teaching a college seminar. It would be more than possible, he suggested, to combine the strengths of both approaches and thereby avoid the weaknesses of each genre when taken to extremes.

My colleague took the time from a busy professorial schedule to meet with me over a long breakfast one morning in order to listen nonjudgmentally to my overwrought story of memoir-terror. I am sure that to him my fears seemed foolish. He had already written such a book himself, and he had done it well. Moreover, I was the recognized authority on personal narrative writing in my college, and scores of students flocked to my course in order to learn more about this type of writing. Why then, I perseverated, was I unable to do what I purported to teach others to do in their theses, dissertations, and scholarly papers? I felt crushed by the self-imposed pressure to exemplify superbly what I explicated to others, to practice well what I preached. I had created a self-destructive narrative of the exposed, deflated expert. In my mind, I was the one who gave new meaning to the canard, "Those who can't do, teach."

Deftly and patiently, my colleague helped me to construct a more realistic, less panicked understanding of personal narrative writing. He was responsive to my feelings. He did this in such a compassionate and sensitive manner that I was more than ready to face the prospect that I could indeed write a self-revelatory, teaching narrative at once restrained yet still engaging. It was all about finding the best balance, doing what I truly believed in, and being thoroughly honest with myself. I can never thank him enough for his kindness, his willingness to listen to my immobilizing anxiety about not being able to start on a major writing project as time was rapidly running out on my sabbatical.

My colleague took the trouble to hear me from the soul of the story that I inhabited: in this case, the story of a teacher who, himself, was frozen in doubt, unable to produce what he taught. He never once berated or belittled my story. Instead, he helped me to transform it into something almost redemptive. He encountered me as a person, living a story of memoir-phobia, and he helped me to find new meaning in the role of personal narrative writer. Although he did not intend to do this, he also became an excellent exemplar for me in my efforts to hear, and respond to, the stories of my students, particularly those stories that might be misfiring.

Let me tell you of one other colleague's timely, narrative intervention in my life that I will treasure for the rest of my days. Once again, let me be very personal. A cherished colleague of mine, a professor of nursing at my university, and a former student in one of my ethics seminars, who, upon sensing my anxiety over an upcoming, fairly routine—but to me cataclysmic—surgical procedure, chose to take time out of her busy schedule to consult with me over a long lunch. Over a deep-dish pizza which we shared, and which I barely touched, she listened nonjudgmentally to my overwrought narrative of surgery-terror. Knowing that I had never faced surgery before, very patiently and very compassionately, she helped me to construct a more hopeful, less panic-stricken narrative understanding of surgery, one based on facts but one also responsive to my feelings.

She did this in such a compassionate and sensitive manner that I was more than ready to face the surgery, indeed to embrace it risks and all, for the restoration of health that I, and she, were convinced it would bring to me. I can never thank her enough for her kindness and wisdom. She exhibited an intuitive, narrative understanding of my surgery-phobia that, in the end, truly liberated me. She took the trouble to hear me from the heart of the anxiety-dread story that I tend too frequently to inhabit. She encountered me as a spiritual being trying to find some meaning in the new and intimidating role of being a patient about to undergo, and having eventually to convalesce from, surgery. Equally as important to me, she showed up unexpectedly in my hospital room the morning after my surgery. Her soothing words of support and comfort, along with the good advice that she gave me as I was about to face a protracted recovery period, got me through the next, harried month.

I believe that, often, what happens within the interstices, or the subtexts, of the formal teacher-student relationship is what really matters in the classroom. While less obvious, and less measurable, than official teaching-advising activities, a teacher's willingness to listen, and to respond compassionately to students' stories frequently has a greater payoff as to whether or not they experience themselves as academic successes.

I readily admit that when a student comes into my office for academic advising, and I am booked solid throughout the day for thirty-minute blocks of time per student in a kind of managed-care pressure cooker, and when I have to rush off to teach a three-hour seminar of tired graduate students making their way, often reluctantly, to my class after a long day's work, I want to advise quickly and effectively, without the frills, and be done with it. I want to move this advisee out the door with the proper information, while leaving us both no less the worse for wear and tear. I have little time for personal counseling or even to know my student as an out-of-classroom human being with significant stories to tell me. I simply cannot spend time hearing about her troubled family, her growing alienation from the church upbringing of her youth, her exuberant hopes for academic success, along with her foreboding fears of personal failure, her nagging concern about an intimate relationship recently gone awry, or her anxious premonitions about an upcoming job interview.

However, truth to tell, as I enter my thirty-fifth year as a professor in the academy, I know full well that these off-task dialogues, these mutual exchanges of personal meaning, these encounters that rarely get officially rewarded (in fact, most are discouraged as pandering to students), are the ones that truly count. I am meeting this student first as a narrative-bearing, narrative-telling, and narrative-interpreting human being, and only second as an assigned advisee in need of specific program advice. The questions that she is asking about the choices she must make regarding her studies and her career options are part of a larger existential narrative that reflects her growing concern about the finitude that she, and all of us, must inevitably confront. Her existential story will indelibly shape her learning in my classroom, whether the subject matter she studies with me is philosophy, ethics, religious studies, or educational theory.

I believe strongly that for me to ignore or to minimize the overall impact of her life's story in favor of staying on professorial task is to treat her, and others like her, unethically. It is to acknowledge that they are not unique and precious individuals who bring their own distinctive narratives of meaning to me and to the class in general. Rather it is to melt them into an undifferentiated mass of learners whose lived educational experiences are no different from anyone else's. It is to discount their singularity, their signature spirituality if you will.

I recently read a very touching story in the Sunday *New York Times Magazine* about a pediatric oncologist, Dr. Michael A. Weiner (Saint Louis 2001), who seems to understand the importance of listening to the stories of his patients. He makes it a point never to discount their existential singularity. I strive to be like Dr. Weiner in my own interactions with students, even though they may not have life-threatening illnesses. He says:

> When parents first hear the word "leukemia," they are absolutely devastated. They think, "Oh, my God, my son is going to die." Their world stops. But during that hour and a half that I sit with them, we go into the nuances of treatment and care. I give families news in a sequence starting from the test results that confirm the diagnosis. I give them particular information. The bad news I mention once or twice, the good news five, six, or eight times so that's what they walk away with. I am hopeful. That's what I want to convey. You have to take your cues from the families. If I am meeting a family that is Orthodox Jewish, I will use messages like "God will take care." With some families, you must sit with them for three hours. It's a strange situation. (p. 22)

In my opinion, Dr. Weiner is a narrative role model par excellence. He is willing to spend whatever amount of time that he needs in order to listen compassionately to parents' narratives of fear and anxiety, of loss and suffering, of devastation and disempowerment regarding their children's illnesses. He doles out appropriate information with exquisite sensitivity and with an impeccable sense of timing. He knows intuitively, based on years of experience, just how much information is necessary, and when and how to deliver it. He tries always to convey a message of hope and understanding to parents and their children. When necessary, he responds to parents' narratives of religious meaning by himself, employing the particular spiritual language of believers in order to soothe them and to make a human connection. He understands all too well that parents look to him as the main protagonist in a narrative of healing that requires him to be therapist, guide, expert, and emotional rock of Gibraltar, all rolled into one. He also realizes that he must disconnect from the hospital, to compartmentalize his own narratives so to speak, in order to return to his work day after day, year after year, reinvigorated and restored.

I wish that every educator I know could have a conversation with Dr. Weiner. For myself, I would be interested to know his own narratives of meaning which sustain him in the work that he does. What gives his life and work focus and purpose? How can he continue decade after decade to meet parents and patients as unique others, with their own characteristic stories to tell? How can he continue year after year to be sensitive to their peculiar ways of hearing the story of healing that they want him to tell, but which he may not be able to deliver in some tragic circumstances? Does he, at some level, recognize his own story in the stories of his parents and young patients? Is he aware that he is actually living out a story that all those parents and patients might see as an extension of their own Jewish, Christian, or Islamic narratives of meaning and hope? From what narrative sources, what spiritual wellsprings, does he himself draw his strength in order to deal humanely with the parents of desperately ill children?

Why is it that some caregivers, and teachers, are crushed under the huge emotional toll that the sometimes contradictory demands for compassion and competence, discretion and honesty, sensitivity and objectivity, exact? Is it only Dr. Weiner's peculiar personality and temperament that keep him from armoring himself against the suffering of his parents and patients by coming across as harsh, cold, and impersonal? Alternatively, is it something far more basic? Is he living out a story, perhaps a spiritual one, that puts his own anxieties about suffering and dying into some kind of metaphysical or cosmic perspective? Is his a secular story that puts great hope and faith in humanity's this-worldly ability to solve its own problems by continually refining its medical science? How important, if at all, is it for parents and patients to know his defining medical story? What, if anything, should his colleagues know about his own spiritual narrative? In the end, does any of this really matter? In my opinion, the answer to this last question is an emphatic yes!

I believe that teachers need to be fastidiously sensitive to the ethical issues that are bound to arise when addressing students' narratives of meaning. There is the danger of violating a student's privacy, and inadvertently exploiting a student's vulnerability. For example, there is the possibility that some students could misread a well-meaning narrative intervention and feel that the teacher is invading their private space. Some students might also feel that they must accept a particular spiritual message as the necessary precondition for remaining on good terms with teachers. Teachers must be very careful not to say or do anything that might come across as coercive to students. There is also the risk of practicing beyond the teacher's competence, by entering a province usually reserved for clergy and therapists. Few teachers whom I know are credentialed ministers or counselors. Fewer still are comparative religions scholars or philosophers of religion.

What I am suggesting, however, is actually a minimal ethical duty: Recognize students as integral human beings who possess spiritual needs in addition to their more obvious psychological and intellectual needs. Treat students as whole persons, many of whom live their lives in all-embracing spiritual narratives. Understand well the significance of the growing body of research which shows that many students, particularly during their college years, want their teachers to talk with them about their religious and spiritual beliefs. Sometimes this entails doing nothing more than asking appropriately sensitive questions about a student's possible faith commitment. This also entails a willingness on the part of the teacher to listen sensitively and respectfully to individual, spiritual stories of fear, hope, anxiety, faith, trust, expectation, courage, meaning, and sacrifice, even when some of these might appear irrelevant, or even bizarre, from an instructional point of view.

Of course, whenever these stories threaten the well-being of students in obvious and harmful ways, then teachers need to know how to address them in such a manner that students can clearly see them to be either compatible or incompatible with the subject matter being studied. Ultimately, of course, the choice to make a particular leap of narrative faith must be left to students, and this needs to be respected. Finally, when listening and understanding are not enough, then teachers must know when to refer students to the services of counselors, ministers, and psychotherapists.

I believe that, if educators are serious about enacting a narrative approach to their work with students, then there are at least three paradoxes in their teaching and learning that will require sustained attention.

1. Educators like myself will need to continue teaching courses on values, virtues, ethics, and spirituality, even though, in the end, there is the likelihood that all of these subject matters may simply be unteachable or unlearnable. There is great wisdom in the old saw that matters related to morality and spirituality, to the will and to the spirit, are better caught than taught. Deeds teach more effectively than creeds, as the Unitarian Universalists point out. There is just not much convincing empirical evidence that didactic teaching methods, or even more nonprescriptive, moral conversations and dialogues like the ones that I try to encourage, end up producing tangible behavior change, or even a less tangible change of mind, in students. If there is such evidence, compiled by researchers outside of particular faith, political, and moral traditions, and with no pet ideological axes to grind, then I have not been able to find it.

Such prescriptive pedagogical tactics as preaching, shaming, demanding attendance at church, chapel, or temple, requiring the reading of sectarian literature, posting the Ten Commandments or a series of moral and spiritual platitudes on the walls throughout a school or college, and, ironically, making volunteer service in the community mandatory, more often than not create a reverse effect on many students. Some will openly rebel at what one of my own students derisively called "forced morality projects." Some will engage in such activities mainly to fulfill an academic or community requirement, and then, later, promptly forget what they were supposed to have learned. Others will opt out entirely, preferring instead to appropriate their moral and spiritual learnings from the most powerful, values curriculum of all, the popular media.

It pains me to tell hard-nosed administrators that courses in character education, religion and spirituality, and applied ethics, even when delivered in the form of unbounded, nonjudgmental dialogues that I find so pleasing, appear to have no measurable effect on the actual formation of students' characters, ethics, and spirituality. As I pointed out in earlier chapters, I have heard some students tell me that their lives have truly been changed as a result of our time together, and I am more than willing, even delighted, to take them at their word. However, as yet, my belief that students do, in fact, undergo an actual sustainable moral and spiritual sea change is largely a leap of faith, a hope beyond indubitable proof. I must hastily add, however, that in the end, whatever teachers do with students in order to modify their behaviors and to transform their worldviews can only come out of a bold leap of faith that the impossible might somehow be possible. There are simply no guarantees, but, to my mind, this journey into the unlikely is what makes teaching and learning such a challenging adventure.

Merely telling students, in settings where they are captive audiences, how they ought to behave both inside and outside school and college walls is hardly enough to conduce them to be people of good moral and spiritual character. If this were true, then no student who comes from a good family, church, or school would ever go wrong. There would be no drug experimentation, sexual promiscuity, unwanted pregnancies, school shootings, gang violence, income-tax cheating, or bullying.

2. The less calculated that teaching is in the areas which I have been discussing throughout the book, the more effective it might actually be. Educators as various as Aristotle, Jean Jacques Rousseau, Mary Wollstonecraft, and John Dewey, each in their own way, have warned us that, for example, while moral character certainly counts, its formation is incredibly complex and unpredictable. Dewey (quoted in Nash 1997) himself said that "moral education is practically hopeless when we set up the development of character as a supreme end...or when it is reduced to some kind of catechetical instruction" (p. 52). To the teacher's dismay, some research suggests that when moral education takes place in isolated family, church, school, and college settings, dramatic, or even subtle, transformations of character are infrequent to nonexistent.

More influential in the shaping of moral character, ethical discernment, and enhanced spirituality, however rare they might be, are those social settings where the values of school, college, family, and community form an almost perfect, intersecting web. This web is one that is mutually reinforcing, consistent, clear, and supportive, such as in military families, extended church groups, and in some highly selective private academies and elite universities attended by many generations of the same family. However, even when this interconnecting moral web exists, I am here to confirm from my experience in the classroom that there is no guarantee students will apprehend morality, ethics, or spirituality in the exact ways that educators would like. From my perspective, however, this is a good thing. I, for one, would worry if any educational site, particularly my seminar room, were part of a perfect intersecting moral and spiritual web which incorporated both inside and outside social settings.

Inspired by William Ellery Channing (cited in Mendelsohn 1995), I believe that "the great end in [any kind of instruction] is not to stamp our minds irresistibly on the young, but to stir up their own; not to make them see with our eyes, but to look inquiringly and steadily with their own" (p. 124). I want to quicken and strengthen students' critical abilities. I want to awaken, and, when necessary, to challenge their moral discernment skills. I want each and every one of my students to compose a coherent narrative about their lives, based on a morality, spirituality, and an ethic which is truly theirs and not mine or others'. Mutually interconnecting and reinforcing moral webs, for all their desirability in a fractured and fragmented culture, scare me. They smack of indoctrination and sectarianism. These latter practices will always be the enemies of efforts to create a vigorous democracy and an autonomous self.

3. An education most suitable for a democracy is not one that teaches a bag of predetermined dispositions, qualities, understandings, devotions, and skills, but rather one that grows out of an indeterminate, democratic dialogue demanding continual compromise and consensus. Democracy, for all its participatory decision making advantages for citizens, can frequently be contentious, messy, and frustrating. Thus, citizens need to know how to work well with others who might think differently from them about how to achieve their shared ends. In the event that shared ends are absent, then people need to engage in what philosophers call deliberative discourse. The purpose of such discourse is to create a democratically sovereign society that is fair, free, and compassionate. To this end, all of us must learn to temper our strong moral and spiritual convictions—even

those regarding the worth of both democracy and sovereignty—with a readiness to compromise, whenever we find our best intentions thwarted by others. The painful irony of democracy is that, like us, our strongest opponents are also motivated by their own best intentions.

The simple truth in a democracy (as in a classroom) is this: We cannot always get what we want, no matter how noble our goals. An indeterminate, democratic dialogue is one that proceeds to wherever the participants wish to take it, and it requires a particular type of person to engage constructively in it. The dialogue calls for commitment and conviction, to be sure, but it also calls for sacrifice, patience, empathy, tolerance, and generosity. The democratic dialogue also asks us, at least initially, to put the best construction on the contributions of others to the dialogue. It obliges us to find the truth in what we oppose and the error in what we espouse, before we go in search of flaws. I would contend that all of these democratic dispositions and processes are profoundly religious and spiritual in nature.

The paradox in this dialogical process is that, when it all goes well, regardless of its concrete outcomes, it has the potential to teach the qualities of self-respect, hope, confidence, courage, honesty, and, above all, friendship and trust. When it does not go well—when participants refuse to attribute the best motive to others—it has the potential to teach those vices that can only endanger democracy: suspicion, self-contempt, hopelessness, powerlessness, cowardice, dishonesty, and, saddest of all, enmity and mistrust. These are the vices that, if left unchecked, guarantee the death of the democratic dream.

As I suggested earlier, no educational content or process, whether my own or others', and no matter how well-intentioned and noble, will insure once and for all the achievement of any type of political system, including a democracy. There is always the likelihood that some students will fail to find the narrative of democracy to be a salient one, just as some students will repudiate a narrative of theism or of secular pluralism. This difference of opinion is both the boon and the bane of any pluralistic democracy. Disagreement is inevitable when politicians and teachers organize their practices around the principle of an unimposed, open-ended consensus-seeking.

"ALL OF US ARE QUESTIONS
TO WHICH THERE ARE NO FINAL ANSWERS"

My pedagogical creed can be summed up in simple terms. I am at the enviable stage in my career when I think of my personal and professional life as an ongoing, lived interpretation whose sentences end with ellipsis points, not exclamation points. I have the late-career freedom of keeping an open mind, abruptly changing my mind, or even losing my mind, if all of this serves in some way to unlock my students' minds. I am under no pressure to provide final answers to any of the political, moral, ethical, or religious questions that I, and they, raise in my courses. In fact, I could not do this if I had to, even under the threat of losing my tenure, or, worse, losing my permanent faculty parking sticker. Nothing in my creed is settled. For a teacher like me, finality is an impediment to learning, while unsettledness is a spur. I find James P. Carse's (1994) insights in this respect highly resonant: "We are always wrong in some essential way about what our story is. We are never living out exactly the story we think we are. Knowing that we don't know the full meaning of our story is not only a higher ignorance. It is the basis for all our hope" (p. 185).

My ultimate direction, if there is one, is unsure. I operate always out of a higher ignorance. I struggle constantly to understand my world, and others', from the vantage point of my unique psychological, cultural, and historical contexts. My deepest beliefs and convictions, like everybody else's, are but reinterpretations of everything that I have read, heard, liked, and disliked throughout my life. I have distilled these beliefs from books, classrooms, personal and professional relationships, houses of worship and houses of commerce, and from all those peaceful places in my life that inspire repose, reflection, and recreation. My creed for teaching and living is a patchwork pastiche of meanings—sometimes consistent, sometimes contradictory—of all that I love and hate, of all that seduces and repels me.

I catch all-too-frequent glimpses of myself both in my friends and in my enemies. I also catch glimpses of my beliefs both in the texts that I cherish and in those I deplore. I myself embody all of these oppositions, and, because I do, I tend to find worth and insight in each of them. In my classroom, I am an open container of colliding and ambivalent meanings.

This frequently upsets those students who are looking for something predictable, even decisive, in their teacher's rants. Most of them have heard that I am a person with strong opinions. I am, of course, but to my students' puzzlement, these opinions often bump up against each other, and on some occasions even cancel themselves out. This leaves everything unbalanced, and the fallout can be very irritating.

Even though we each have our personal idiosyncracies that make us truly unique, my students and I are similar in one sense: Each of us must eventually address the confounding anomalies in a human situation that is inexorably finite and marked by continual uncertainty. This human situation features indescribable moments of mystery, transcendence, and joy, along with heartbreak, suffering, and remorse. What binds all of us together in this human situation of mixed curses and blessings is that we are each hermeneutes trying to make meaning. We are mediators and redactors, asking our perpetual questions, forever reinterpreting the answers, constantly revising the "texts" that we read and critique, carefully reediting our life stories, and cautiously forging provisional responses to the challenges of living happy, satisfying, and productive lives. In the quotation of the atheistic philosopher, Thomas Sheehan (1986), which heads this section, "We are all questions to which there is no final answer" (p. 226).

I personally find the words of the theist, John Updike (1997), less salient in capturing the essence of the human situation than do many of my more devout, Christian students. However, I deeply respect the meanings conveyed by these words, and I do find considerable truth in them. At times, I, too, feel their bite: "We are in a state of fear and trembling, separated from God, haunted by dread, twisted by the conflicting demands of our animal biology and our human intelligence, of the social contract and the inner imperatives, condemned as if by otherworldly origins to perpetual restlessness" (p. 9).

My own taste, in contrast to Updike's, runs more toward E. B. White's sentiments concerning the human situation: "If the world were merely seductive, that would be easy. If it were merely challenging, that would be no problem. But I arise in the morning, torn between a desire to isolate myself from the world, and a desire to fully enjoy and savor the world. This makes it hard to plan the day" (Quoted in Mendelsohn, 1995, p. 8). What both Updike and White agree on, of course, is that the human situation leaves all of us "perpetually restless." This makes it all the more important for each of us to find those spaces where we are able to tell our stories of perpetual restlessness to one another.

Here are the thoughts of Rabbi Mordechai Gafni (2001), and they capture well everything that I have tried to say in this last chapter about the complementarity of passion and spirituality, teaching and learning, narrative and meaning:

> We need to know that in the details of our lives dangle the keys to heaven. No corner of our story is created in vain; we have never been down any dead-end street, never met an unnecessary face, never heard a senseless song. Every nuance, event, image, and incident of our lives is a source of vital psychological and spiritual information. Telling our autobiographies, we forge a coherent narrative out of our life stories, shedding light on the meaning of our lives.... There are simply no men and women of little interest and no distinction existing in the world. Indeed, it is far from certain that the anecdotes of the famous...have the most to teach us. In fact, it is certain that they do not. (p. 39)

One Hundred Breakfasts

I close my spiritual-pedagogical narrative with a brief, personal account of how far I think I have come from those early days of teaching high school English some forty years ago. I made the decision before I applied for my most recent (and probably last) sabbatical that, because I was going to be at home spending a full year writing, I would try to maintain face-to-face contact with some of my present and former students. To this end, at a nearby restaurant equidistant from my home and the university, I scheduled a few breakfasts to begin in the early fall. Initially, my reasons were selfish ones: I wanted to carry on conversations with them in order to punctuate my manuscripts with real-life examples of students' stories. I also wanted to be kept abreast of the political gossip that surrounds and enlivens undergraduate and graduate work in any major research university. These breakfasts soon took on a life of their own, however.

I discovered, before too long, that I actually looked forward to hanging out with students for an early morning meal. Sometimes these breakfasts would consume two to three hours of enjoyable, meandering, agenda-free chatter. Often they produced intense soul-searching. Always they ended up being mutually satisfying encounters between a veteran faculty member who was missing the classroom more than he knew, and students who desired a different kind of relationship with a professor, one that could be intimate without being illicit. Before my sabbatical year ended, I was shocked to learn that I had met with over one hundred students, counting repeaters. What was more, the vast majority of these breakfasts, and occasional lunches, were initiated by students. Word had gotten out early on that I was in a relaxed mood, I wanted to talk, I was available to listen, and, most of all, I was less the scholar and professor in this setting and more the older friend.

A community of scholars is many things, of course, but before it is anything, I believe that it must be a gathering of friends. As I said in the first chapter, a philosopher is perforce a lover—someone who has a passion for wisdom, but also someone who has a tender regard for all of those who want to be wise. Many writers (see, for example, John Henry Newman 1986) on the nature of the university have made the case that learning communities need to be places where the pleasures of friendship are combined with the challenges of scholarship. I think it is true that what students remember most about the academic component of their college studies are the personal relationships they were able to form both in and out of classrooms with particular professors.

While the power imbalance between professors and students, and the possible exploitation that could result, might justifiably make many academicians suspicious of these kinds of relationships, I believe that Aristotle had it right. *Philia,* or friendship affection, is the source of the greatest learnings in the academy, both for students and for us, their teachers. In Schwehn's (1993) thoughtful terms: "The deepest intimacy between human beings arises in the process of conversation. For Aristotle, human beings were most fully and truly themselves when they were thinking together. Thus, thinking and speaking together are expressions of a kind of virtuous love" (p. 62). I unexpectedly found this kind of virtuous love during those scores of breakfasts with my students. Without this *philia,* I am convinced that I would not have been nearly as productive as I was during what turned out to be the most satisfying of all the sabbaticals I have taken throughout my long career.

I came to understand with a clarity I had not truly known before that, like me, students were also living lives of perpetual restlessness. In the language of Rabbi Gafni (2001), each of them, in their own unique ways, was desperate to understand that in the details of their lives dangled the keys to some kind of meaning. They wanted some assurance from me that, somehow, their stories were not in vain, their journeys were not dead ends, their faces were not forgettable, and their songs were not senseless. As I listened to their impromptu tales of success and failure, sadness and joy, hopes fulfilled and hopes dashed, love and hate, faith and faithlessness, dreams and nightmares, wisdom and ignorance, and optimism and pessimism about their futures, I realized that I was being granted a great privilege. I was standing on holy ground, in that I was being asked to participate directly in the soul-stories that were altering my students' lives.

I will not recount any specifics of these stories here, out of respect for the sacred zone of privacy that protected our precious encounters each morning. Permit me only to say that my own story grew richer, more nuanced and satisfying, and, most of all, more lucid to me as I listened day after day to their stories. Our friendships, forged together in that cozy little restaurant in Williston, Vermont, gave the lie to the myth that learning must be a solitary and competitive experience, if anything worthwhile is ever to come of it. My students and I had no need for argumentative hot seats during those early A.M. meals. Moreover, our texts were the ones that we constructed out of our common, lived experiences.

There is a new identity problem in the United States, and it goes by the name of "quarterlife crisis" (see Marin 2001). Unlike the typical midlife crisis that I and most people my age experienced, triggered by too much stability, predictability, and security, the quarterlife crisis is the direct opposite. Underlying all the conversations I had during the course of my sabbatical year with students in their twenties and thirties were feelings of intense self-doubt, endless self-questioning, and, for some, a gnawing regret over opportunities lost and relational roads not taken. All of my breakfast companions were experiencing varying degrees of John Updike's "perpetual restlessness," but not, I believe, in any classical Christian sense. Their restlessness, as far as I could tell, had its roots in what I would call a meaning vacuum that few religions, philosophies, or political ideologies could fill at this particular time in their lives.

Most of the young people whom I got to know well on those fall, winter, and spring mornings began to open up almost immediately, over a cup of coffee and a scone. They talked about whether the sacrifices they were making to insure their futures were, in the long run, worth what they were losing. Many were in varying stages of despair over the prospect of ever finding a stable and secure meaning to their lives. Everything seemed to be so up in the air to them. Few were willing to give themselves over to a single, avocational passion for fear of being sidetracked from their career goals. Those who did choose to spend a little time fostering relationships outside of their professional orbits, and pursuing hobbies and other personal activities unrelated to their academics, frequently found themselves marginalized and criticized by their peers and supervisors. They were the secessionists from the career rat race, and, thus, they were perceived to be uninterested in establishing, and pursuing, serious work expectations.

These expectations included a straight-ahead, no-detour route to finding the perfect job, partner, colleagues, clients, income status, more advanced degrees, and lifestyle. Sadly, these goals were set at so unreasonably high a level that, for many of the students who broke bread with me, they created extraordinary conditions of psychological distress. Much of the identity turbulence experienced by pre- and early-career adults is, of course, predictable and normal today. However, I think that this developmental shibboleth too often diminishes the intensity, and the distinctiveness, of young people's restlessness at the present time. The quarterlife crisis generation that I got to know firsthand, with its guard down, during my casual breakfasts with them, is caught between pulls of independence and interdependence, isolation and community, passion and apathy, and, perhaps most seriously, spirituality and materialism. This, in my language, adds up to a unique crisis of meaning, and it illustrates well the paradox of poverty amidst abundance. The loss of meaning is what the worm has nibbled away in the apple of heightened American expectations.

Thus, I listened carefully and respectfully to each and every student. I took to heart the advice of Saint Ignatius of Loyola, the founder of the Society of Jesus, at the beginning of the *Spiritual Exercises:* "Let it be presupposed that every good Christian is more ready to save his neighbor's proposition than to condemn it" (cited in Komonchak 2001). I made it a point for an entire sabbatical year to save rather than to condemn my students' propositions about learning, loving, living, and, at times, loathing. I affirmed their feelings as real and significant, and when I identified or differed with students, I acknowledged this honestly. I gently questioned what

I thought might be all-or-nothing, black-or-white thinking, particularly when this might have been self-destructive. I made it a point to advance no pet political, educational, philosophical, or religious agendas. If any character education and ethical discernment did, in fact, happen, they occurred only in the subtext of our open and warm human encounters.

I have since had a number of my young breakfast confreres tell me that those meetings provided the best education they ever had. I do not think it a coincidence that, for the first time in my entire professorial career, I shut my mouth (well, not entirely) and opened my ears. I sometimes chuckled when a student would exclaim at the end of our time together: "What a great conversation!" Our verbal interactions were two-way, to be sure, but only in the sense that I was the riveted receiver of their messages, and they were the excited senders. One wonderful payoff of genuinely listening and receiving was that I was often the recipient of many uninitiated embraces from people of both sexes, most of them half my age. This made me something of a celebrity among other patrons who frequented the Williston restaurant each morning, as well as among the waitstaff, owners, and chefs. Once, a waitperson who got to know me well, approached me to ask with tongue in cheek: "Are you the leader of a cult or something? Where do all these young people come from? Why do they want to spend so much time with an old guy?" I was not insulted by her questions; in fact, I was delighted. When I told her that I was a professor meeting with students, she only half believed me. I did not care.

For my part, what I found there for an entire year in that comfortable little breakfast restaurant was the affirmation that in my sixth decade I am on the right track in my efforts to become a good teacher. I relearned that my life is worthwhile because it is purposeful. I continue to have something important to offer students of all ages, something they want to hear, even outside my classroom and my office. I recognized that my vocation is intellectually and emotionally satisfying because I accept, at this late date, that I am as much the taught as I am the teacher. My spirituality, while still forming, really comes to life when I am with others, sharing in their stories nonjudgmentally, and trying ever so hard to grasp resonant lessons for my own life-narrative. I know, at the deepest level, that all of this somehow matters, even though I cannot prove it to doubters. This, I suppose, is my faith. For now, this is more than enough. I am grateful to be a teacher.

REFERENCES

Allison, D. (1994). *Skin: Talking about sex, class, and literature.* Ithaca, NY: Firebrand Books.

Armstrong, K. (1993). *A history of God: The 4000-year quest of Judaism, Christianity, and Islam.* New York: Knopf.

Barnes, H. (1967). *An existentialist ethics.* New York: Vintage.

Barnes, H. (1997). *The story I tell myself: A venture in existentialist autobiography.* Chicago: University of Chicago Press.

Bellah, R. N., R. Madsen, W. M. Sullivan, A. Swidler, & S. M. Tipton. (1985). *Habits of the heart: Individualism and commitment in American life.* Berkeley: University of California Press.

Bennett, W. J. (1993). *The book of virtues: A treasury of great moral stories.* New York: Simon & Schuster.

Berger, P. L. (1992). *A far glory: The quest for faith in an age of credulity.* New York: Free Press.

Bloom, A. (1987). *The closing of the American mind.* New York: Simon & Schuster.

Brameld, T. (1965). *Education for the emerging age: Newer ends and stronger means.* New York: Harper & Row.

Brameld, T. (1971). *Patterns of educational philosophy: Divergence and convergence in culturological perspective.* New York: Holt, Rinehart and Winston, Inc.

Brameld, T. (2000). *Education as power.* San Francisco, CA: Caddo Gap Press. Original work published 1965.

Brandom, R. B., ed. (2000). *Rorty and his critics.* Malden, MA: Blackwell.

Bromwich, D. (1992). *Politics by other means: Higher education and group thinking.* New Haven, CT: Yale University Press.

Bruffee, K. A. (1993). *Collaborative learning: Higher education, interdependence, and the authority of knowledge.* Baltimore, MD: Johns Hopkins University Press.

Carse, J. P. (1994). *Breakfast at the victory: The mysticism of ordinary experience.* San Francisco: Harper.

Channing, W. E. (1986). *Unitarian Christianity.* Boston, MA: Beacon Press. Original work published 1819.

Clouser, K. D. & B. Gert (1990). A critique of principlism. *Journal of Medicine and Philosophy* 15: 219–236.

Cone, J. H. (1997). *God of the oppressed.* Maryknoll, NY: Orbis.

Cupitt, D. (1997). *After God: The future of religion.* New York: Basic Books.

Cupitt, D. (1998). *Mysticism after modernity.* Oxford, UK: Blackwell.

Cupitt, D. (2000). The radical Christian worldview. *Cross Currents* (Spring/Summer) 64.

Dewey, J. (1897, January 16). My pedagogic creed. *The School Journal,* 77–80.

Dewey, J. (1960). *The quest for certainty: A study of the relations of knowledge and action.* New York: G. P. Putnam's Sons. Original work published 1929.

Dillard, A. (1999). *For the time being.* New York: Alfred A. Knopf.

Easterbrook, G. (1998). *Beside still waters: Searching for meaning in an age of doubt.* New York: William Morrow and Company, Inc.

Eck, D. L. (1993). *Encountering God: A spiritual journey from Bozeman to Banaras.* Boston: Beacon.

Eliot, T. S. (1933). *T. S. Eliot: The complete poems and plays.* New York: Harcourt Brace Jovanovich.

Engelhardt, H. T. Jr. (1986). *The foundations of bioethics.* Oxford: Oxford University Press.

Fish, S. (1980). *Is there a text in this class? The authority of interpretive communities.* Cambridge, MA: Harvard University Press.

Gafni, M. (2001, May-June). Live your story. *Tikkun,* 39.

Glover, J. (1999). *Humanity: A moral history of the twentieth century.* New Haven: Yale University Press.

Goleman, D. (1995). *Emotional intelligence.* New York: Bantam.

Gordis, D. (1995). *God was not in the fire.* New York: Scribner.

Greeley, A. M. (1990). *The Catholic myth: The behaviors and beliefs of American Catholics.* New York: Charles Scribner's Sons.

Habermas, J. (1988). *The philosophical discourse of modernity.* New York: Political Press.

Halberstam, J. (1993). *Everyday ethics: Inspired solutions to real-life dilemmas.* New York: Penguin.

Hanh, T. N. (1995). *Living Buddha, living Christ.* New York: Riverhead.

Hauerwas, S. (1977). *Truthfulness and tragedy: Further investigations into Christian ethics.* Notre Dame, IN: University of Notre Dame Press.

Haught, J. A. (1996). *2000 years of disbelief: Famous people with the courage to doubt.* Buffalo, NY: Prometheus.

Higgins, R. (2001). Combating the ungodly violence that stains many religions. *Boston Sunday Globe,* September 16, D8.

Hirsch, E. D., Jr. (1987). *Cultural literacy: What every American needs to know.* Boston, MA: Houghton Mifflin.

Hobbes, T. (1962). *Leviathan.* Edited by M. Oakeshott. New York: Macmillan. Original work published 1651.

Hollingdale, R. J., ed. (1977). *A Nietzsche reader.* New York: Penguin.

hooks, b. (1994). *Teaching to transgress: Education as the practice of freedom.* New York: Routledge.

Hume, D. (1902). *Enquiry concerning the principles of morals.* Edited by L. Å. Selby-Bigge. New York: Oxford. Original work published 1752.

Hunter, J. D. (1991). *Culture wars: The struggle to define America.* New York: Basic Books.

Johnson, F. (1998). Beyond belief: A skeptic searches for an American faith. *Harper's,* (September): 8.

Kaufmann, W. (1961). *Critique of religion and philosophy.* New York: Doubleday.

Kilpatrick, W. (1992). *Why Johnny can't tell right from wrong: Moral illiteracy and the case for character education.* New York: Simon & Schuster.

Kohlberg, L. (1984). *The psychology of moral stages.* San Francisco: Harper & Row.

Komonchak, J. A. (2001). All dressed in scarlet. *Commonweal,* (February 23): 9.

Lama, D. (1999). *Ethics for the new millennium.* New York: Riverhead.

Lawrence-Lightfoot, S. (2000). *Respect: An exploration.* Cambridge, MA: Perseus.

MacIntyre, A. (1984). *After Virtue.* Notre Dame, IN: University of Notre Dame Press.

Magee, B. (1997). *Confessions of a philosopher.* New York: Random House.

Marin, R. (2001). 20-somethings suffer "quarterlife crisis." *The Burlington Free Press,* 25 June, 7.

May, R. (1969). *Love and will*. New York: W. W. Norton & Company.

McLennan, S. (1999). *Finding your religion: When the faith you grew up with has lost its meaning*. San Francisco: Harper.

Mendelsohn, J. (1995). *Being liberal in an illiberal age*. Boston, MA: Skinner House.

Midgley, M. (1991). *Can't we make moral judgements?* New York: St. Martin's Press.

Nash, R. J. (1996). *"Real world" ethics: Frameworks for educators and human service professionals*. New York: Teachers College Press.

Nash, R. J. (1997). *Answering the "virtuecrats": A moral conversation on character education*. New York: Teachers College Press.

Nash, R. J. (1999). *Faith, hype, and clarity: Teaching about religion in American schools and colleges*. New York: Teachers College Press.

Nash, R. J. (2001). *Religious pluralism in the academy: Opening the dialogue*. New York: Peter Lang.

Natoli, J. (1997). *A primer to postmodernity*. Malden, MA: Blackwell.

Newman, J. H. (1986). *The idea of a university*. Notre Dame, IN: University of Notre Dame Press. Original work published in 1899.

Nielsen, K. (1990). *Ethics without God*. Amherst, NY: Prometheus Books.

Nietzsche, F. (1989). *On the genealogy of morals*. Translated by W. Kaufmann & R. J. Hollingdale. New York: Vintage. Original work published 1887.

Noddings, N. (1993). *Educating for intelligent belief or unbelief*. New York: Teachers College Press.

Nord, W. (1995). *Religion & American education: Rethinking a national dilemma*. Chapel Hill: University of North Carolina Press.

Oakeshott, M. (1950). The idea of a university. *The Listener* 43: 420–450.

Ostling, R. N. (2001). Scholars debate 'just war.' *The Burlington Free Press*, 20 October 2D.

Palmer, P. (1983). *To know as we are known: A spirituality of education*. New York: HarperCollins.

Perry, W. G. (1970). *Forms of intellectual and ethical development in the college years: A scheme*. New York: Holt, Rinehart and Winston, Inc.

Plato. (1956). *Great dialogues of Plato*. Translated by W. H. D. Rouse. New York: Mentor.

Pojman, L. P. (1995). *Ethics: Discovering right and wrong*. Belmont, CA: Wadsworth.

Postman, N. (1996). *The end of education: Redefining the value of school*. New York: Vintage.

Rawls, J. (1971). *A theory of justice.* Cambridge, MA: Harvard University Press.

Reeves, T. C. (1996). Not so Christian America. *First Things* (June): 16–21.

Roof, W. C. (1993). *A generation of seekers: The spiritual journeys of the baby boom generation.* New York: HarperCollins.

Roof, W. C. (1999). *Spiritual marketplace: Baby boomers and the remaking of American religion.* Princeton, NJ: Princeton University Press.

Rorty, R. (1979). *Philosophy and the mirror of nature.* Princeton, NJ: Princeton University Press.

Rorty, R. (1982). *Consequences of pragmatism.* Minneapolis: University of Minnesota Press.

Rorty, R. (1989). *Contingency, irony, and solidarity.* New York: Cambridge University Press.

Rorty, R. (1998). *Truth and progress.* New York: Cambridge University Press.

Rorty, R. (1999). *Philosophy and social hope.* New York: Penguin.

Russell, B. (1957). *Why I am not a Christian.* New York: Simon and Schuster.

Saint Louis, C. (2001). What they were thinking: How to deliver bad news. *New York Times Magazine,* 8 April, 22.

Sandel, M. (1982). *Liberalism and the limits of justice.* Cambridge, England: Cambridge University Press.

Schwehn, M. R. (1993). *Exiles from Eden: Religion and the academic vocation in America.* New York: Oxford University Press.

Sheehan, T. (1986). *First coming: How the kingdom of God became Christianity.* New York: Random House.

Smart, N. (2000). *Worldviews: Crosscultural explorations of human beliefs.* Upper Saddle River, NJ: Prentice-Hall, Inc.

Smith, B. H. (1997). *Belief & resistance: Dynamics of contemporary intellectual controversy.* Cambridge, MA: Harvard University Press.

Spong, J. S. (1998). *Why Christianity must change or die: A bishop speaks to believers in exile.* San Francisco, CA: HarperCollins.

Stout, J. (1988). *Ethics after Babel: The languages of morals and their discontents.* Boston: Beacon.

Tannen, D. (2000). Agonism in the academy: Surviving higher learning's argument culture. *Chronicle of Higher Education,* (March 31): B7-B8.

Tillich, P. (1948). *The shaking of the foundations.* New York: Charles Scribner's Sons.

Tivnan, E. O. (1995). *The moral imagination: Confronting the ethical issues of our day.* New York: Simon & Schuster.

Updike, J. (1997). A disconcerting thing. *America*, (May): 8–9.

Wilson, E. (1998). *Consilience: The unity of knowledge*. New York: Alfred A. Knopf.

Wolfe, A. (1998). *One nation after all: What middle-class Americans really think about*. New York: Viking.

Wolfe, A. (2001). *Moral freedom: The search for virtue in a world of choice*. New York: W. W. Norton & Company.

Woodward, K. L. (2001, September 24). A peaceful faith, a fanatic few. *Newsweek*, 67-68.

Wright, R. (1995). *The moral animal: Why we are the way we are*. New York: Vintage.

Wuthnow, R. (1998). *After heaven: Spirituality in America since the 1950s*. Berkeley: University of California Press.